Financial Statement Analysis Under IFRS
Sixth Edition

by

Kenneth Lee and Deborah Taylor

Published by Financial Edge Training (a trading name of IBHero.com Ltd.) News Building, 3 London Bridge Street, London, SE1 9SG, UK

Visit us online at: www.fe.training

Other credits
Publishing and formatting: Robert Smith

ISBN: 978-1-9165028-0-2

Foreword

Is accounting important? After many years of teaching, researching and discussing accounting issues, we hardly need to clarify our position on this! If you want to work in finance, in all its forms from investment banking to professional accounting to industry, a working knowledge of financial statement analysis is a vital tool in your armoury. We designed this text specifically for those wishing to gather the analytical tools required to become a competent user of accounting information.

The book is suitable for self-study or as a complement to instructor-led education. It has been prepared specifically with the user in mind, from investment and sell side analysts to those working in corporate treasury and finance. Accountants working in practice or other professionals who deal with accounting information, or are interested in how it is used, will also find the text of interest. The text is based on a completely updated version of a book originally written solo by Ken in 2001 and which enjoyed a run of 5 editions. Having joined forces with Deborah for this update, our experience from the previous editions alongside our knowledge of the many recent (and upcoming!) accounting changes has allowed us to hone and focus the book to maximise its learning potential.

For context

Despite its supposed reputation as a dry subject, accounting remains a critical information set for those seeking to understand companies. In many ways it is the only representation of a company that is subject to a comprehensive independent check. This check is on the form of the annual audit, during which the financial statements are examined by an independent expert audit firm. Contrast this to other sources such as media or direct interaction with management. All of these avenues suffer from potentially undesirable levels of bias. However, when reviewing financial statements, even after an audit, it should be borne in mind that financials contain a vast amount of judgement and subjectivity. The issues are not black and white. Never has an appreciation of this seemed more important than in the current environment.

Students and practitioners alike should resist reducing accounting to a mere technical exercise. To some degree this is understandable as, to appreciate the impact of accounting, you need to master the concepts, many of which are highly technical in nature. Indeed, the objective of this text is to help with such an endeavour. Nonetheless, I want to emphasise how important it is to acknowledge the significance of accounting to society. In western economies we have chosen to measure the success or otherwise of institutions by examining profits, costs, market share, leverage, returns etc. These are all firmly based on accounting and financial statement analysis.

We *could* live in a world where performance assessment focused on taxes paid, employment generated and environmental impact. Despite an increased focus on these matters, we do not live in a world where they are the main focus. The emphasis accounting places on, say, reported earnings in turn influences corporate behaviour across the world with real consequences for people and society in general. Nobody should forget that decisions about accounting have far reaching consequences even if, at a surface level, they take on the appearance of abstract debates about technicalities.

October 2018

About the Authors

Kenneth Lee

Kenneth's career has steadfastly remained centred around finance, research and education. Kenneth is an Associate Professorial Lecturer at the London School of Economics and Political Science, where he lectures on financial analysis and equity valuation, as well as being the programme director for the MSc Accounting and Finance and MSc Accounting, Organisations and Institutions.

Before academia Kenneth was a Managing Director & Head of European Equity Research at Barclays Capital, where he worked for 8 years before leaving in August 2017 to take up a number of academic positions. Prior to this he was also a Managing Director and a ranked accounting and valuation analyst at Citi Investment Research in London. During this time Kenneth published extensively on accounting and valuation topics for investors and was ranked in the top 3 in the Institutional Investor Survey over more than a continuous 10-year period.

In the lead up to his investment banking career, Ken was a professional trainer for many years both in professional practice and financial markets. This love of training was behind his decision to leave his banking career for roles in academia and professional training.

Kenneth graduated from Trinity College Dublin/Dublin Institute of Technology with a degree in Management Science. He is a Fellow of the Institute of Chartered Accountants, a member of the Institute of Taxation, a CFA Charterholder and a member of the Securities Institute. He holds a doctorate from Aston University on how analysts make stock recommendation decisions.

He lives just outside London on a farm where, despite his best efforts, his children show no interest whatsoever in matters of accounting or finance!

Deborah Taylor

Deborah Taylor is a Director in Barclays Equity Research and is co-head of Sustainable and Thematic Investing. She joined Barclays in 2009 and for a number of years she focused on accounting and valuation research, whilst working with her co-author Kenneth, and where they were one of the top ranked teams in their sector. In recent years, Deborah has broadened her remit to include research on corporate governance issues, including corporate taxation and regulation.

Deborah is a Chartered Accountant, having qualified at Deloitte where she worked in the Financial Services audit division for 8 years. Prior to training as an accountant, she graduated from the Queen's College, Oxford University with a Master's degree in Physics.

It should be noted that the views expressed in this book are the authors' own, and do not necessarily represent or reflect those of Barclays plc.

Acknowledgements

Many people were involved in the production of this new, extensively revised edition. First, we would like to thank those analysts who gave their time to look at specialist chapters. In particular, we wish to thank Rohith Chandra-Rajan and Alan Devlin for reviewing the banks and insurance chapters respectively. Also, Nick Antill contributed much to early editions and it is telling that his 'analysis focus' boxes appear almost unedited from their original text in the first edition. Next, a huge thanks to Rob Smith of Financial Edge who has worked tirelessly on the formatting and publication mechanics, which has allowed us to focus on the content. Lastly, this revision has benefited from the help, encouragement and critical comments of hundreds of investors, analysts and students over the years. Thanks to all of you for your input.

Ken and Deborah

October, 2018

Table of Contents

Chapter 1: Basic Concepts Bootcamp

Always look for the bottom line

"A girl writes home from her boarding school to her parents. Her letter tells them that there has been a fire in her dormitory. Her parents are obviously worried by this news. But the letter goes on to say that she was rescued by the school handyman. She has forged a strong friendship with the handyman as a result. So strong in fact that she is pregnant by him and they have eloped. Her parents are aghast until they read the postscript which says: "None of the foregoing actually happened. I just failed my history GCSE and wanted you to get it in perspective." [1]

[1] Joke told by Sir David Tweedie, Chairman of the ASB. The punchline is always to 'look for the bottom line' (reported in Accounting for Growth by Terry Smith). You will notice throughout the text that many of these quotes are a few years old, but I have avoided replacing those which still resonate. This quote is a great reminder how companies might try to distract with all sorts of underlying numbers but that the bottom line is always an important input to a user's thinking.

1 Introduction to Financial Analysis

This chapter provides an initial insight into the importance of financial statements and the basic concepts that underpin them. It raises the issue of different accounting treatments across different countries. It also provides an introduction to the income statement and balance sheet as well as an insight into double entry book keeping. The subsequent chapters provide an in-depth examination of the preparation and analysis of financial statements from an analytical perspective relevant to a wide range of users in investment management, valuation and investment banking. The text has been prepared in accordance with International Financial Reporting Standards (IFRSs). These standards form the basis of preparing group accounts in the European Union. However, key international accounting differences are also addressed.

1.1 How to Use This Chapter

This chapter uses many worked examples and can itself be used as a basic accounting course (or 'bootcamp'). For those who already have a good foundation in accounting this chapter can be bypassed.

2 Purpose and Nature of Accounting

Accounts are prepared in order to provide useful information about a business to various groups including management, shareholders, employees, suppliers, banks and financial analysts. Essentially, the accounts contain a historical record of the financial transactions of a company for a specific period, usually one year. The idea is that gaining an understanding of past performance assists with the prediction of future performance.

Although the basic concept is straightforward, preparing accounts for large companies can be a very complex process. Therefore, there are regulations and principles governing how to prepare financial statements.

These can and do vary from country to country, but a typical framework would be:

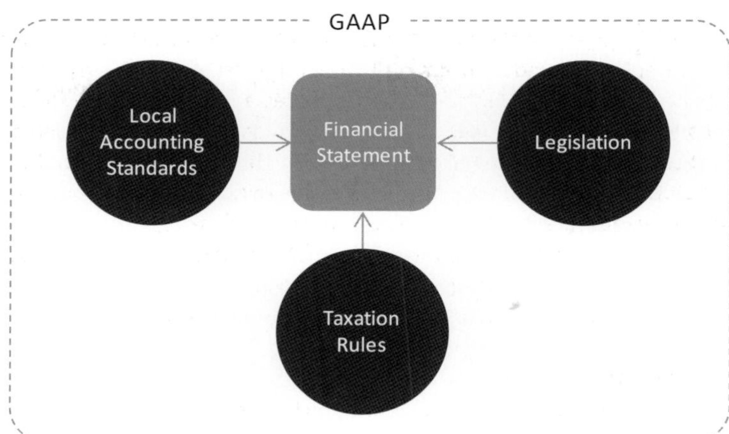

All of the rules governing financial statement preparation in a particular country are called GAAP or Generally Accepted Accounting Practice. Given that there are different rules in each country we end up with terms such as US GAAP, UK GAAP or Japanese GAAP.

This text uses International Financial Reporting Standards (IFRSs) as its basis for the examination of financial statements. These are often referred to as International GAAP.

By way of background, the International Accounting Standards Committee was established in 1973. Since its formation, the IASC has been responsible for the issuance of a large number of accounting standards. The IASC has two key objectives.

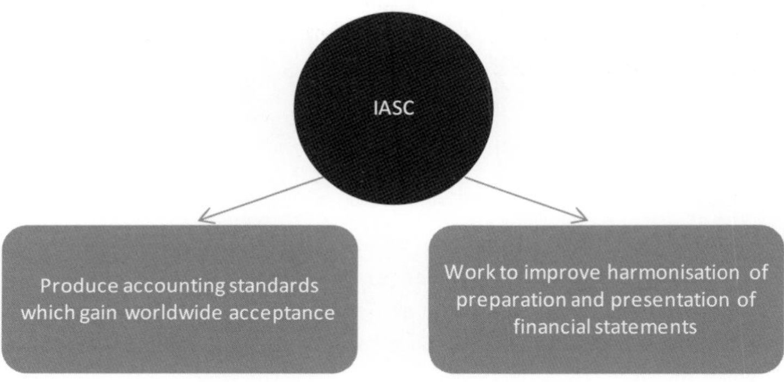

The role of the IASC has now been taken on by the International Accounting Standards Board (IASB). It is vital to recognise that international accounting differences do exist. Such differences can have a major impact on the earnings of a company. These issues are considered in detail in subsequent chapters. Most commentators are of the opinion that a single GAAP for all markets would be highly desirable.

Since 2005, the European Union (EU) has required all EU listed companies to prepare their financials under International GAAP. This means that, given the moves towards IFRS in many parts of the world (e.g. Asia Pacific region) two major GAAPs exist; US and International. In general, US GAAP standards tend to be much more specific than IFRS. The latter tend to outline general principles and leave management freedom to apply them. The argument is that, with some creative thinking, it is relatively straightforward to circumvent a detailed rule. However, attempts to get around a general principle would be much more challenging.

3 Financial Statements and Fundamental Concepts

3.1 Terminology

The terminology employed in accounting often causes difficulty. For example, accounts are more commonly known as financial statements. IAS 1 *Presentation of Financial Statements* addresses the component parts of financial statements.

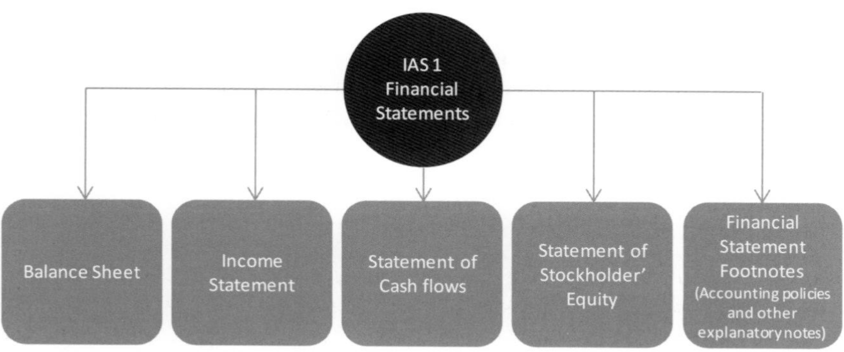

Note that we have retained the term 'balance sheet' here despite accounting standards using the much more formal 'Statement of Financial Position'. Consistent with many areas of accounting you will need to come to terms with a diverse lexicon of terms, many of which mean precisely the same thing. This is the first!

Before addressing the make-up of these different elements, it is useful to examine the fundamental accounting concepts. These underpin the calculations and rules that are included in all financial statements.

Accounting has, in essence, developed as a pragmatic art. Unlike science or mathematics, it has no accepted set of theoretical principles. Therefore, for many years accounting practice has developed in a piecemeal and fragmented fashion. However, attempts have been made to address this seemingly significant gap. From the perspective of the IASB, this resulted in the publication of a framework for the preparation and presentation of financial statements. This document gives important clues as to how the IASB will tackle various issues in the future. The framework is complex and so it is not appropriate to analyse it in depth at this juncture. However, it is useful to examine the objective of financial statements as set out in the framework.

The objective of financial statements is:

'to provide information about the financial position, performance and changes in the financial position of an enterprise that is useful to a wide range of users in making economic decisions'.

This view of accounting puts forward the decision utility paradigm, i.e. accounting information exists to help economic decision making. Also note the wide range of users that are within this definition, e.g. shareholders, analysts, employees, government bodies (including tax collection bodies). Various aspects of the framework are covered throughout the text.

3.2 Fundamental Concepts

Although the framework document sets out various complex issues as underlying concepts, there are certain concepts that are enshrined in accounting. The following are the key internationally recognised concepts used in the preparation of financial statements:

Conservatism

Essentially this means prudence i.e. when preparing financial statements it is acceptable to anticipate losses but gains should, in general, not be recognised until they are reasonably certain to occur. The application of this concept encourages the recognition of a lower profit figure.

For example, a publishing house signs a new innovative band to its record label for $3m. A prudent or conservative approach to accounting for this might require the entire $3m to be recognised as a cost. This concept is considered in more detail at the end of the chapter. It should be noted that the framework document places less emphasis on this principle than previous standards.

Accruals

Expenses are included in the income statement in the period to which they relate. This may or may not be the period in which such expenses are paid in cash. Another way of thinking about this is to imagine that we are trying to link or match sales with all the costs of making these sales. This concept attempts to calculate a 'fair' profit figure.

For example, the phone bill for the last quarter of a specific accounting period may not have been paid by the cut-off date (i.e. end of the accounting year). The accruals concept would still require this cost to be estimated and included in the financial statements for the year just finished as it relates to this period.

Going Concern

When drawing up financial statements we assume that the business will continue in operational existence for the foreseeable future. Historic cost is therefore the accepted accounting convention for recording transactions in financial statements. Where going concern is in doubt, the balance sheet of an entity is prepared on a "break up" basis instead. For example, assets are reflected at their realisable value rather than cost.

Consistency

Similar items should be treated in a similar manner from year to year. This aids comparability of the performance of the entity. Any changes in the methods used to prepare financial statements should be disclosed (see Chapter 2).

Separate Entity

When preparing the accounts of a business, the business is treated separately from the owners. This means that it will exclude the personal assets and personal transactions of the owners. Thus, if a company was set up with €100,000 cash then this would be reflected as:

Assets	€	Liabilities	€
Cash	100,000	Owed to owners	100,000

4 Structure

A balance sheet (also known as 'The Statement of Financial Position') is simply a list of the assets and liabilities of a business at a point in time. Formal definitions of assets and liabilities are included below. The objective of a balance sheet is to show the resources available to a corporate's management and how such resources are funded. This can be illustrated as follows:

Given that there are two main sources of funding, debt (loans) and equity (shares), we can add these to the diagram:

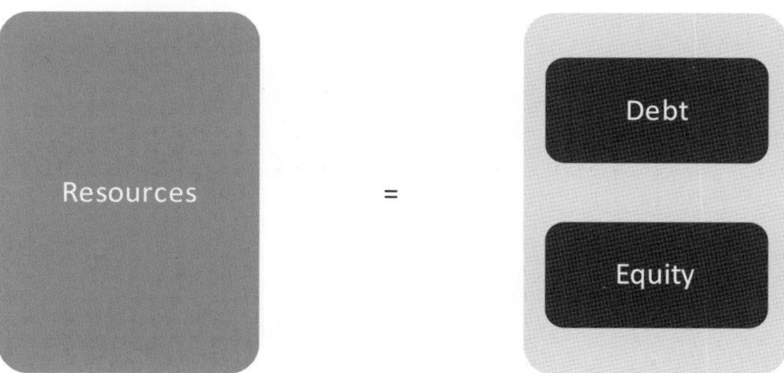

Furthermore, certain resources (e.g. inventory) may effectively be funded by suppliers as they have not yet been paid. We would call these particular liabilities trade payables. However, let us simply refer to these as liabilities for the moment.

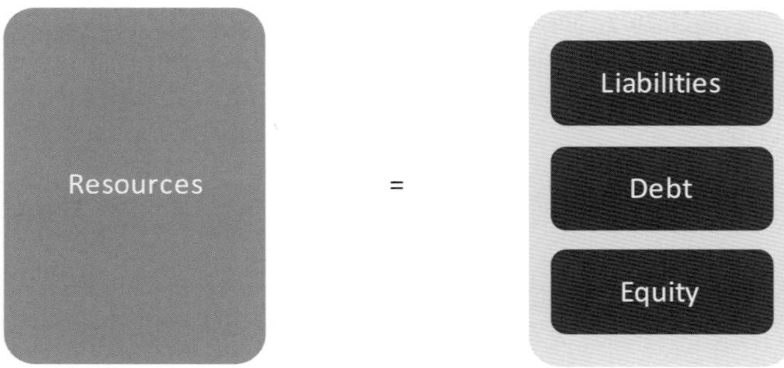

Resources can then be broken up into current (e.g. inventory) and longer term non-current (e.g. plant, see later). This leads us to the complete diagram:

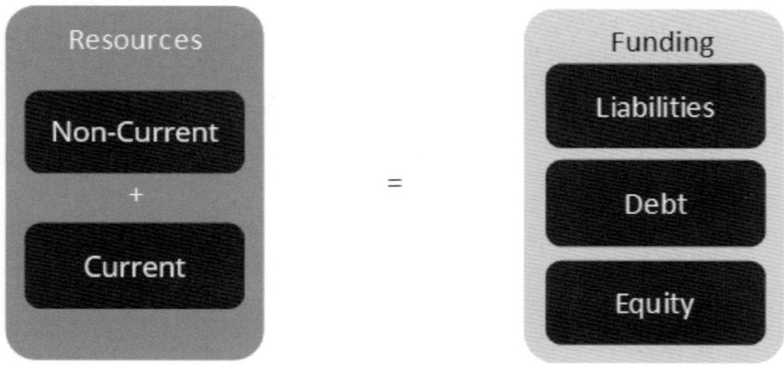

Alternatively, in equation form:

		Resources	=	Funding
Non-current assets	+	Current assets	=	Liabilities + Debt + Equity

This latter expression is called the accounting equation. It can take various forms which are considered in more detail on the following page.

A typical balance sheet under IFRS is simply a more formal representation of these diagrams and the accounting equation. A typical example might be presented as follows:

ABLE S.A. Balance Sheet as at 31 December Year 2

	Year 2	Year 1
Assets	**€'000**	**€'000**
Current Assets		
Inventory	20,000	10,000
Accounts receivable	40,000	40,000
Investments	2,000	500
Cash	12,000	13,000
Total Current Assets	**74,000**	**63,500**
Non-Current Assets		
Intangible	100,000	105,000
Tangible	500,000	400,000
Investments	50,000	40,000
Total Assets	**724,000**	**608,500**
Liabilities and Stockholders' Equity		
Current Liabilities		
Accounts payable	28,000	41,000
Non-current Liabilities		
Long-term debt	181,992	94,500
Non-controlling interests	20,000	18,000
Stockholders' Equity		
Called up common stock (€1 par value)	200,000	200,000
Additional paid in capital	100,000	100,000
Retained earnings	194,008	155,000
Total Financing	**724,000**	**608,500**

Note that the top of the balance sheet illustrates the resources available while the lower part relates to the funding. The statement is prepared on a specific date, in this case 31 December Year 2. As we shall see this is different from income statements and cashflow statements which are prepared for periods of time rather than a specific date.

We shall address each section of the balance sheet briefly in the next section of the chapter.

5 Assets

5.1 Definition and Classification

IAS 1 defines assets as:

> *"Probable future economic benefits obtained or controlled by a particular entity as a result of past transactions or events."*

The balance sheet starts with assets which can be subdivided as follows:

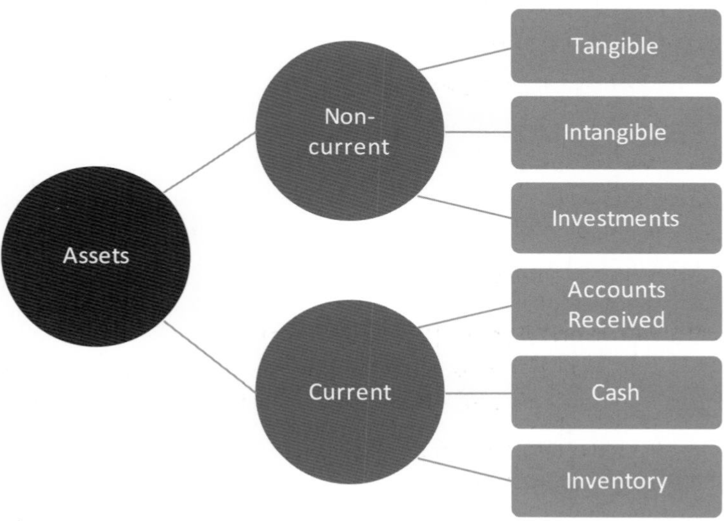

Exercise: Asset Classification

Indicate which category of assets the following would be recorded in:

		Current Assets (✓)	Non-Current (✓)	Not an Asset (✓)
1	Machinery	☐	☐	☐
2	Telephone bills	☐	☐	☐
3	Vehicles	☐	☐	☐
4	Patents	☐	☐	☐
5	Non-purchased goodwill	☐	☐	☐
6	Debtors (Accounts receivable)	☐	☐	☐
7	Creditors (Accounts payable)	☐	☐	☐
8	Closing stock	☐	☐	☐
9	Equipment	☐	☐	☐
10	Computers	☐	☐	☐

The solution to this exercise can be found on page 435.

5.2 Non-Current Assets (Fixed Assets)

These are assets acquired for use on a continuing basis. Such assets are often called fixed assets. As the diagram above shows they are split into three categories:

- Tangible: assets with a physical presence such as buildings, vehicles, plant and equipment, and computers.
- Intangible: assets with no physical presence such as brands, goodwill, patents, research and development, and trademarks.
- Investments: investments bought with the intention of holding for a long period.

Generally, assets are only recognised if purchased. This is especially important with intangibles. This means that many key assets are not recognised on the balance sheet. For example, in most businesses people are not explicitly purchased (note, sports such as football would be notable exceptions to this example!).

Whilst investments are generally held at market value, other fixed assets must be recorded at cost and then depreciated (tangible) or amortised (intangible) over their useful economic life. This means that as the asset is used up, a portion of its cost is written off as an expense in the income statement (referred to as the depreciation charge or expense) with a corresponding reduction in the asset's value. Therefore, in the balance sheet such assets are stated as:

	€
Cost	X
Less cumulative depreciation or amortisation	(X)
Book value	X

Note: land is not normally depreciated.

We shall explore these concepts in detail in later chapters.

5.3 Current Assets

These are assets which are not acquired with the intention of using them on a continuing basis. Typically one would expect them to be converted into cash within an operating cycle, typically assumed to be one year.

The key examples are:

- Inventory: effectively goods purchased for resale that remain in the warehouse at the balance sheet date.
- Accounts receivable: represents the amount customers, who have bought goods on credit, owe at the balance sheet date.
- Investments: any investments not intended to be held for the long term.
- Cash

Note that current assets are normally valued at cost. However, if market conditions change then cost may exceed the monies that these assets could generate in the future (referred to as net realisable value). Conservatism would require a write-down to this lower figure. Therefore, the overall valuation rule is:

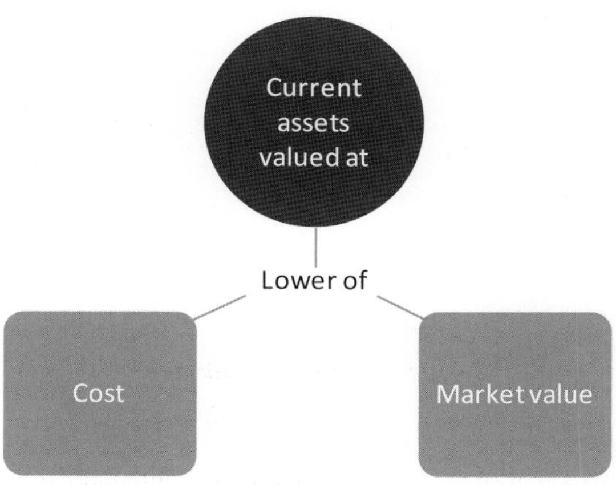

6 Liabilities

IAS 1 defines these as:

> *"Probable future sacrifices of economic benefits arising from present obligations of a particular entity to transfer assets or provide services to other entities in the future as a result of past transactions or events."*

Essentially, at its most basic level a liability depends on future cash outflow. Examples include, accounts payable, taxation and loans (debt finance). Typically, liabilities are classified as current and non-current. Chapter 4 addresses this area in detail.

7 Statement of Stockholders' Equity

This part of the balance sheet lists the ownership interest in order of preference upon liquidation. In other words, it explains who owns the business and these items are listed according to the order in which they would be paid back on the dissolution of a company.

IAS 1 defines equity as:

> *"The residual interest in the net assets of an entity that remains after deducting its liabilities. In a business enterprise, the equity is the ownership interest."*

Equity essentially consists of:

Called up capital + Reserves

7.1 Called Up Capital

This consists of two major types of stock; common and preferred. The key differences are as follows:

Issue	Common Stock	Preferred Stock
Who gets priority repayment in a liquidation?	Subordinated to preferred stock	Paid in preference to common stock
Dividend priority	Paid after preference dividend	Paid in preference to common stock
Can the shares be converted into common stock?	N/A	Potentially
Can the shares be repurchased (redeemable)?	May be repurchased	May be repurchased/ redeemed

You should note the following terminology.

- **Authorised share capital** – the maximum number of shares a company can issue.
- **Issued or called up share capital** – the actual number of shares in issue.

The terminology in this area can be confusing so note the following:

- Common stock is the same as ordinary share capital
- Preferred stock is the same as preference shares
- Additional paid in capital is the same a share premium

Example

X Inc. issues 250,000 units of common stock (par value €1) at €1. Par value is also known as nominal or face value. It has little or no analytical importance.

Here, we can see that X is issuing stock at par. Therefore, the called up common stock will rise by €250,000.

Additional Paid in Capital

It is far more normal for a company to issue common stock at a premium. The premium represents the excess of the issue price over the nominal value or par.

Example

Y Inc. issues 200,000 units of common stock (par value €1) at €1.50.

Here, called up common stock would increase by €200,000 and additional paid in capital (also known as share premium) would increase by €100,000 (i.e. 200,000 × €0.50).

7.2 Reserves

These can be thought of as undistributed gains of a company.

The major reserve for almost all profitable companies is retained earnings. This figure represents the total accumulated profits of the company that have been retained rather than distributed to shareholders as dividends. In order to decide if dividend payments can be made, reference is made to the balance of the retained earnings reserve **not** just the retained earnings for the year as disclosed in the income statement. Additional paid in capital, or share premium, is also technically a reserve, although normally it cannot be used to pay dividends.

8 The Balance Sheet and the Accounting Equation

Now that we have looked at the major elements of balance sheets it is worthwhile to return to a core aspect of financial statements – the accounting equation.

The basic form of the accounting equation (replacing resources in our previous example with assets) is:

Assets = Liabilities + Capital

PTW Inc

Assets	**€**	**Liabilities and Stockholders' Equity**	**€**
Cash	4,000	Common stock	4,000
	4,000		4,000

This can be viewed as a simple balance sheet as follows:

The above balance sheet might be for a company that has raised €4,000 by issuing some common stock. Notice two things:

- The balance sheet balances
- The accounting equation holds, i.e.

Assets = Capital + Liabilities

€4,000 = €4,000 + 0

In other words:

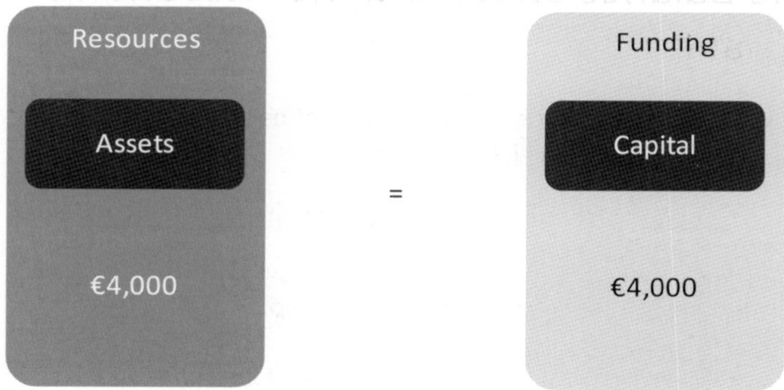

Example

If PTW undertook the following transactions the balance sheet assets and liabilities would change as follows:

Transaction 1 Borrow €1,000

↑ Loans €1,000 ↑ Cash €1,000

Transaction 2 Buy inventory at a cost of €500 paid for in cash

↑ Inventory/purchases €500 ↓ Cash €500

Transaction 3 Sell inventory which had cost €400 for €400. All sales made on credit

↓ Inventory €400 ↑ Accounts receivable €400

Transaction 4 Received €200 from customers owing money to the company

↓ Accounts receivable €200 ↑ Cash €200

Transaction 5 Bought more inventory for €500 on credit

↑ Inventory/purchase €500 ↑ Accounts payable €500

Note

When choosing the entries, remember that the balance sheet must still balance after the transaction!

The balance sheet after these transactions would look as follows:

PTW Balance Sheet

Assets	€	Liabilities and Equity	€
Cash (4 + 1 − .5 + .2)	4,700	Loans	1,000
Inventory (.5 − .4 + .5)	600	Accounts payable	500
Accounts receivable (.4 − .2)	200	Common stock	4,000
	5,500		5,500

Exercise: Building Balance Sheets

City and Co. deposits €20,000 in a bank account on 1 March in order to commence business. Let us assume that the cash is supplied by the owner (€6,000) and an outside party (€14,000).

a) Draw up a balance sheet on 1 March.

We can see from the balance sheet that the total claims are the same as the total assets.

Assets	€	Liabilities and Equity	€
Cash at bank	20,000	Capital	6,000
		Liability – loan	14,000
	20,000		20,000

Thus:

Assets = Capital + Liabilities

b) Consider some further possible transactions for City and Co. Assume that, after the €20,000 had been deposited in the bank, the following transactions took place:

2 March	Purchased a motor van for €5,000 paying by cheque.
3 March	Purchased stock-in-trade (or inventory) on one month's credit for €3,000.
4 March	Repaid €2,000 of the loan from outside party.
6 March	Owner introduced €4,000 into the business bank account.

Draw up a balance sheet after each day in which transactions have taken place. Check the answer in appendix 1.

c) Let us assume that, on 7 March, the business managed to sell all of the stock for €5,000 and received a cheque immediately from the customer for this amount. Draw up the balance sheet on 7 March, after this transaction has taken place. Again, check appendix 1 for the answer.

The solution to this exercise can be found on page 436.

The Income Statement

9 Elements of the Income Statement

In the example above, the sale on 7 March was made at a profit. Essentially what happened was that:

Inventory decreased by	€3,000
Cash increased by	€5,000
Retained earnings increased by	€2,000

Therefore, the profit made has increased assets by €2,000 and this is reflected as retained earnings on the balance sheet. In reality, analysts need far more information on the revenues and costs of a business than one line in the balance sheet. Therefore, a separate statement is used to reflect this information.

This statement captures the financial performance of the enterprise. It explains the changes in the assets, liabilities and equity of a business (e.g. in the above example the increase in equity of €2,000). For many years, it is the income statement that has interested investors, creditors and analysts, mainly because it is used to predict future performance and earnings. The financial press and media are very much focused on earnings as a measure of financial performance.

The key elements of an income statement include:

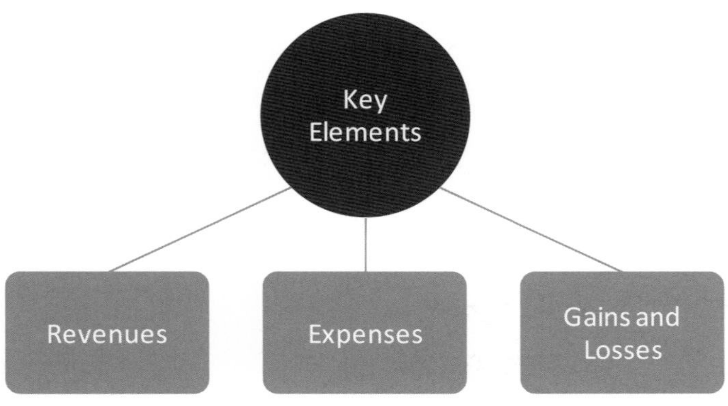

IFRS does prescribe the key headings to be disclosed on the face of the income statement, but it does not prescribe a specific format. Users will see different presentations at both a national and international level. There are various elements to income statements:

Item	Comments
Revenue or Turnover	The sales figure for a particular period. There are specific rules about when revenue should be recognised. These are covered in chapter 2.
Operating Profit	The income earned from the core activities of the business. It is independent of capital structure.
Unusual or Infrequent Items	Analysts are concerned with ongoing profits from ordinary activities and less with abnormal earnings. Therefore, how such items are disclosed is important.
Income Tax Expense	This expense is outside the control of management and hence is disclosed separately.
Net Income	The net earnings figure after all expenses but before dividends.

A typical income statement might look as follows:

ABLE S.A. Income Statement for the Year Ended 31 December Year 2

	€'000	€'000
Revenues		100
Cost of Goods Sold		(50)
Gross Profit		50
Expenses:		
Selling	(5)	
General	(3)	
Administrative	(2)	
Other expenses:		
Amortisation	(6)	
Miscellaneous	(3)	
Unusual items (sale of fixed assets)	(5)	
Infrequent items (restructuring)	(5)	(29)
Operating profit		21
Interest	(1)	
Profit before tax	20	
Taxes		(10)
Income from Continuing Operations		10
Other items (e.g. discontinued segment)		(3)
Net Income		7

The income statement is described as 'for the year ended year 2'. This is in contrast to the balance sheet which is described 'as at' a particular date. The income statement is a flow statement as it reflects activities that have flowed through a period. At the end of the period everything is reset to zero for the start of the next period. In contrast the balance sheet is a cumulative statement.

Linkages

The income statement and the balance sheet are explicitly linked. The accumulated retained earnings is shown in the balance sheet as retained earnings (sometimes called the profit and loss account reserve). Retained earnings, as you have already seen, is a reserve and is shown in the funding part of the balance sheet. So, the income statement shows the annual increase (or decrease if a retained loss) in retained earnings. The balance sheet shows the cumulative position.

Example

Build up the accounting equation for XYZ plc as it does the following transactions:

1. XYZ issues one hundred €1 ordinary shares for cash at a price of €2 each.
2. XYZ borrows €200 from a bank all repayable after 5 years.
3. XYZ buys €400 worth of flowers ready to sell on to customers.
4. XYZ sells all these flowers for €800 cash.
5. XYZ buys and resells another stock of flowers for €2000 cash at the same mark up on cost.

Continuing the theme of interchanging technical terms that have the same meaning here we use 'Fixed Assets' in place of 'Non-Current Assets' and Long-term liabilities instead of 'Non-Current Liabilities'. In addition, we have rearranged the accounting equation. In its original form in paragraph 4, it was shown as:

Fixed Assets (FA) + Current Assets (CA) = Current Liabilities (CL) + Long Term Liabilities (LTL) + Share Capital (SC) + Reserves

Rearranging this equation is something you will have to do and should understand. For example, we will use the following form:

FA	+ CA	− CL	− LTL	=	SC		+Reserves		
1.	+€200	cash		=	€100	SC	+€100	Share premium	
2.	+€200	cash	−€200	=	€100		+€100		
	€400		−€200	=	€100		+€100		
3.	−€400	cash							
	+€400	stock							
	400		−200	=	100		+100		
4.	−€400	stock						+400	profit
	+€800	cash							
	+800		−200	=	100		+100	400	
5.	−1000	cash							
	+2000	cash						+1000	profit
	1800		−200	=	100		+100	+1400	

This exercise should help bring the various issues together.

Exercise: Impress Inc.

Impress Inc. deposits €40,000 in a bank account on 1 September as seed capital for a business. The cash is invested by the owner (€12,000) and a bank (€28,000).

a) Draw up a balance sheet on 1 September.

b) The following further transactions occurred during September.

2 September	Purchased a van for €10,000 paying by cheque
7 September	Purchased stock on credit for €6,000
14 September	Repaid €4,000 of the loan from the bank
26 September	Owner invested an extra €8,000 into the business

Draw up a balance sheet after each day in which transactions have taken place.

c) On 27 September, the business sold all of the stock for €10,000 and received a cheque immediately from the customer. Draw up the new balance sheet on 27 September.

The solution to this exercise can be found on page 438.

Cash Flow Statements

10 Purpose and Content

Financial statements are prepared in accordance with the accruals concept. An alternative might be to reflect cash transactions. However, if cash inflows and outflows were used results could be distorted purely due to the timing of a receipt or payment. Instead, financial statements apply the accruals concept and so reflect transactions when earned or incurred in a period. This means that a more consistent presentation of earnings is given. However, it should be noted that profitability does not necessarily mean liquidity. For this reason, companies are also required to prepare a cash flow statement.

These statements provide cash-based information regarding operations and are of importance because they are used to assess an enterprise's ability to generate and meet future cash flows (loan repayments, dividends).

It is a useful statement given that it provides information about an entity's ability to generate cash as well as its ability to meet cash outflows.

The statement is considered in more detail in Chapter 5, but a typical statement might look as follows:

Cash Flow Statement of PTW Inc. for Year Ended 31 December Year 1

	€'000	€'000
Net cash flows from operating activities		200
Cash flows from investing activities		
Purchase of property plant and equipment	150	
Sales of equipment	(25)	
Net cash used in investing activities		(125)
Cash flows from financing activities		
Proceeds from issuance of share capital	250	
Repayment of long term debt	(70)	
Net cash provided by financing activities		180
Net increase in cash and cash equivalents		255
Cash and cash equivalents at beginning of the year		73
Cash and cash equivalents at the end of the year		328

Essentially, the cash flow statement attempts to explain the movement in cash and cash equivalents (assets readily convertible into cash) between the current and prior accounting periods. It categorises the cash flow into three key areas:

- Operating activities
- Investing activities
- Financing activities

Other Components of Financial Statements

11 Statement of Stockholders' Equity

We have already seen that most gains and losses go through the income statement and are therefore apparent to investors and users. However, certain gains and losses bypass the income statement. These tend to be the more obscure items. In order to clearly show these items (and changes in related captions), there is a separate working of opening and closing equity.

12 Footnotes

The balance sheet, income statement and statement of cash flows are all highly summarised statements. For any business of even moderate complexity these numbers need to be disaggregated to provide the analyst with useful information. These disaggregations happen in the various notes or, as they are often referred to, footnotes in the financial statements. You almost always need to examine such notes if undertaking detailed analysis.

Recording Transactions

13 Dual Effect and Double Entry

So far, we have considered the key components of financial statements and addressed some of the mechanics of the numbers themselves. Transactions are reflected in the financial statements using the system of double entry which recognises that a transaction has a dual effect. We have, in effect, seen this with the various increase/decrease examples. The formal double entry system is recorded in terms of debits and credits. For each transaction there is both a debit and credit entry in the accounting records. This is the one area of international consensus. The real issues are which account do we debit/credit and by how much?

Analysis Focus

The Mysteries of Double Entry

Accountants are very concerned with double entry. For analysis and valuation an appreciation of the dual effect of a transaction is important but the application of double entry rules is unlikely to be essential. However, it may be useful for impressing the accountants working on a deal!

13.1 A Systematic Approach to Identifying Double Entries

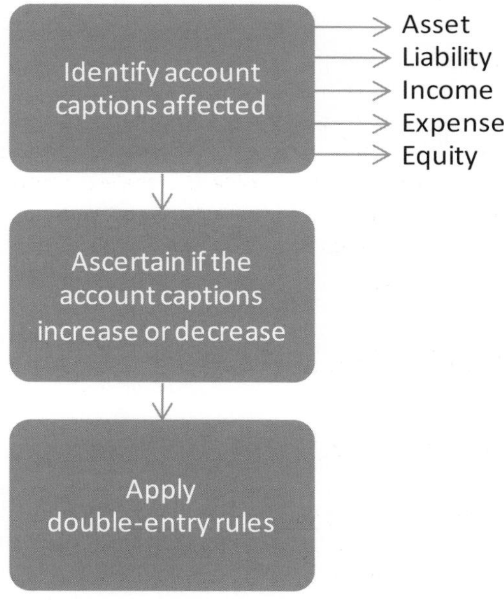

13.2 Double-Entry Rules

These can be summarised as follows:

Item	Increase	Decrease
Asset	Debit	Credit
Liability	Credit	Debit
Revenue Item	Credit	Debit
Expense Item	Debit	Credit

In reality, this is simply terminology. A debit of itself means nothing. It is just the accounting term used for *inter alia* an increase in an asset.

13.3 Double-Entry Exercises

What are the appropriate double entries for the following transactions?

- Issue of shares for cash

  Debit **Cash**
  Credit Common stock

- Raising debt

  Debit **Cash**
  Credit **Loans**

- Capital expenditure

  Debit Long-lived assets
  Credit **Cash**

- Purchases (cash & credit)

  Debit Purchases
  Credit Cash/accounts payable

- Sales (cash & credit)

  Debit Cash/accounts receivable
  Credit **Sales**

- Paying for overheads

  Debit Expenses
  Credit **Cash**

13.4 Example

A business begins operations on 1 January. Identify the double entries for each of the following transactions that occur during the month of January, and the overall effect on profit and cash balances of these transactions. You should assume that all transactions for 'cash' go via the bank account. Cover the columns to assess your performance.

		Debit	Credit	Impact on Net Income	Impact on Cash Balance
1	The payment of cash wages for January of €3,000	Wages	Cash	↓ €3,000	↓ €3,000
2	Issue of a sales invoice for €15,000	Accounts receivable (debtors)	Sales	↑ €15,000	–
3	Receipt of cash from debtors of €12,000	Cash	Accounts receivable	–	↑ €12,000
4	Receipt of cash from cash sales of €2,000	Cash	Sales	↑ €2,000	↑ €2,000
5	Purchase of stock items for €14,000 on credit	Purchases	Accounts payable	↓ €14,000	–
6	Payment to creditors of €10,000	Accounts payable	Cash	–	↓ €10,000
7	Payment of rent of €500 by debit transfer	Rent expense	Cash	↓ €500	↓ €500
8	Purchase of a car for €18,000 for cash	Vehicles	Cash	–	↓ €18,000
9	Receipt of an invoice for electricity of €300	Electricity	Accounts payable	↓ €300	–

Adjustments at the end of an accounting period to recognise that:

10	€100 of insurance costs already paid but relate to next financial year	Prepaid expenses	Insurance	↑ €100	–
11	€1,000 of debtors are probably uncollectable	Bad debt expense	Accounts receivable	↓ €1,000	–
12	Depreciation of €300	Depreciation expense	Accumulated depreciation	↓ €300	–

Points to Note

- The entries for transactions 4 and 5 might prove confusing. Essentially when a sale is made, it goes straight into profit. The cost of purchases also ends up hitting profit. At the end of the accounting period, an adjustment is made to ensure that only the cost of those items actually sold goes through the income statement.
- Transaction 10 is an example of applying the accruals or matching concept. The insurance expense, whilst paid during the current accounting period, relates to the next one. The expense is therefore transferred to prepayments where it is shown as an asset on the balance sheet. It will then be released in the next accounting year to the income statement and matched against the revenue it has generated.
- Transaction 11 is an example of applying the concept of conservatism. Accounts receivable (or debtors as they are sometimes known) represent an asset and as a result should be indicative of future benefit (i.e. cash inflow). If the asset is doubtful, then it should be written off.
- Transaction 12 is also an example of the matching concept. The car will benefit more than one accounting period and so its cost should be spread over the accounting periods that will benefit. This cost is referred to as depreciation (see Chapter 3).

Note that these issues are considered in more detail in later chapters.

14 Understanding Accounting Numbers and Linkages

Two issues tend to cause significant difficulties for those analysing financial statements: first is the concept of accruals or matching, second is the linkages that exist between the various statements. These are considered below.

14.1 Understanding Accruals

As mentioned earlier, the accruals at matching concept means that costs and revenues are matched in the periods to which they relate. So, for example, the rent for the year 1 accounting period would relate to year 1 and so should be included in operating costs irrespective of whether it has been paid in cash or not. In practice, expenses are recorded as paid, i.e.

Then, at the period end (cut-off point), the accountant will apply the matching concept by identifying accruals (expenses enjoyed but not yet paid) and prepayments (expenses paid but not yet enjoyed). Adjusting entries will then be made.

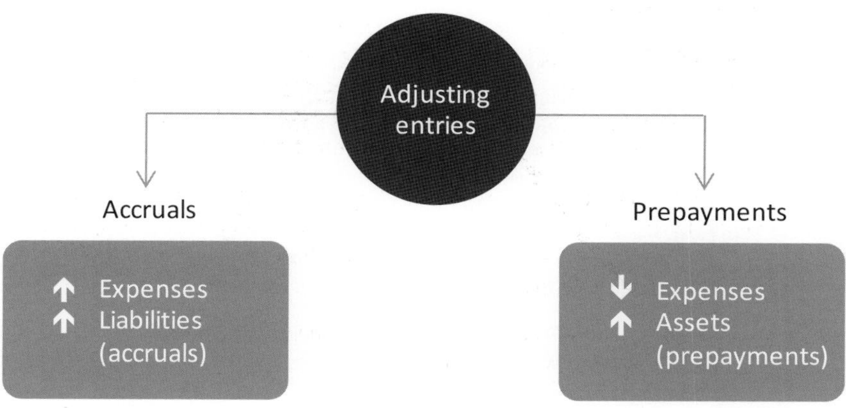

These entries are then reversed out at the start of the next period and (for example) the rent paid is recorded as normal.

Employing the matching or accruals concept means that profits rarely equal cash. Although there are a multitude of reasons for this the matching concept is a crucial differentiating factor. The following example illustrates this point.

Exercise: Professional Services Inc.

Consider the following information for Professional Services Inc.

General information

Sell Lots, a major client, called Murtin Humbug, a senior employee of Professional Services Inc. Sell Lots want to secure the services of Professional Services Inc. for a project. The work will be done in the first six months of the year. Sell Lots are willing to pay €240,000 for the work and are happy to be invoiced monthly a month in arrears. For example, the January work will be paid for in February. Murtin, a closet accountant, estimates that the costs of providing the services will be €60,000 wages and €120,000 overhead. This will accrue evenly over the six months of the project.

Key issues

1. What is the overall profit on this transaction?
2. What is the net cash inflow by the end of the contract?

Use the following schedules to support your calculations:

3. Prepare a schedule showing the monthly net profit on this transaction for the six months (see page 35).
4. Murtin knows that the overheads and wages are paid promptly during each month. Assuming these are spread evenly over the six months prepare a schedule of the cash outflows each month (see page 36).
5. Prepare a schedule of the cash inflows from Sell Lots Limited assuming timely invoicing and payment (see page 36).
6. Combine the results of 5 & 6 above to prepare a schedule of the net cash flow each month (see page 36).
7. Compare the cash flows and profit numbers – what do you notice? What does the cash flow statement tell you about the financing requirements of Professional Services Inc.?

The solution to this exercise can be found on page 439.

Professional Services Inc.

Monthly Net Profit

	January €	February €	March €	April €	May €	June €	July €	August €	Total €
Sales									
Costs:									
Wages									
Overheads									
Profit									

Professional Services Inc.

Cash Flows

	January €	February €	March €	April €	May €	June €	July €	August €	Total €
Cash in flows									
Cash out flows									
Wages									
Overheads									
Net cash flows									

15 Linkages

A source of enduring confusion is the various linkages that exist between different financial statements and within different numbers of the same statement. As mentioned in the foreword, throughout the text such linkages are illustrated by the link graphic.

However, it is useful to outline some basic aspects of linkage before continuing to more specific linkages in the rest of the text. Some crucial linkages can be illustrated as follows:

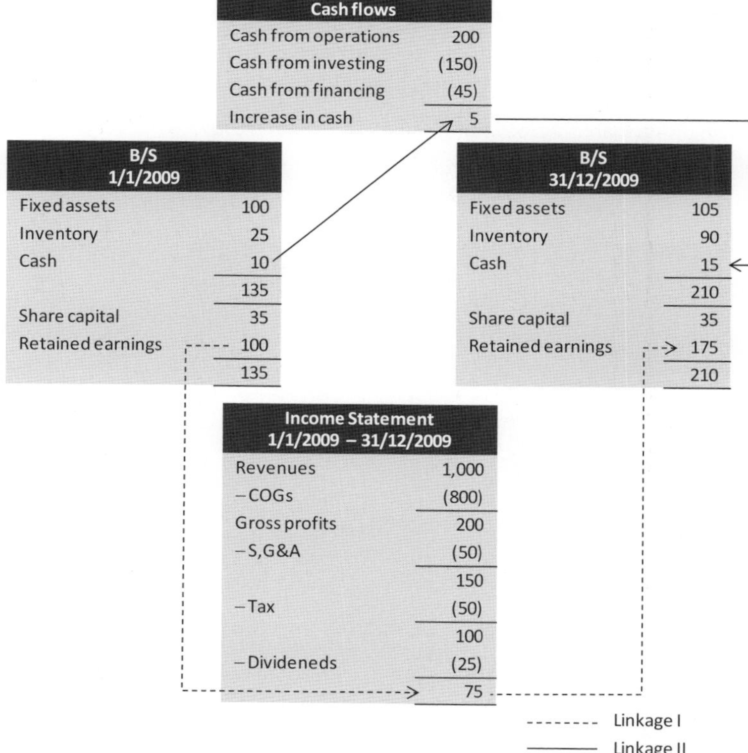

* Dividends are included in this 'mock' income statement for illustration only, as it allows us to see the retained earnings more clearly. In a real set of financial statements you would need to go to other statements and notes to gather this information.

15.1 Linkage I – Balance Sheet Income Statement

The retained earnings from the Income Statement flow through to the retained earnings line in the balance sheet. Therefore, the income statement describes (part of) the change in the balance sheet. An interesting observation to make is that the only way to increase the size of a balance sheet (in net asset terms) is to:

1. Earn and retain profits, and/or
2. Issue share capital

Note borrowing monies has no impact on net assets, (assets increase but so do liabilities).

15.2 Linkage II – Balance Sheet Cash and Cash Flow Statement

If we ignore cash equivalents (see Chapter 5), then the purpose of the cash flow statement is merely to explain the increase or decrease in the cash balance figure. Cash flows, as well as income statement numbers, change balance sheet figures.

(e.g. paying off a loan naturally reduces balance sheet debt).

15.3 General Model of Linkages

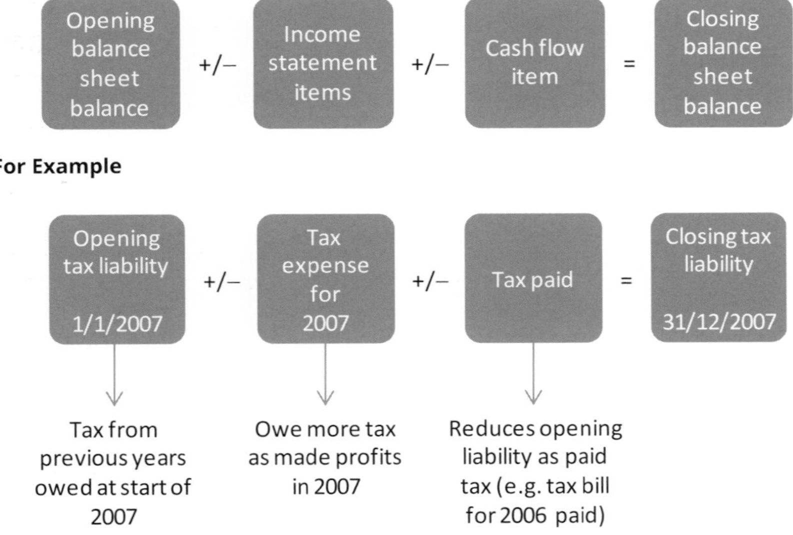

Exercise: IFS Company

Below is presented a balance sheet at start of Year 1, a profit and loss account for Year 1, a statement of cash receipts and expenditure for Year 1 and a balance sheet at end of Year 1, for IFS Company.

Calculate the amounts for each of the missing items labelled **(a)** to **(n)**. The amounts **(NR)** are not required.

Balance Sheet START Year 1

	Assets	**Liabilities & Shareholders' Equity**
	€'s 000	**€'s 000**
Fixed asset	600	
Cumulative depreciation		(250)
Stocks	300	
Debtors	200	
Cash	50	
Accounts payable		(180)
Wages payable		(30)
Taxes payable		(20)
Loans		(200)
Retained earnings		(345)
Share capital		**(a)**
Total assets	**(b)**	**(c)**

Income Statement for Year 1	€'s 000
Sales	2000
Cost of goods sold	**(d)**
Gross profit	**(e)**
Wages	(400)
Depreciation	**(f)**
EBIT	(NR)
Interest	(10)
Tax	(35)
Net income	(NR)
Dividend	(15)
Retained earnings	(NR)

Statement of Cash Receipts and Expenditure	
Collections from customers	1700
Purchases	(1300)
Wages	**(g)**
Tax	(40)
Interest	(10)
New Building	(100)
Loan repayment	(120)
Dividend	(15)
Shares issued	400
Increase in cash	**(h)**

Balance Sheet END Year 1

	Assets	Liabilities & Shareholders' Equity
	€'s 000	**€'s 000**
Fixed asset	**(i)**	
Cumulative depreciation		(300)
Stocks	400	
Debtors	**(j)**	
Cash	**(k)**	
Accounts payable		(220)
Wages payable		(40)
Taxes payable		(15)
Loans		(80)
Retained earnings		(595)
Share capital		**(l)**
Total Assets	**(m)**	**(n)**

(Reproduced with the kind permission of the Securities Institute.)

The solution to this exercise can be found on page 442.

Final Exercise

This chapter covered a wide range of fundamental issues of concern to analysts examining financial statements. A significant part of many analysts' time is spent using, forecasting and reading annual reports.

Throughout the text we shall refer to the recent (2017) financials statements at Lufthansa. The following exercise uses these real statements. Please access the report online, just type the following into your browser's address bar to download the PDF:

bit.ly/lufthansa2017

15.4 Accounts Commentary

Basic Concepts – Income Statement Test

1. Why is turnover (i.e. revenue) broken down into traffic and other?
2. Distinguish operating profit from gross profit.
3. How might you measure whether the 'Cost of materials and services' costs are 'out of control'?
4. What would interest normally arise on? Why is it referred to as net interest?
5. Why is the tax figure negative?
6. Why is depreciation and amortisation included in operating expenses?
7. What is EPS?

Basic Concepts – Balance Sheet Test

(i) Distinguish between tangible and intangible fixed assets?

(ii) Would aircraft be classified as fixed or current assets?

(iii) What are provisions? Where are they disclosed in these financials?

(iv) Distinguish between issued share capital and capital reserve.

(v) Identify the numbers for: -Net assets -Total assets -Equity

- Net assets
- Total assets
- Equity

The solution to this exercise can be found on page 444.

Chapter 2: The Income Statement

The Deadly EBITDA Virus

"In assessing a business, the starting point should be the bottom line, and every move away from that should be viewed with suspicion. Valuations based on EBITDA reflect only part of a business's financial performance and can only be right by coincidence" [2]

[2] Brian Singleton-Green Accountancy Magazine, 2001. This is an older quote but the sentiment remains important even if the language is a little dramatic. Looking at measures such as EBITDA is fine so long as the costs reversed out are not forgotten.

1 Introduction

This chapter provides insight into the structure and nature of the income statement. It examines the issues of revenue and cost recognition, classification of ordinary and unusual items. In addition, it focuses on the calculation of Earnings before Interest, Tax, Depreciation and Amortisation (EBITDA) and the crucial issue of earnings management. Advanced issues are also addressed including the accounting treatment of share options, employee share schemes and pension costs.

2 The Income Statement

As mentioned in Chapter 1, the income statement is a key element of an enterprise's financial statements. It provides the analyst with information on the financial performance of a company over a specified period of time.

Although most users are familiar with the general concept of profit, the concept of income in accounting terms must be clarified before we can proceed further. The net asset position of an enterprise will change year on year and so too the book value of stockholders' equity. Assuming the movement is upwards, then it is referred to as income. Therefore, income can be conceptualised and defined in terms of a change in the balance sheet.

The more formal IFRS definition of income is as follows:

> *"Increases in economic benefits during the accounting period in the form of inflows or enhancements of assets or decreases of liabilities that result in increases in equity, other than those relating to contributions from equity participants. The definition of income encompasses both revenues and gains."*
>
> *(Source: IASB)*

The income statement is a calculation of the retained earnings for a particular period. It should not always be considered to be a comprehensive statement of all sources of income during the accounting period, although it is typically used as such.

Although an historic statement, it is widely acknowledged that understanding an enterprise's past performance can assist with the prediction of future performance.

3 Elements of an Income Statement

3.1 Overview

At its most basic level, the income statement is a calculation of revenue minus expenses for the accounting period as illustrated below.

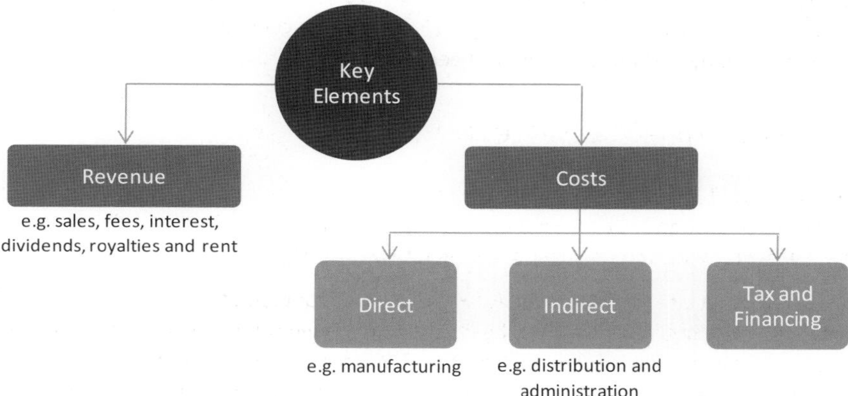

3.2 Format

IAS 1 requires that the **minimum** disclosure in the income statement is as follows:

- Revenue
- Results of operating activities
- Finance costs
- Share of profits and losses of associates and joint ventures accounted for by the equity method.
- Tax expense
- Profit or loss from ordinary activities
- Non-controlling interests
- Net profit for the period

There are several key issues which are fundamental to analysing income statements:

- When should revenue be recognised?
- When should costs be recognised?
- When should an item be classified as ordinary or exceptional?
- How should analyst specific measures be calculated (e.g. EBITDA)?
- What discretion does management have in the calculation of earnings?

Each of these issues is considered in turn in the rest of the chapter.

Recognition of Revenue

4 The Traditional Approach to Timing and Measurement

This section aims to address the issue of when revenue should be recognised in the income statement. The subsequent section addresses some of the contemporary issues surrounding revenue recognition. This is a significant accounting issue as incorrect recognition could lead to a misstatement of income.

Let us examine the sales cycle for a basic transaction involving the sale of goods.

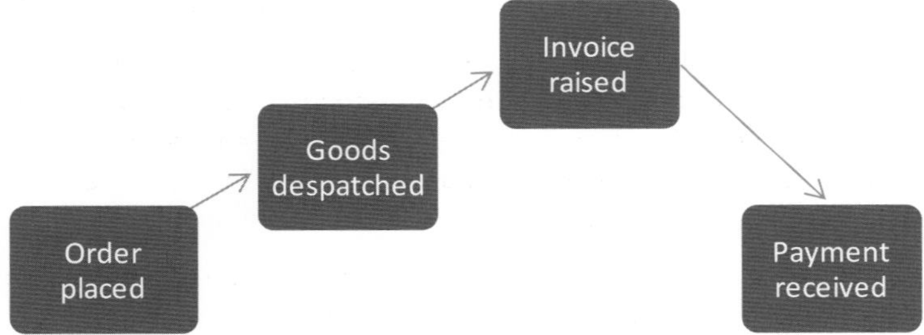

Timing

At which stage of the above cycle should the sale be recognised as revenue?

IFRS 15 - Revenue from Contracts with Customers provides guidance on this accounting issue. It states that revenue should be recognised when control of a promised good or service is transferred to a customer. For the sale of goods, transferring control to the customer would ordinarily occur when most (but not necessarily all) of the following conditions are met:

- The vendor has a right to payment for the goods sold
- The customer has legal title of the goods
- The customer has physical possession of the goods
- There has been a significant transfer of risks and rewards of ownership from the vendor to the customer.
- The customer has accepted the goods

In many cases, most of the above criteria are satisfied at the point of despatch (typically, goods are transferred using 'free on board' shipping point terms, where the buyer is deemed to have taken delivery at the point of despatch). It can therefore be assumed that normal practice is to record the sale once the goods have been despatched. Section 5 of this chapter provides further illustration of applying the principles of IFRS 15.

The accounting issue of cut off should also be considered at this point. Financial statements are prepared using the accruals or matching concept. This means that all revenues earned, and all costs incurred during the accounting period should be reflected in the financial statements regardless of date of cash receipt or payment.

At the end of the financial year, particular attention should be given to the matching of goods despatched pre-year end and the corresponding sales invoices. The sales invoices for these goods should be accounted for in the current financial year in order to match revenue and costs. Even in this apparently straightforward situation, there is significant room for error and manipulation.

The timing of revenue recognition is therefore a significant accounting issue and IFRS 15 provides instruction and guidance to help address this.

Measurement

Measurement of revenue for the sale of goods is a less contentious issue than for long-term contracts. In general, revenue is based on the transaction price, which is defined as:

> *"the amount of consideration to which an entity expects to be entitled, in exchange for transferring promised goods and services to a customer"*

However, there are a few key areas of complexity that should be considered and where IFRS 15 provides some guidance:

- Variable consideration – offering discounts, rebates or even a right of return to customers will cause some uncertainty as to the amount of consideration that the vendor eventually receives. The vendor is required to recognise revenue based on an estimate of the net amount they expect to receive (i.e. after adjusting for discounts, rebates and returns).
- Non-cash consideration –payment by the customer may be in the form of other goods or services. If this occurs, the vendor needs to estimate the fair value of the goods and services received, and include them in the amount of revenue recognised.
- The existence of a significant financing component – if a significant period of time elapses between payment by the customer and transfer of the goods, the vendor needs to consider whether the consideration includes a financing component (e.g. the amount payable by the customer has been adjusted to reflect payment being made significantly before or after the goods are transferred). If this is identified then the amount of revenue recognised needs to exclude any estimated interest income or expense (and the interest income or expense separately presented in earnings).

5 Revenue Recognition and Long-Term Contracts

So far, we have considered transactions which are completed within the accounting period. In practice, that is not always the case. The area of long-term contracts is a particular revenue recognition "grey area". Long-term contracts are contracts that straddle a year end.

Example

The accounting issues which arise from this scenario are:

- When should the revenue on the contract be recognised?
- When should the costs on the contract be recognised?

In practice, there are two possible approaches for recognising the revenues (and costs) as demonstrated in the diagram below:

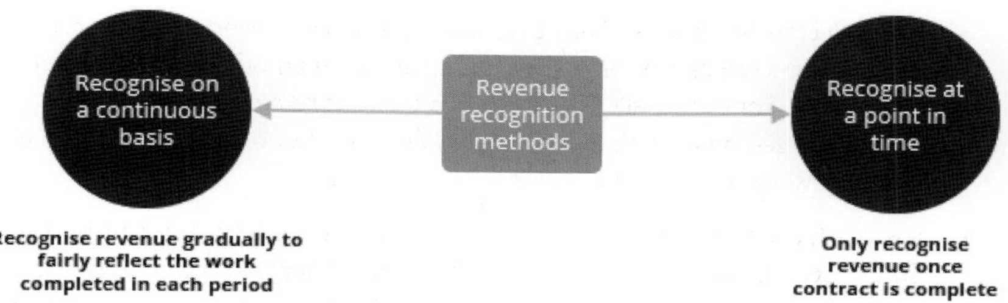

As mentioned in Section 4, IFRS 15 requires revenue to be recognised when control of a promised good or service is transferred to a customer. For a long-term contract, this transfer of control can occur either on a continuous basis (and therefore revenues would be recognised over time) or at a point in time (and therefore revenues would be recognised at that point in time).

Although the concept of 'transferring control' on a continuous basis might seem unusual, it essentially means that the vendor is providing a service to the customer, even where this service results in the construction of a physical asset. The accounting rules provide some guidance on how to determine when control is transferred over time:

- The customer simultaneously receives and consumes the benefits of the vendor's efforts (e.g. can the customer enjoy the benefit of any work performed to date?).
- The vendors efforts create (or enhance) a physical or intangible asset that the customer controls (e.g. the customer bears the risks and rewards of ownership of the asset).
- The vendor has a right to payment for work completed to date and any asset created has no alternative use (e.g. the work is sufficiently bespoke that the vendor could not sell the item to another customer).

In reality, determining whether these criteria can be satisfied will depend on the detail contained within the customer contracts.

Assume the following:

	€m
Contract value	20
Total estimated costs	(16)
Profit	4

If it is determined that the control transfers only on completion of the contract:

- Revenue will be accounted for on completion.
- Costs recorded as 'contract assets' (i.e. part of current assets).

This would result in the following:

	Year 1 €m	Year 2 €m	Year 3 €m
Revenue	–	–	20
Costs	–	–	(16)
Profit	–	–	4

Although this example demonstrates a prudent approach to the accounting, it is questionable whether it is particularly relevant for users. It does not assist the users in their understanding of how the profit of €2m was earned, nor what was happening in Year 1 and 2.

Fortunately, for the majority of long-term contracts, revenue recognition over time will be the most appropriate method. This method does however raise the question of how to measure progress on the contract, since this will determine how much revenue is recognised each year:

$$\text{Revenue recognised} = \%\ \text{progress on contract} \times \text{total contract revenue}$$

IFRS 15 addresses this issue and stipulates that one of the following two methods should be used to determine contract progress:

- Output method: expert survey of work to date is used to determine value of work completed relative to total value of contract.

- Input method: compare the input costs incurred to date (e.g. labour and materials) relative to the total expected input costs for the contract. This is also known as the 'cost-to-cost' method.

Returning to the example from above, we now determine that control transfers on a continuous basis and the company decides to use the input method to determine contract progress. 25% of input costs are incurred in Year 1, 50% in Year 2 and the remainder in Year 3.

This would result in the following:

	Year 1 €m	Year 2 €m	Year 3 €m
Revenue	5	10	5
Costs	(4)	(8)	(4)
Profit	1	2	1

This approach can only be adopted if there is reasonable certainty as to the outcome of the contract and at a point where progress under the contract can be measured with reasonable certainty. Where this is not the case, then revenues are only recognised to offset any costs recognised (i.e. no profit is recognised). Once there is sufficient certainty on the outcome and progress, the approach described above would then be applied.

This again illustrates the play off between the fundamental concepts of prudence and accruals.

Comprehensive Long-Term Contract Example

The following information relates to a particular contract of Vern Construction S.A. The total contract price is €110 million. Total costs are estimated to be €50 million.

Actual Results (€m)

	2005	2006	2007
Cost incurred and paid in each year	15.3	23.7	11.0
Cumulative costs	15.3	39.0	50.0
Cash received during the year	21.5	48.9	39.6
Estimated costs to completion	34.7	11.0	–

Solution

Income statement (extracts)

	2005	2006	2007
Revenue recognised over time	**€m**	**€m**	**€m**
Revenue recognised	33.66	52.14	24.20
Costs recognised	(15.30)	(23.7)	(11.00)
Income	18.36	28.44	13.2
Revenue recognised at completion			
Revenue recognised	0	0	110
Costs recognised	0	0	(50)
Income	0	0	60

Revenue recognised over time – Balance sheet (extracts)

	2005	2006	2007
	€m	**€m**	**€m**
Cash (asset)	6.2	31.4	60
Contract assets	12.16	15.4	0
Equity	18.36	46.8	60

Revenue recognised at completion – Balance sheet (extracts)

	2005	**2006**	**2007**
	€m	**€m**	**€m**
Cash (asset)	6.2	31.4	60
Contract liabilities	6.2	31.4	0
Equity	0	0	60

Workings

Cash (both methods)

As this is a balance sheet item, it is cumulative. Furthermore, accounting methods normally do not impact on net cash flows. An exception to this might be when the accounting treatment impacts on taxation.

2005	**€m**
Opening balance	0
+ cash received	21.5
– costs paid	(15.3)
	6.2

2006	**€m**
+ cash received	48.9
– costs paid	(23.7)
	31.4

2007	**€m**
+ cash received	39.6
– costs paid	(11.0)
	60

Contract Assets/Liabilities	2005	2006	2007
	€m	€m	€m
Revenue recognised over time			
B/fwd	0	12.16	15.4
Cash received during year	(21.5)	(48.9)	(39.6)
Costs incurred	15.3	23.7	11.0
Profit recognised	18.36	28.44	13.2
Contract asset	12.16	15.4	0
Revenue recognised at completion			
B/fwd	0	6.2	31.4
Cash received during year	(21.5)	(48.9)	(39.6)
Costs incurred	15.3	23.7	11.0
Profit recognised	0	0	(60)
Contract asset	6.2	31.4	0

Equity

Simply the cumulative profit.

Points to Note

- Recognising revenue at completion, in general, introduces more volatility and distortion of results due to the 'lumpy' nature of revenues and costs.
- Recognising revenue at completion, in general, produces smaller net worth in the balance sheet during the contract period as no profit is recognised until the last year.
- Recognising revenues over time involves various estimates and is heavily dependent on subjective estimates of costs incurred relative to costs to completion (which are often inaccurate).

6 Further Thoughts on Revenue Recognition

There are a number of different sources of revenues that a company might have. For example, these might include:

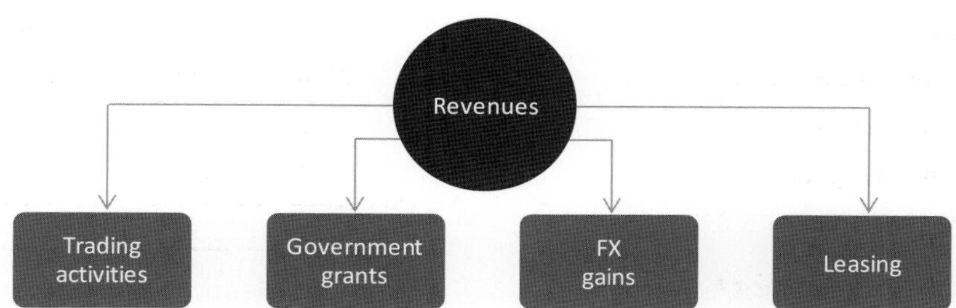

The importance of accounting rules governing revenues cannot be overstated. Revenues directly impact on earnings. In addition, revenue figures, in particular relating to growth therein, and whether they arise from organic or acquisitive growth, are particularly important for making a realistic assessment of corporate performance.

Given the importance of revenue, it may be surprising to learn that until the introduction of IFRS 15 (and its US equivalent, Topic 606) in 2018 there was a dearth of accounting standards on revenue recognition in many countries. In fact, only US GAAP had well developed, substantial rules on revenue recognition, and even these rules differed widely by industry. The introduction of IFRS 15/Topic 606 therefore represented a significant development in accounting by introducing a single, core principle which determines how revenues are recognised, regardless of industry and contract type:

> *"Revenue [shall be recognised] to depict the transfer of promised goods and services to customers, in an amount that reflects the consideration to which the company expects to be entitled in exchange for those goods and services."*

This principle means that similar transactions in different industries would result in the same pattern of revenue recognition.

We shall now look at how this principle is applied in more complex situations relating to revenue recognition.

Multiple element contracts

In recent years, companies have increasingly sold goods and services together, under a single contract. These contracts often have payment schedules requiring both upfront and on-going payments from the customers, with the timing of the payments often unrelated to the timing of when the goods and services are delivered. This is particularly the case in the software and telecoms industry where hardware, licenses and data may all be included in the customer contract. These 'multiple element contracts' present a significant accounting challenge, in determining how and when the revenue for each element should be recognised.

IFRS 15 has introduced a five-step framework which explains how revenues should be recognised for all the goods and services promised in a single contract:

1. The contract determines the rights and obligations of a company and customer.
2. Performance obligations are distinct goods and services promised to a customer.
3. The total payments the company expects to receive from the customer, including an estimate of any uncertain amounts or discounts.
4. Allocation is made based on the estimated relative standalone values of the goods and services.
5. Revenue is recognised as each good or service is delivered to the customer.

One of the most important steps in this framework is that companies must allocate revenue to each of the goods and services, based on their **relative standalone values;** this means allocating revenue based on how much they are worth if they were to be sold separately. It should be noted that this allocation occurs even if the goods are *never* sold separately, and in that situation the company would need to make an estimate of the values (e.g. based on the value of similar goods and services or based on cost plus a mark-up).

Principal Verses Agent

Companies can either be acting as a principal (on their own behalf) or as an agent (on behalf of a third party). This is an important distinction for revenue recognition as it determines whether the company is required to present the gross revenues and costs in relation to a customer contract (if they are acting as principal) or just the net fees or commissions that they derive from the contract (if they are acting as agent).

Indicators that a company is acting as an agent would include where the company:

- Does not have the primary responsibility for fulfilling the contract.
- Does not take on significant inventory risk or credit risk (i.e. would not incur losses from inventory damage or non-payment by customer).
- Does not have discretion in setting prices for the goods and services.

If these indicators apply, then the company would recognise only their fees or commissions as revenue, rather than including the total value of goods and services delivered to the customer.

Warranties

Companies frequently provide warranties to customers in connection with the goods and services they provide. The question therefore arises as to whether the warranty is a 'distinct service' and therefore whether revenue should be separately allocated to the warranty (thus reducing the amount of revenue allocated to the underlying goods or services).

The accounting rules distinguish between warranties which provide assurance to the customer that the goods or services will function as expected (which are not considered a distinct service) from warranties which provide the customer with additional assurance or services (which are considered a distinct service).

Where warranties are not considered a distinct service, then they do not impact on revenue recognition; instead the company would need to recognise a provision (i.e. liability) for any expected warranty claims.

Where warranties are considered a distinct service, then the company would need to allocate revenue to the warranty and recognise the allocated revenue over the warranty period.

Consignment Sales

Companies may transfer inventory to a third party (dealer) but retain ultimate control for the inventory. This is known as a consignment sale and an example of this would be where any unsold inventory is returned to the company at the end of a specified period.

No revenue is recognised by the company until the inventory is sold by the dealer to the ultimate customer, as this is the point where control is transferred.

Non-refundable Upfront Fees

Companies may require customers to pay a non-refundable upfront payment at the start of a contract; examples would include joining fees for a health club or set up fees in service contracts.

Upfront fees cannot be recognised at the start of the contract except where the payment relates to a good or service which is being provided at that point. In practice, this is rarely the case so these fees are usually deferred and recognised when the underlying goods and services in the contract are delivered.

Summary of Probable Treatment for a Range of Sources of Revenues

Understanding accounting rules for revenue recognition is a real challenge for analysts: businesses (and their contracts with customers) are complex and often difficult to understand as an outsider. The following table should provide a starting point for analysing the revenue recognition rules for a range of activities.

Issues	Commentary/Treatment
Subscriptions	Revenue is recognised as service is delivered. Treat as deferred (unearned) income until then.
Media revenues	Advertising revenue is recognised on publication or transmission of the advertising. Production revenues (e.g. television production) are recognised on delivery of content and acceptance by the customer. License and distribution revenues are recognised in full as soon as the customer is able to benefit from the license or content.
Software revenues (how to account for those in the vendor's financials)	If the company is not required to provide any material updates or hosting, revenue is recognised in full at the start of the licence period (even if the licence is for a fixed term). If the software and hosting are provided together (software-as-a-service or cloud services), revenue is recognised as service is delivered. If significant customisation is required, then follow a 'long term contract' approach. If multiple elements exist (e.g. sale of standard software with support) then generally, the fee should be allocated to software and support services, and recognised as earned.
Real estate transactions	Revenue could be recognised at either: Exchange of contracts Completion of the transactions
Barter transactions (exchange)	IFRS 15 provides that: If the exchange is like for like (i.e. similar goods/services) then no revenue is generated If dissimilar goods/services are exchanged, then revenue will be recognised at the fair value of the goods/services received

Analysis Focus

Traps for the Unwary

What the extensive content on revenue recognition shows is that, for certain types of company, there may be a big difference between revenue and cash receipts from customers. This means that the commonly used 'EBITDA' figure (see later) is not a real measure of cash flow – even though it looks like one. Also, whereas we might expect revenue to be a simple matter, this is a complete misconception outside of a few sectors. It should be remembered that historically we have had many companies go back and restate revenues that turned out to be incorrect. Therefore, a deep understanding of the revenue policies and judgements is an important part of analysing financial statements.

Recognition of Costs

7 Approaches to Cost Recognition

As has been noted, the issue of cost recognition will often follow the approach to revenue recognition. This is no surprise as the overriding principle is matching or accruals, i.e. costs should be 'matched' with the revenue those costs helped generate.

Once again, let us examine the purchase cycle for a basic transaction involving the purchase of goods.

At which point should the expense be recorded?

The IFRS framework for the Preparation and Presentation of Financial Statements provides the following guide.

> *"Expenses are decreases in economic benefit during an accounting period in the form of outflow or depletions of assets or incurrences of liabilities that result in depletions of equity, other than those relating to distributions to equity participants." (Source: IASB)*

Taking the above transaction cycle, the expense will be recorded in the accounting records on receipt of goods from the supplier (with a corresponding increase in liabilities).

The issue of cut off at the year-end will need to establish that for all goods received pre-year-end the relevant invoice has also been recorded. Once the expense has been recorded, application of the matching concept will ensure that it is expensed to the income statement to match with the revenue it has generated.

Normal practice would allow for costs to be expensed in the period in which they occur. It should be noted that some expenses help to generate revenue over more than one accounting period (example, non-current assets such as buildings, plant and machinery). These items are expensed to the income statement over the period of their useful economic life (see Chapter 3).

Example

1. A subscription of €100 is received in advance payment for the next ten issues of a magazine.

   Revenue recognition approach: as delivery is made

   Cost recognition approach: as delivery is made

2. A long-term contract is 20% complete. However, total cost estimates are highly unreliable. Total contract costs (and therefore contract profitability) is uncertain.

   Revenue recognition approach: revenues recognised to the extent the costs are incurred

   Cost recognition approach: as incurred

3. As per 2 above except cost estimates are reliable.

   Revenue recognition approach: over time (cost to cost method)

   Cost recognition approach: as incurred

Non-recurring Items

8 Introduction

So far, we have examined the issues of revenue and cost recognition in the income statement. We will now examine the issue of presentation of revenue and expenses. Among the major tasks of most analysts are the valuation of assets and the prediction of future earnings. When attempting to predict earnings analysts require income measures that are persistent, i.e. will recur. Abnormal sources of income and expense are not relevant in the forecasting process. It is therefore vital to identify which items of revenue and expense will occur on an ongoing basis (ordinary activities) and which do not. This process is often referred to as 'cleaning' earnings.

Analysis Focus

Uses and Abuses

The idea of separately disclosing restructuring costs is justified by the need on the part of the user of the accounts to understand underlying, ongoing profitability. But it is very easily abused. This 'cleaning' exercise is an important analytical task. The objective is to derive a normalised set of historic earnings numbers that will be a better basis for future prediction. For example, consider a company where profits have been boosted by the sale at a large gain of the head office. Clearly this will not re-occur and so it should be removed. However, if a company regularly reports operating costs within the charges, it may well be flattering its apparent underlying profits. Furthermore, gains or losses on disposals can be selectively treated as usual.

There is a simple, if brutal principle to apply: check that on average there is no great proportion of negative over positive 'one-off' items!

9 Types of Non-recurring Items

There are three distinct types of non-recurring item:

(i) Separate disclosure items

(ii) Discontinued operations

(iii) Accounting changes

10 Overview

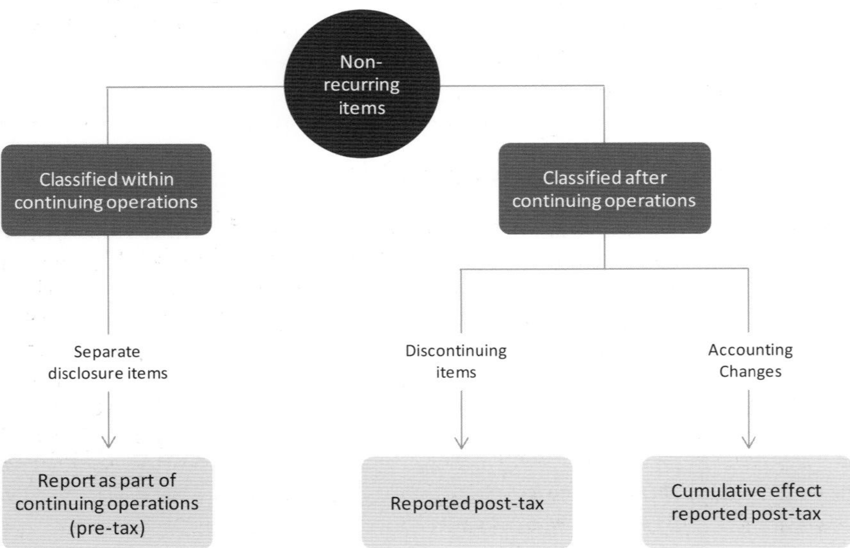

11 Separate Disclosure Items

IAS 1 recognises that some items, whilst occurring as part of the ordinary activities of the entity, require additional disclosure due to size, nature or incidence.

Examples

- Provisions for making good environmental damage
- Impairments, write-offs and restructuring costs

Disclosure Requirements

- Included in continuing operations
- Appear as a separate line item
- Reported above the line, i.e. pre-tax basis

12 Discontinued Operations

IFRS 5 *Non-current Assets Held for Sale and Discontinued Operations* sets out specific guidance on the requirements for these items. A 'discontinued operation' is a part of a business that either has been disposed of or is classified as held for sale. It could be a subsidiary that was acquired exclusively for resale, a major line of business or a major geographical area of operations.

In order to allow meaningful analysis and assessment of the entity's future results, discontinued operations are presented separately in the income statement. The SUM of the post-tax profit/loss of the discontinued operation AND the post-tax gain/loss on disposal must be shown as a single amount on the face of the income statement. This single amount must then be disaggregated either on the face of the income statement or in the notes to the financial statements.

13 Accounting Changes

Finally, one should also be aware of two other key items which have an impact on income. These are summarised below:

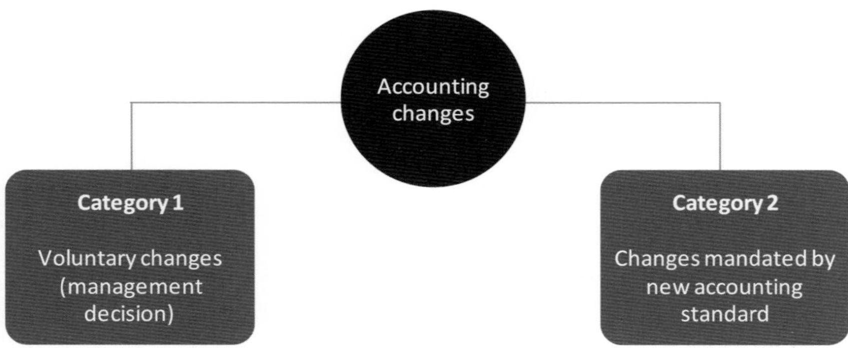

Accounting Treatment

In the case of a change in accounting principle by management (for example, a change to capitalising a cost to expensing it), it is important that the users are made aware of the impact on earnings of such changes.

IAS 8 describes the key way of dealing with these changes:

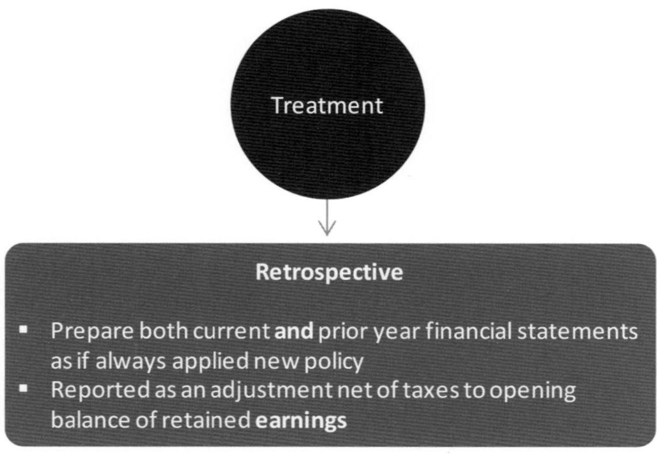

14 Suggested Pro-forma Income Statement

Although no specific presentation approach is specified by IFRS, the following would be typical of good practice. You should also examine the Lufthansa financials available online, just type the following into your browser's address bar to download the PDF:

bit.ly/lufthansa2017

Excerpt S.A. Income statement for the year ended 31 December Year 8

	€
Revenues from the sale of goods and services	1,500,000
Operating expenses	(200,000)
Operating income from continuing operations (independent of the firm's capital structure)	1,300,000
Other income and revenues (interest/dividend income; gains/losses from sale of fixed assets not requiring separate disclosure)	(260,000)
Recurring income before interest and taxes	
from continuing operations	1,040,000
Financing costs (interest expenses)	(300,000)
Recurring (pre-tax) income from continuing operations	740,000
Separate disclosure items (e.g. gains or losses related to the impairment of investments)	150,000
Pre-tax earnings from continuing operations	890,000
Income tax expense (provision for taxes)	(300,000)
Net income from continuing operations	590,000
Income from discontinued operations (reported net of tax)	(50,000)
Net income	540,000

15 Analysis of Income Statements, Management Discretion and Earnings Management

15.1 Analysing Income Statements

Now that we have obtained a basic understanding and appreciation of the issues of cost and revenue recognition, disclosure of recurring and non-recurring items and impact of changes in accounting policy, we are able to look at the income statement as a tool to understand financial performance.

Key areas of the income statement used by analysts and investors are as follows:

- Operating Income
- Earnings Before Interest and Tax (EBIT)
- Earnings Before Interest, Tax and Amortisation (EBITA)
- Earnings Before Interest, Tax, Depreciation and Amortisation (EBITDA)
- Net income (used for Earnings Per Share – see Chapter 6)

Operating Income and EBIT

Operating income is the profit generated from the core activities of the enterprise. It is income that would be expected on a recurring basis and would be compared to:

- Operating income of the same enterprise over a number of years to calculate growth or contraction rates;
- Operating income of different enterprises in the same industry to compare the growth/contraction rates;
- The calculation is used in analysis as it gives an indication of profitability regardless of how the company is financed. However, operating profit is not without its problems:
  - Operating profit includes both depreciation and amortisation. As we shall see in Chapter 3, these are areas of significant discretion for management. The existence of such items inhibits true 'peer' comparisons
  - Operating profit may include separate disclosure items which, in all likelihood, will be of a non-recurring nature and so should be excluded by an analyst in calculating sustainable earnings

EBITDA

The calculation of EBITDA is often referred to as the process of "normalising earnings". The calculation of EBITDA involves stripping amortisation, depreciation and separate disclosure items from earnings in order to facilitate meaningful analysis. Another benefit is that EBITDA can be used as a proxy for operating cash flows although it is not the same number.

Even though EBITDA exhibits attractive qualities for use in valuation (see Chapter 6), it is not without its problems. For example, this short article appeared in an edition of Accountancy magazine many years ago, but its message remains very important to this day.

The deadly ebitda virus

Until quite recently ebitda was almost unknown. Then rare, isolated cases of it appeared, and now it's all over the place, endangering rational thought about accounts and company valuations across the civilised world.

In case you've been fortunate enough to escape contact with it, ebitda is earnings before interest, tax, depreciation and amortisation. Some elements of it make sense in certain circumstances. If you want to check a company's operating performance, then it's perfectly reasonable to ignore tax, interest and amortisation of goodwill. If you want to assess a company's value, while keeping an open mind about how it's financed, then it's sensible to ignore interest.

What does not make sense is a comment such as: 'At 12 times ebitda, Z plc is out of line with its peers. Sell it and buy X and Y instead.' Unfortunately, that's exactly the kind of comment that you will see daily (except of course that no analyst who wants to keep his job ever actually tells you to sell anything).

There are two major problems with using ebitda. The first is that no assessment of a business should ever ignore the cost of its fixed assets. Fixed assets are as much an operating cost as any other. The only difference between them and other operating costs is that their consumption is spread over more than one accounting period. It beggars belief that serious commentators should be ignoring these costs for any purpose whatever, let alone for making valuations.

The second big objection to ebitda is that it is miles away from the bottom line. Depreciation, interest and tax are all real costs. They should be taken into account in assessing a company's performance and its value. (Amortisation of goodwill is arguably a real cost too, but as there's some doubt about it we'll leave it aside). The further you get from the bottom line, the easier it is to kid yourself about how well a company is really doing. Even chronic loss-makers can be made to look like healthy investments by focusing on ebitda.

Maybe analysts think that ebitda is free from accounting judgments. As our Accounting Solutions page this month shows, that would be a mistake. The focus on ebitda has simply made it into a target for manipulation, like any other accounting figure. There is no escape from Strathern's law – that 'when a measure becomes a target it ceases to be a good measure'. The sensible course of action is to decide what figure would ideally provide the best measure and then put in place appropriate defences to ensure its integrity, such as audits, accounting standards, and so on.

In assessing a business, the starting point should be the bottom line, and every move away from that should be viewed with suspicion. Valuations based on ebitda reflect only part of a business's financial performance and can be right only by coincidence.

Brian Singleton-Green

Reproduced with kind permission of Accountancy Magazine
www.accountancymagazine.com

15.2 Management Discretion and Earnings Management

It must not be forgotten that management has some degree of control over the income statement. The key motives for this potential management of earnings are:

- Management's remuneration (bonus or earn-out linked to earnings).
- Potential takeover bids.
- Maintain constant level of earnings; low volatility may give the impression of low risk.
- Meeting the earnings forecasts expectations of analysts, especially in UK and US.

The main areas where management has potential input into the reported earnings figure are as follows:

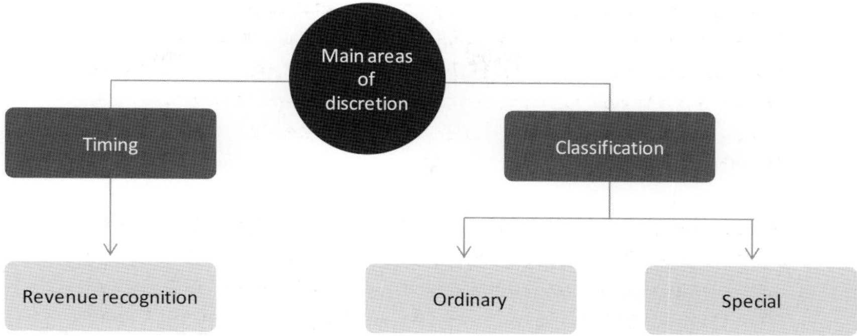

Revenue Recognition Timing

As we have explored in this chapter, there is considerable discretion regarding the timing of revenue recognition. Therefore, management could make judgements that accelerate revenue recognition in comparison to peers. As those faced with analysing the financial statements, we must carefully analyse the policies around revenue. It can be very difficult as an 'outsider' without access to contracts and other documents to question these decisions. One cross-check would be the analysis of accounts receivable vs. sales for the company in question over time and against the competition. Material deviations might indicate something is amiss!

Classification

In the knowledge that analysts typically exclude non-recurring items from their analysis, management will often follow a simple principle; classify losses as non-recurring (i.e. separate disclosure) and gains as ordinary. Note that analysts and others might potentially treat recurring exceptional items as normal given their frequency.

There are other areas of management discretion such as the use of provisions which will be covered in Chapter 4. Judicious review of the notes, in particular accounting policies, is the only way to try to identify potential problems.

16 Advanced Issues

Almost every item you might see in an income statement will be governed by the general principles enunciated in this chapter. However, there are several advanced issues that require further consideration. The following provides an explanation of these issues.

Deferred Taxation

This is a complex issue which impacts of the tax charge in the financial statements. The tax charge itself is an amalgam of a number of different numbers and is not a simple transcript from the tax computation. One of the main reasons for this is that deferred taxation arises because of timing differences between recognition rules for taxation purposes and those for financial statement purposes. This issue is addressed in detail in Chapter 4.

Stock Options

IFRS 2 *Share-based Payment* is the current International Financial Reporting Standard on stock options. The basic issue is, should a charge be made for granting a stock option to, say, an employee? Previously, most GAAPs required a charge for such compensation to be made. However, the charge tended to be merely the intrinsic value of the option, i.e. exercise price less market value of the stock rather than the fair value of the options. The result of using the intrinsic value approach is that the charge for stock options is probably too low for many entities. This is one reason that such schemes have proved so popular with profit starved start-up technology companies. IFRS 2 now requires expensing of stock options at fair value. A detailed analysis of stock options is included in Chapter 15.

Retirement Benefits

Providing benefits on retirement is an important source of employee compensation. The accounting treatment is dependent on the type of scheme. For defined contribution schemes (i.e. a scheme whereby monies are invested in a fund with no guarantee of future benefits), there are few accounting problems. The contributions are reflected in the income statement as an expense. Defined benefit schemes (where benefits are guaranteed) are much more complex. The entire pensions issue is addressed in detail in Chapter 15.

Chapter 3: Balance Sheet – Assets

"Financial Statements are pieces of paper with numbers on them, but it is important to think about the real assets that underlie the numbers." [3]

[3] Fundamentals of Financial Management, Brigham and Houston (2015)

1 Introduction

The income statement provides information on the financial performance of a company during the accounting period. The balance sheet on the other hand is a snapshot of the net asset position at a given point in time which reflects its financial position. The next two chapters focus our attention on the balance sheet and in particular examine associated accounting issues relating to assets (this chapter) and liabilities (Chapter 4). The topic of Investments is dealt with in Chapter 7.

In general terms, there are four major accounting issues of importance for assets:

- Should the asset be recognised on the balance sheet?
- How should it be classified?
- If so, at what value?
- What happens to subsequent changes in value?

As seen in Chapter 1, assets can be classified as current and non-current. We shall address current assets prior to moving on to non-current (fixed) assets.

2 Current Assets – Accounting Treatment Overview

The areas of inventory and non-current assets each have their own accounting complexities. The following diagram summarises the key accounting rules:

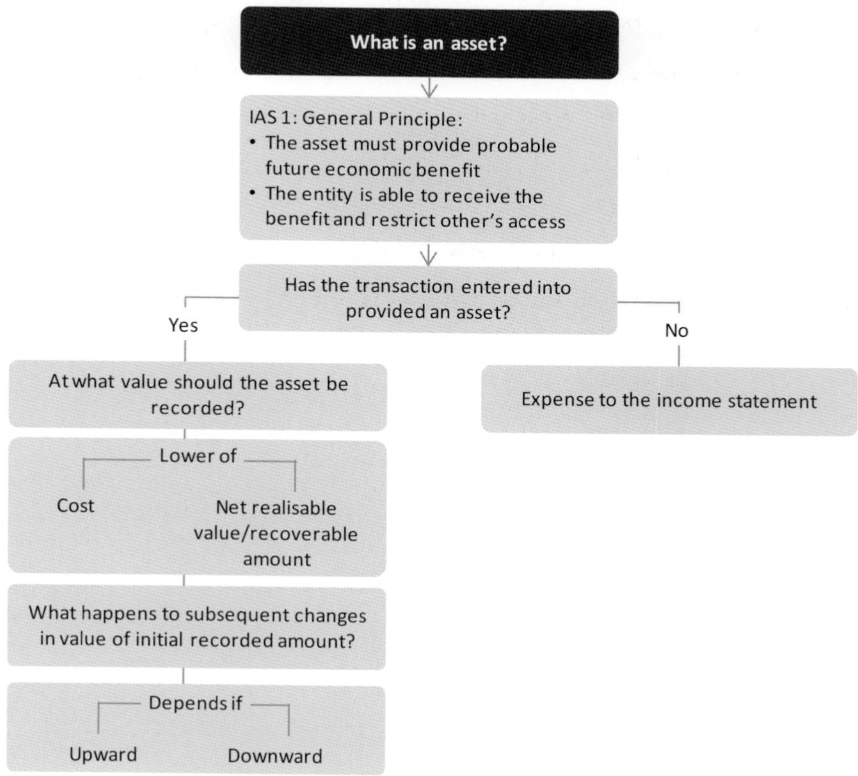

At its most basic level, the fundamental concepts of conservatism (avoid an overstatement of the balance sheet by inclusion of assets that do not exist and/or are overvalued) and matching (costs of assets aligned with revenues generated) are applied in the accounting treatment of assets.

3 Analysis of Inventories

3.1 Basic Principles

Inventories are defined by IAS 2 *Inventories* as items that are:

> *"held for sale in the ordinary course of business; in the process of production for such sale, or in the form of materials and supplies to be consumed in the production process or in the rendering of services."*

In other words, at a basic level:

Ending inventory, or closing stock, is arrived at in the balance sheet as follows:

Inventories = Quantity on hand × Value

Establishing the quantity of inventories held is not especially problematic given the widespread use of computer-based systems. The two main ways of quantifying inventories are:

- Physical count
- Perpetual inventory records (e.g. using software)

It should be noted that issues of cut off (i.e. dealing with sales and purchases around the accounting year-end), goods in transit (ensuring such goods are counted, but only once) and consignment stock (inventory held by a business but legally owned by a third party) must also be specifically addressed when quantifying inventory.

4 Valuation

Inventory valuation is always based on the fundamental valuation rule:

Inventory is valued at the lower of cost or net realisable value (NRV)

This is in accordance with the concept of conservatism as the lower value is recognised in the balance sheet (not overstating assets position). We therefore need to understand how cost and net realisable value are determined.

IAS 2 provides general principles on these areas.

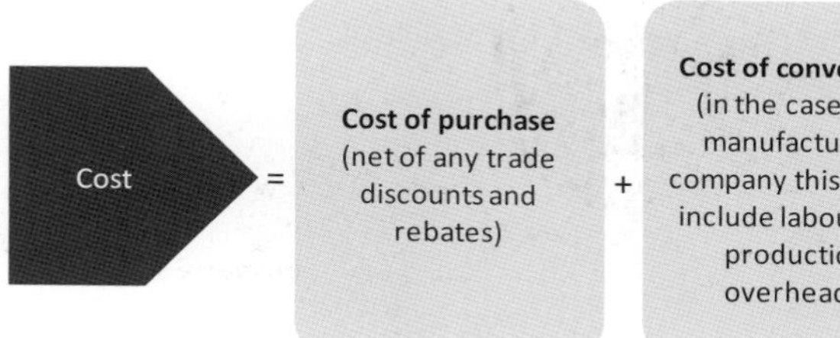

Net Realisable Value = Selling price less estimated costs necessary to make the sale (costs of amendment, selling, etc.)

Example

Zaragoza S.A. has three products in stock, details of which are as follows:

	Quantity	Cost per unit €	NRV per unit €
A	100	10.00	12.50
B	150	11.50	9.50
C	120	8.50	10.50

What is the value of inventory?

Solution

			€
A =	100 × 10.00	=	1,000
B =	150 × 9.50	=	1,425
C =	120 × 8.50	=	1,020
			3,445

Points to Note

The principle of lower of cost and net realisable value should be applied on an item by item basis. If not, then we would compare total NRV and cost:

Total cost		€	vs.	**Total NRV**		€
100 × 10.00	=	1,000		100 × 12.50	=	1,250
150 × 11.50	=	1,725		150 × 9.50	=	1,425
120 × 8.50	=	1,020		120 × 10.50	=	1,260
		3,745				**3,935**

This gives a higher (less conservative) value. The valuation principle aims to ensure two things:

- Losses are accounted for when foreseeable.
- Profits are not anticipated on an item by item basis.

Conservatism is also applied to the valuation of items A and C as profits are not anticipated.

5 The Inventory Equation

The basic calculation for ending inventory (closing stock) is as follows:

Ending Inventory (EI) = Beginning Inventory (BI) + Purchases (P)
– Cost of Goods Sold (COGS)

This can be shortened to: EI = BI + P – COGS

This is more commonly rearranged to calculate COGS directly:

Alternatively rearranged as: COGS = BI + P – EI

The cost of the units sold (COGS) is the inventory at the start of the period, plus additions, less what remains in the inventory at the end of the period.

Whereas the inventory at the end of the period reflects what was there at the beginning, plus purchases made during the period less what was sold.

Example

Justice Inc. had a beginning inventory of 42,000 units. During the year, it purchased 150,000 units. Sales amounted to 108,000 units. If the cost of these units remained constant at €15 and sales prices at €25, what is a) the ending inventory and b) gross profit?

Solution

a) EI = BI + P – COGS

EI = 42,000 + 150,000 – 108,000

∴ EI = 84,000 units

∴ Value = 84,000 × €15 = €1,260,000

b) Gross profit

	€
Revenue (108,000 × 25)	2,700,000
Cost of sales (108,000 × 15)	(1,620,000)
	1,080,000

A more complete income statement would look as follows:

	€	€
Revenue		2,700,000
Beginning Inventory	630,000	
(42,000 × 15)		
Purchases	2,250,000	
(150,000 × 15)	2,880,000	
Ending inventory	1,260,000	
Cost of goods sold		1,620,000
Gross profit		1,080,000

Points to Note

Ending inventory has its own 'dual effect':

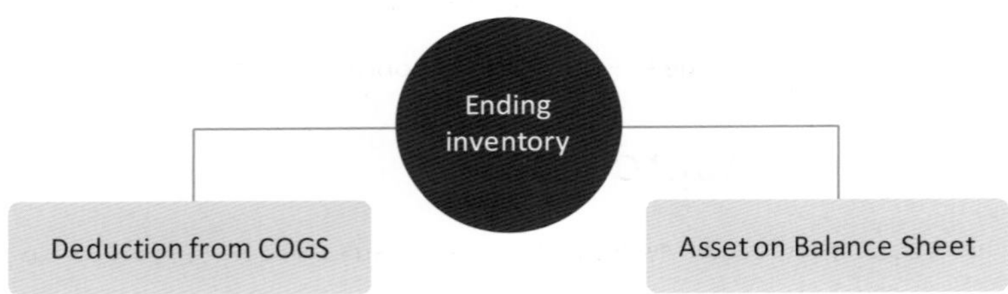

i.e. once the value of ending inventory has been determined, it is simply deducted in arriving at the calculation cost of goods sold and carried forward on the balance sheet to the next period.

6 The Cost Allocation Problem

So far, we have considered basic examples where the cost of inventory is known. If costs were constant, then inventory accounting would not be too onerous. However, prices are rarely stable. This is now the focus of our attention.

Example

Lee S.A. started to trade on 1 January. Goods were purchased for resale during the period to 31 March as follows:

Purchase 1 – 2,000 units at cost €10 per unit
Purchase 2 – 3,000 units at cost €12 per unit

During the period, 1,500 units were sold for €25,000.

The accounting problem is twofold:

- What is the cost of goods sold?
- What is the cost of what is left (i.e. ending inventory or EI)?

The solution depends upon the stock accounting approach used.

7 The Three Approaches

There are three possible approaches to arriving at a suitable cost figure:

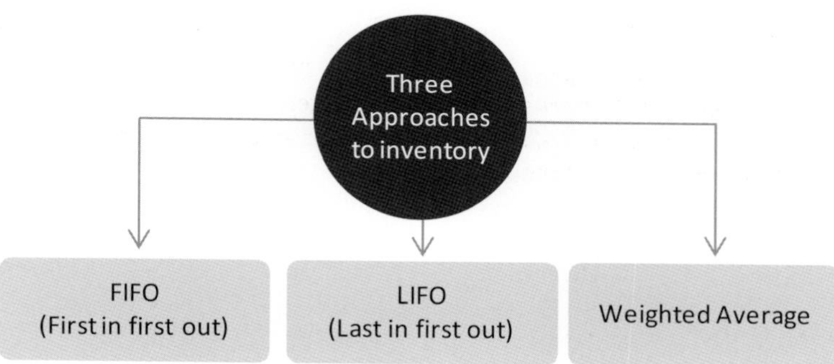

FIFO and LIFO arrive at costs looking at the flow of inventory through the system and making a simplifying assumption about inventory that has been sold and inventory that remains.

FIFO assumes that the first goods in are the first to be sold. This means that ending inventory comprises the most recent purchases and therefore will reflect the most up to date costs.

LIFO assumes on the other hand that stock turnover is the opposite to that of FIFO, i.e. sell our most recent purchases first. Closing inventory is therefore valued at older costs.

Weighted Average as its name suggests involves averaging. It is often used in situations when it is not possible to ascertain with sufficient accuracy the stock flow.

$$\frac{\text{Total Cost (BI+Purchases)}}{\text{Total Units}}$$

Both FIFO and Weighted Average are permitted under IFRS. LIFO is still allowed under US GAAP but not under IFRS. The impact of these methods on the income statement is illustrated by the comprehensive example below.

8 Comprehensive Example

Deep Inc. had the following stock transactions in Widgets at the end of its second year of trading.

Date	Transactions	Units	Total cost/sale proceeds €
2 Jan	Sold	50	350
5 Jan	Purchased	80	424
8 Jan	Purchased	90	495
10 Jan	Purchased	120	708
15 Jan	Sold	200	1,400
25 Jan	Purchased	20	120

Beginning inventory was 100 units valued at €5 per unit. Ending inventory was 160 units.

Required

(i) Calculate the Ending Inventory under FIFO, LIFO and Weighted Average.

(ii) Calculate the impact on cost of goods sold and hence gross profits.

Solution

Units remaining

Opening stock	100
Purchased	310
Sold	(250)
	160

Ending Inventory (FIFO)

The ending inventory will consist of the latest purchases:

Purchases

		BI	5/1	8/1	10/1	25/1
Sales		100	80	90	120	20
2 Jan	50	(50)				
15 Jan	200	(50)	(80)	(70)		
Balance				20	120	20

Stock value based on the above:

Date	Units	Costs per Unit	Total
25 Jan	20	€6.00	€120
10 Jan	120	€5.90	€708
8 Jan	20	€5.50	€110
	160		€938

Ending Inventory (LIFO)

The ending inventory will consist of the earliest purchases:

Purchases

		BI	5/1	8/1	10/1	25/1
Sales		100	80	90	120	20
2 Jan	50	(50)				
15 Jan	200			(80)	(120)	
Balance		50	80	10	-	20

This would produce an inventory valuation of €849 (50 × €5 + 80 × €5.30 + 10 × €5.5 + 20 × €6).

In the US this calculation is normally simplified to the oldest units. In this case, this would be the oldest 160 units as follows:

Date	Units	Costs per Unit	Total
1/1	100	€5.00	€500
5/1	60	€5.30	€318
	160		€818

Ending Inventory (Weighted Average)

The ending inventory will consist of inventory valued at the average cost of acquiring the units of stock.

Total purchases	= 500 + 424 + 495 + 708 + 120
	= €2,247
Total units	= 410
Average	= €5.48
Stock	= 160 × €5.48 = €877

Impact on Costs of Goods Sold (COGS)

	FIFO	LIFO	Weighted Average
	€	**€**	**€**
BI	500	500	500
+ P	1,747	1,747	1,747
– EI	(938)	(818)	(877)
= COGS	1,309	1,429	1,370

Impact on Gross Profit

	FIFO	LIFO	Weighted Average
	€	**€**	**€**
Revenue (350 + 1,400)	**1,750**	**1,750**	**1,750**
COGS	**(1,309)**	**(1,429)**	**(1,370)**
Gross profit	**441**	**321**	**380**

9 Analytical Impact

FIFO charges old units to COGS and so this approach results in a stock valuation at more recent prices. Therefore, FIFO produces a more accurate, or relevant, balance sheet.

LIFO charges new units to COGS and so this approach produces a more realistic income statement.

If we assume prices are rising and inventory is consistent or growing:

Measure	LIFO	FIFO
Net income	Lower	Higher
Inventory balance	Lower	Higher
Taxes	Lower	Higher

Implications for Cash Flow and Profits

In a rising market, FIFO accounters will show higher profits than LIFO accounters, though cash flows will be the same (because there will be an offsetting expansion in the working capital of the FIFO accounters). Under some accounting and fiscal regimes, those that opt to account in this way will incur more tax. Analysis has shown that despite this higher profit, they are valued at relatively low levels by the equity market, which correctly values cash flows, not profit streams. It seems that in this sense markets are efficient.

10 Adjusting from LIFO to FIFO

This might be required for comparative purposes and in a US context is a common issue facing analysts. Entities using LIFO to value inventory often have a figure which is out of date compared to that if FIFO basis had been applied. In order to arrive at a FIFO figure in the balance sheet, a LIFO reserve (mandatory to disclose in the US if using LIFO) is added to the LIFO amount.

$EI_{FIFO} = EI_{LIFO}$ + LIFO reserve

$COGS_{FIFO} = COGS_{LIFO}$ − LIFO reserve increase

$Profit_{FIFO} = Profit_{LIFO}$ + LIFO reserve increase

These calculations are best illustrated with an example.

Example

The year-end LIFO inventory figure is €14,000 and the year-end LIFO reserve is €10,000. The current year's LIFO cost of goods sold is €40,000. The previous year's LIFO reserve was €8,000. The profit before tax is €2,400.

Required

Calculate the following under FIFO:

(i) Ending inventory

(ii) Cost of goods sold

(iii) Profit before tax

Solution

(i) FIFO = LIFO + LIFO reserve

FIFO = €14,000 + €10,000

FIFO = €24,000

(ii) COGS = €40,000 – €2,000

COGS = €38,000

(iii) Profit = €2,400 + €2,000

Profit = €4,400

Points to Note

- The balance on the LIFO reserve represents the difference between inventory valued on a LIFO basis versus on a FIFO basis
- The cost of goods sold adjustment only reflects the movement on the reserve because:

Opening inventory	X
Purchases	X
	X
Ending inventory	(X)
COGS	X

We only need to adjust COGS sold for the change in inventory. If the reserve moves upwards, then ending inventory must be higher by €2,000 and so COGS is reduced by €2,000. If COGS is reduced by €2,000, then profit must increase by €2,000. If sales volumes exceed purchases or production, then a LIFO liquidation has occurred.

The impact of LIFO liquidations must be disclosed in the US, otherwise analysts might be misled by the high margins.

11 Accounts Receivable and Prepaid expenses

As the vast majority of sales are on a credit basis, most corporates will have amounts due from customers, known as accounts receivable, as a current asset. As mentioned earlier, sometimes these amounts are referred to as debtors. If there are doubts about the recoverability of monies from customers, then adjustments must be made to reflect concerns about recoverability. This is termed writing off bad debts or providing for bad debts based on specific circumstances. This has a direct impact on profits.

Prepaids are prepaid expenses. These are classified as an asset as the insurance, rent or whatever service that has been paid in advance is 'owed' to the company in the future. The recognition of prepaid expenses reflects the matching concept.

In a similar way to all current assets, accounts receivable should be valued at the lower of its original amount ('cost') and the amount of monies that can be recovered ('NRV'). However, there are a number of approaches to achieving this which complicate the treatment somewhat.

11.1 Write-Offs and Provisions

In applying the prudence concept, debts that are highly unlikely to be paid, must be removed from the trade receivables account. These are debts that are no longer an asset as they have gone 'bad'.

To make the accounting equation balance, the amount removed must also be reflected in the income statement as an expense.

Writing off a bad debt:		
B/S	↓	Accounting receivable
P&L	↑	Expenses

Specific Provisions

If there is uncertainty about the recoverability of a debt, a company should still be prudent but rather than completely removing the debt the company will make a specific provision (or allowance) against it.

Recognising a specific doubtful debt:		
B/S	↑	Provision for doubtful debt
P&L	↑	Expenses

The provision is set off against the accounts receivable balance on the balance sheet.

Note that it is only on initial recognition of the doubtful debt that the income statement reflects an expense. The provision may then sit there from one year to the next with no additional effect on profit or on the balance sheet. However, adjustments upwards or downwards to the provision amount would be reflected in the income statement as 'updates' until the debts is received or goes bad.

If subsequently a doubtful debt goes bad (i.e. it is now definitely not recoverable), there is no effect on profits. Simply reduce provisions (no longer required) and reduce accounts receivable (debt now bad and so needs to be removed).

General Provisions

After all specific write-offs and provisions have been considered, a company may decide to account for the fact that, from experience, a proportion of remaining accounts receivable may not pay up. This is a general provision and is usually a percentage of remaining net debts. As with specific provisions, it is only the change in the provision that is reflected in the P&L as an expense.

General provisions, where a company provides for say 2% of all receivables because 2% of all receivables typically go bad, are no longer permitted under IFRS. In order to book a provision, there must be objective evidence that the recoverability of a debt is in doubt.

Long-Lived Assets

12 Capitalisation or Write Off?

12.1 Introduction

Long-lived assets are categorised as follows:

- Intangible
- Tangible
- Investments

This chapter concerns itself with the first two categories. Investments are specifically examined in Chapter 7. Before examining each category of long-lived asset in detail let us familiarise ourselves with some fundamental accounting issues of importance for this area.

Expenditure incurred by a business will either result in an asset in the balance sheet (capitalise) or expense in the income statement.

Capitalised means recognise on the balance sheet and spread the cost. Write-off means recognise the entire cost now in the income statement. It is therefore essential to identify whether expenditure should be capitalised as 'capex' and written off as revenue expenditure. Long-lived assets are those assets that are expected to benefit more than one accounting period. As a result, their respective accounting treatment differs from that of current assets.

12.2 Core Accounting Treatment

The costs of acquiring such assets should be spread over the period to which they relate as illustrated below for an asset with a 4-year life.

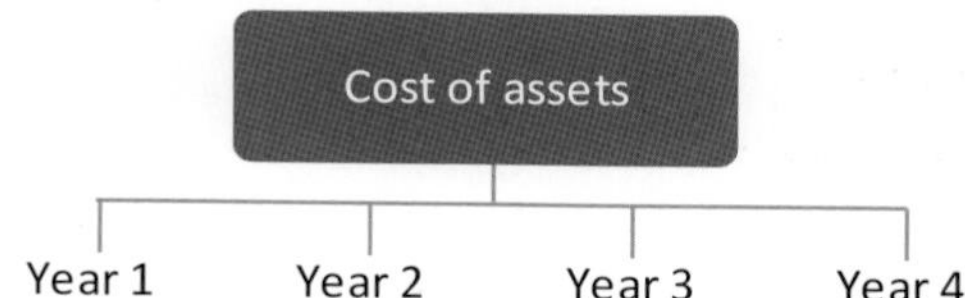

Two questions need to be addressed:

- What is meant by cost?
- How is this cost then allocated?

First, let us address the issue of cost. This should include all costs incurred in bringing an asset into its location and working condition. These costs may include purchase price, freight costs and installation. Costs incurred subsequent to purchase are generally classified as repairs or maintenance. Such costs are generally expensed to the income statement unless it could be argued that they have enhanced the asset (e.g. extended its useful economic life or improved capacity).

In relation to allocation, the cost of the asset is allocated as an expense to the income statement of the accounting periods expected to benefit from its use.

Example

Numerate Inc. has incurred the following items of expenditure.

1. €10,000 on the acquisition of an advanced computer including €1,000 on import duties and €2,000 on installation costs.
2. €15,000 on a new set of windows to replace the existing ones which were rotten.

How should each amount of expenditure be treated?

Solution

For Scenario 1, the acquisition cost of the computer should be capitalised assuming that it will benefit more than one accounting period. In addition, the import duty and installation costs should also be capitalised. These costs were necessary to getting the asset to its location and putting it into a working condition. Total costs capitalised are €13,000.

In the case of Scenario 2, this expenditure could be written off to the income statement if it is classified as repairs and maintenance, otherwise it would be capitalised.

12.3 Interest Capitalisation

One of the more controversial aspects of the capitalisation decision relates to interest.

Under IAS 23 *Borrowing Costs* it is mandatory to capitalise interest when it is incurred on financing an asset under construction by the company and when certain conditions are met. The principle behind this is that interest, in this case, is a cost of getting an asset into a useable condition. Therefore, it qualifies under the general capitalisation rule. This represents a relatively recent change to IFRS as until 2009 companies could choose whether to capitalise or expense these interest costs. The change brings IFRS in line with US GAAP.

The amount of interest which must be capitalised depends on whether or not it relates to:

- A loan specifically taken out to finance the production of the asset.
- A pool of finance which was made available for several projects some of which may relate to the asset under construction.

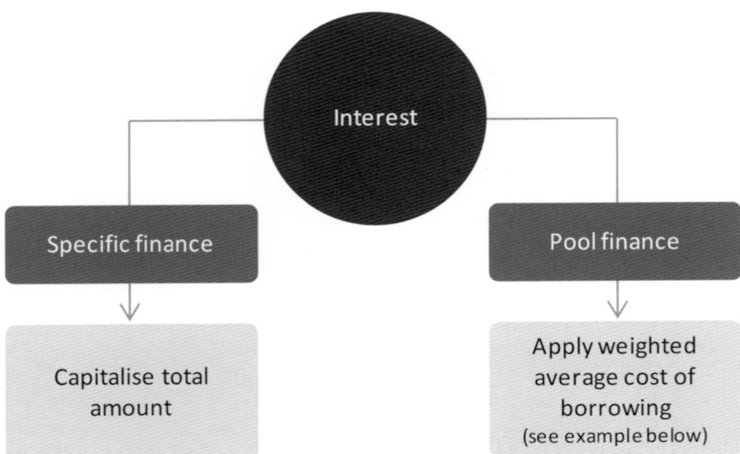

Example

Construct Inc. is constructing a canteen for its production staff. The cost of the partially constructed building is €3,000,000.

Construct Inc. has borrowed €1,000,000 at 5% to finance the project. It also has €6,000,000 of 10% bonds and €1,200,000 of 8% bonds.

How much interest will be capitalised?

Solution			€
Interest on specific debt	€1,000,000 × 5%	=	50,000
Interest on debentures	€2,000,000 × 9.67%*	=	193,332
			243,332

*weighted average interest of bonds in issue:

$$\frac{(10\% \times 6{,}000) + (8\% \times 1{,}200)}{7{,}200} = 9.67\%$$

Points to Note

- The €2,000,000 balance of finance is assumed to be in the form of bonds.
- The interest relating to the canteen project is calculated on a weighted average basis.

12.4 Analysis Implications

Below is a summary of the key analytical issues affected by the capitalisation of assets on the balance sheet.

Firms that capitalise costs will have a smoother earnings trend

This is due to the fact that the income statement will be affected by annual depreciation charges as opposed to one off expense items.

Firms that capitalise may appear more profitable

The annual depreciation charge is less than the total cost of the asset and hence less expense is charged to the income statement. This is a result of the matching concept and the cost of the asset is expensed over its useful economic life.

Firms that capitalise will have higher stockholders' funds

This is largely due to the cost of the asset being expensed to the income statement over the asset's life rather than when it is incurred which would immediately reduce net assets.

Interest capitalisation results in higher subsequent depreciation charges

This is due to the higher cost to be depreciated. During the period of construction of the asset, the income statement will benefit from the capitalisation of interest. Once the asset is in use the amount to be depreciated will be:

Cost + Total Capitalised Interest

Interest capitalisation can have an impact on cash flow statement presentation

The issue in this situation is whether or not the finance charge should be classified as an investing activity (relates to purchase of an asset) or as a financing activity.

Normally adjustments are made by an analyst to remove the impact of interest capitalisation

Given the above, it will facilitate meaningful analysis if this adjustment is made (if the amount is substantial) especially if the analyst wishes to undertake meaningful comparable company analysis.

13 Intangible Assets

13.1 Introduction

An intangible asset is an asset with no physical presence. Typically, such assets pose difficulties for accountants and analysts. These mainly arise because it is:

- Very difficult to measure value
- Very difficult to establish a meaningful useful economic life

Essentially, these matters are so significant that they call into question whether or not an asset really exists. However, the capitalisation of intangibles is a highly relevant issue when analysing financial statements. It is important to understand whether or not all the resources available to the entity to generate income have been disclosed. Furthermore, intangibles have become increasingly important for valuing companies as physical assets become less important for more businesses (for example Apple, Google and Amazon). Reliability of accounting information is an issue purely due to the difficulties involved in establishing cost and then determining useful economic life for the purpose of amortisation.

13.2 Examples and Accounting Treatment

The table below summarises the accounting treatment of key intangibles.

Example	Accounting Treatment
Research and development (see below)	Split: Research ↓ Expensed; Development ↓ Must capitalise (see below)
Goodwill (see below)	Purchased ↓ Capitalise
Other intangibles: ▪ Patents and Copyrights ▪ Brands and Trademarks	Capitalise and amortise over useful economic life once acquired. Generally, no recognition of non-purchased items although certain legal and set up costs can be capitalised

13.3 Research and Development

Research and development expenditure is an analytically important and high-profile issue in many sectors. For accounting purposes, the expenditure can be analysed into:

- Research (i.e. original work)
- Development (i.e. using existing research to improve products, processes, etc.)

These costs are specifically dealt with under IAS 38 *Intangible Assets*. There are a number of ways to rationalise the accounting treatment. Here we shall explain the treatment based on the concepts of conservatism and matching.

Research expenditure is required to be expensed immediately. This is in accordance with the concept of conservatism. The research being carried out may not lead to a probable future income stream and as such it is unlikely to represent an asset.

Development expenditure on the other hand **must** be capitalised as long as certain criteria are met. This is in accordance with the matching concept. The capitalised costs are then expensed to the income statement as amortisation and matched with the revenues they have hoped to generate.

The criteria themselves are based on the concept of conservatism – does an asset really exist? They are summarised as follows:

- The product is technically feasible and can be sold.
- Management intend to complete the intangible assets (i.e. complete the development).
- Management is able to use or sell the asset.
- Management can demonstrate that there is a mechanism by which the intangible will generate future economic benefits.
- Adequate resources exist to complete and sell the intangible asset.
- The costs associated with developing the asset can be reliably measured.

13.4 Goodwill

Definition of Goodwill

Goodwill only emerges in financial statements if there has been an acquisition. The process for recognising goodwill is addressed in the chapters on consolidated accounts. At this stage we need to know that is represents the difference between what a company pays to acquire another company and the market value of that target company's individual assets. Typically, the excess would represent brands, customer loyalty, future synergies amongst other things.

13.5 Analysis Implications

Choice of Economic Life

This is at the discretion of management and as a rule will directly impact the income statement. The longer the useful life, the smaller the amortisation charge and the higher the earnings figure. Analysts often use EBITDA as the basis for their analysis, given the managerial flexibility in relation to amortisation periods.

Valuable Assets Off Balance Sheet

IAS 38 specifically prohibits the capitalisation of internally generated assets such as brands, publishing titles, customer lists, etc. as it is unlikely they will meet recognition criteria. However, such assets are critical to many companies. Consider the importance of the Apple trademark! A related issue here is the write-off of research and development expenditure. Most users would expect companies that have a high 'R&D' spend to have lots of potential for future growth. However, the accounting treatment would often result in high losses and low assets. An analyst might choose to capitalise such expenditure when undertaking comparable company analysis.

Analysis Focus

Economic Versus Accounting Definitions

Section 13 makes clear the reasons why companies are unhappy capitalising intangible assets. But from the economic viewpoint, operating costs are just the expenses incurred in producing, distributing and selling the firm's **existing** products. All research costs, or costs associated with creating new brands, are really discretionary investments, on which managers (and shareholders) expect to see a return. To understand the real size of a company's balance sheet, and how profitable it really is, it is essential to capitalise and amortise intangible assets.

14 Tangible Assets

This category of long-lived assets presents fewer accounting problems. Useful lives, although still requiring the exercise of judgement, are much more straightforward due to the physical nature of most tangible assets.

Examples

- Vehicles
- Buildings
- Computer equipment
- Equipment

Tangible long-lived assets should be capitalised at the costs incurred in bringing them into use. These will include costs such as import duties, installation costs and, as seen above, interest.

Depreciation and Impairment of Long-Lived Assets

15 The Principle of Long-Lived Assets

Matching requires that all costs incurred in generating revenues for a particular period be charged in that period. Given that, in general, the use of an asset will reduce its value and future earnings potential, this is a real cost to the company.

For example, take an asset purchased at €10,000 which in three years' time will have a residual value of €4,000. The cost of its use is €6,000. In accounting terms, this cost is called depreciation.

Management have to decide how best to allocate the depreciation of €6,000 to the accounting periods benefiting from use of the asset. This is a very subjective area.

16 Methods of Depreciation

There are three main methods of depreciation.

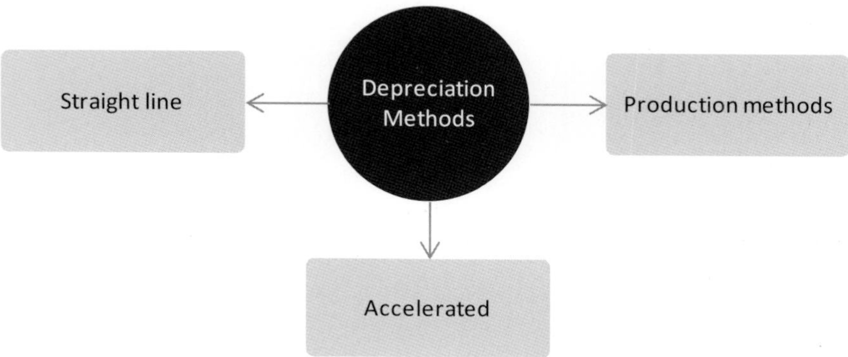

They all have the same aim but have different impacts on the income statement. Furthermore, the value of an asset on the balance sheet is net book value (NBV). NBV is defined as:

Carrying value – Accumulated depreciation

The following examples show the calculations.

16.1 Straight Line

As its name suggests, this method charges the same amount of depreciation each year.

Example

Juice Inc. purchases an industrial orange peeler for €100,000. Installation costs were €16,000. The expected useful life is eight years. The residual value at the end of Year 8 is expected to be €8,000.

Required

Calculate the annual depreciation charge and book value for each year of its useful life.

Solution

$$\text{Annual charge} = \frac{(100{,}000+16{,}000)\text{-}8{,}000}{8 \text{ years}} = €13{,}500$$

Year	Annual Charge Income Statement	Accumulated Depreciation	Net Book Value Balance Sheet		
	€	€	€	€	€
1	13,500	13,500	116,000 –	13,500 =	102,500
2	13,500	27,000	116,000 –	27,000 =	89,000
3	13,500	40,500	116,000 –	40,500 =	75,500
4	13,500	54,000	116,000 –	54,000 =	62,000
5	13,500	67,500	116,000 –	67,500 =	48,500
6	13,500	81,000	116,000 –	81,000 =	35,000
7	13,500	94,500	116,000 –	94,500 =	21,500
8	13,500	108,000	116,000 –	108,000 =	8,000

Point to Note

- The assumption underlying this method is that the asset provides the same level of benefit to each accounting period

16.2 Accelerated Methods

These methods seek to charge more in the earlier years and less in the later years of an asset's useful life.

There are three main accelerated methods:

- Sum Of the Year's Digits (SOYD)
- Declining balance
- Double declining balance

SOYD

$$\text{Cost - Salvage value} \times \frac{\text{Years remaining}}{\text{Sum of the digits}}$$

Example

Using the information in the example of Juice Inc. above, calculate the annual depreciation charge over the useful life of the asset together with the book value for each year of the asset's useful life.

$$(\text{Cost - Salvage value}) \times \frac{\text{Years remaining}}{\text{Sum of the digits}} = (116{,}000 - 8{,}000) \times \frac{\text{Years remaining}}{\text{Sum of the digits}}$$

Sum of the digits = 8 + 7 + 6 + 5 + 4 + 3 + 2 + 1 = 36

Alternatively, the sum of year's digits can be calculated by using the formula:

$$\text{n} \times \frac{\text{n} + 1}{2}$$

In this case, that would be 8 × 8[8 + 1]/2 = 36

Year	Depreciation Charge					Accumulated	Net Book Value
	€				€	€	€
1	108,000	×	8/36	=	24,000	24,000	92,000 (=116k − 24k)
2	108,000	×	7/36	=	21,000	45,000	71,000
3	108,000	×	6/36	=	18,000	63,000	53,000
4	108,000	×	5/36	=	15,000	78,000	38,000
5	108,000	×	4/36	=	12,000	90,000	26,000
6	108,000	×	3/36	=	9,000	99,000	17,000
7	108,000	×	2/36	=	6,000	105,000	11,000
8	108,000	×	1/36	=	3,000	108,000	8,000

Declining Balance (DB)

This uses the following formula to calculate the annual charge:

Constant % × Net book value*

* NBV = Cost less cumulative depreciation

The relevant percentage can be calculated using the formula:

$$\sqrt[n]{\frac{\text{Residual value}}{\text{Original cost}}} - 1$$

Where n is the useful life.

Example

Using the information for Juice Inc. and assuming a depreciation rate of 25%, calculate the annual charge together with the book value for each year of the asset's useful life. In this example, for ease of calculation, assume that the residual value is €11,613 approximately.

Solution	**€**
Cost	116,000
Year 1 depreciation @ 25%	(29,000)
Year 1 net book value	87,000
Year 2 depreciation @ 25%	(21,750)
Year 2 net book value	65,250
Year 3 depreciation @ 25%	(16,313)
Year 3 net book value	48,937
Year 4 depreciation @ 25%	(12,234)
Year 4 net book value	36,703
Year 5 depreciation @ 25%	(9,176)
Year 5 net book value	27,527
Year 6 depreciation @ 25%	(6,882)
Year 6 net book value	20,645
Year 7 depreciation @ 25%	(5,161)
Year 7 net book value	15,484
Year 8 depreciation @ 25%	(3,871)
Year 8 net book value	11,613*

*This is the residual value

Double Declining Balance Method

This method uses another more accelerated method to calculate depreciation:

$$\text{Net book value} \times \frac{2}{\text{Useful life}}$$

Often, this is driven by tax regulations and corporates swap between various methods to maximise the depreciation charge and, hence, minimise taxes. However, beware that in many jurisdictions accounting and tax issues are not governed by the same rules. Therefore, increasing the accounting depreciation charge may have no impact whatsoever on taxes.

Example

Using the information from the Juice Inc. example directly above, calculate the annual depreciation charge together with the net book value in each year.

Solution

NBV* = (Cost – Accumulated depreciation)

*Ignore salvage value

Year	Depreciation					Accumulated	Net Book Value
	€				€	€	€
1	116,000	×	2/8	=	29,000	29,000	87,000
2	87,000	×	2/8	=	21,750	50,750	65,250
3	65,250	×	2/8	=	16,313	67,063	48,937
4	48,937	×	2/8	=	12,234	79,297	36,703
5	36,703	×	2/8	=	9,176	88,473	27,527
6	27,527	×	2/8	=	6,882	95,355	20,645
7	20,645	×	2/8	=	5,161	100,516	15,484
8	15,484	×	2/8	=	3,871	104,387	11,613

16.3 Other Methods

This method uses an economic approach to define the depreciation amount. The underlying assumption is that the asset generates constant cash flows over time. If this is so, then this method will adjust the asset's value to achieve a constant rate of return over time. The result is low depreciation in the earlier years and higher depreciation in the later years.

It is a highly subjective approach and is rarely used in practice. It is not allowed under US/UK GAAP or US tax law.

Production Method

Some asset's lives reflect the usage of that asset. For example, consider a machine that has a total useful life of 20,000 hours. It costs €250,000 to purchase. Estimated usage over its useful life is as follows:

Year	Hours
1	1,000
2	8,000
3	7,000
4	2,000
5	2,000

What would be the depreciation charge for each year?

Solution

$$\text{Depreciation per hour} = \frac{€250{,}000}{20{,}000\text{ hrs}} = €12.50$$

Year	Hours	Depreciation per hour	Annual charge	Accumulated charges	NBV
		€	€	€	€
1	1,000	12.50	12,500	12,500	237,500
2	8,000	12.50	100,000	112,500	137,500
3	7,000	12.50	87,500	200,000	50,000
4	2,000	12.50	25,000	225,000	25,000
5	2,000	12.50	25,000	250,000	-

17 Further Considerations About Depreciation

17.1 Choice of Depreciation Method

The choice of depreciation method is a management decision. They should select the method that best reflects the manner in which benefit is obtained from the asset during its useful life. Given the choice of methods available, it is possible that different methods are used across entities and across nations. In order for meaningful analysis to be made, we have already discussed the cleaning of earnings by the calculation of EBITDA (Chapter 2). In order for this to happen, financial statements should make full disclosure of the methods chosen. In addition, IFRS requires that the method of depreciation be reviewed on a periodic basis.

17.2 Change of Depreciation Method

If on reflection management decide that one method of depreciation is more suitable than another, then this is a change in accounting policy. In accordance with GAAP, as noted in Chapter 2, changes in depreciation methods are accounted for as a change in accounting estimate. This means that the prior year financial statements are not restated as if the new method had always been adopted. Instead, just the current and/or future financial statements will report the change.

17.3 Revision of Useful Life

In addition to a periodic review of the method of depreciation, management must also review the useful life of an asset. This is affected by repairs and maintenance policy, pace of technological innovation, market demand for goods produced and sold.

Just as the decision on which method of depreciation to use is a subjective area, so too is the decision about an asset's useful life. There remains a risk that management will get the estimate of useful life materially wrong. This risk would be highest for a new type of long-lived asset which management are less familiar with.

If it transpires that the useful life is longer or shorter than previously anticipated, then the change is accounted for as a change in accounting estimate, i.e. in the same manner as a change in the method of depreciation. The change is accounted for in the current year and then all subsequent years.

If a company decides to change the useful life of an asset, then it will calculate the subsequent annual depreciation based on writing off the net book value over the new remaining useful life.

Example

John Inc. purchased an asset on 1.1.05 for €200,000. The straight-line method was applied using a useful life of seven years and a residual or salvage value of €60,000. On 1.1.08, John Inc. revised the remaining useful life to two years.

Required

Calculate the annual depreciation charge for each year of the asset's life.

Solution

Step 1 Find the book value at point of change in useful life.

$$\text{1.1.05 Annual charge} \quad \frac{200{,}000 - 60{,}000}{7} = €20{,}000$$

Applied for 3 years = €60,000

Net book value = €200,000 – €60,000

= €140,000

Step 2 Write the remaining net book value over the new useful life.

$$\frac{140{,}000 - 60{,}000}{2} = €40{,}000$$

18 Analysis Implications

There are three key areas that should be noted:

- Possibility of Income Manipulation
  - Given the impact of different methods of depreciation on earnings, the income statement can be manipulated.
- Comparability problems
  - This is simply due to the fact that depreciation is a subjective area. It is an estimate based on management judgement and expertise which may vary from entity to entity.
- Impact of method on depreciation charge on earnings.

Below is a summary of the impact on earnings of the three key methods of depreciation:

	Straight Line	**Accelerated**	**Sinking Fund**
Earlier years	Average	High	Low
Later years	Average	Low	High

Analysis Focus

Economic and Straight-Line Depreciation

When a project is analysed, it is conventional to use discounted cash flow (DCF) methods. It is implicit in a DCF that the impairment of value to an asset during the year is the fall in its net present value (NPV) over the period. This usually implies small declines in value early in the asset's life, with much bigger falls as the end of its life approaches. This is clearly not what happens if straight-line depreciation is used, and the distortion resulting from accelerated depreciation is worse still.

This has the unfortunate effect of reducing the returns on capital of growing companies, and increasing it for shrinking companies – a perverse incentive for managers

19 Subsequent Changes in Value

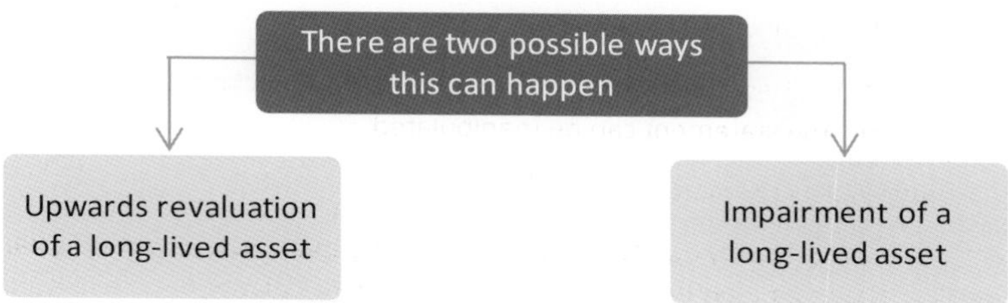

19.1 Revaluations

IAS 16 *Property, Plant and Equipment* allows upward revaluation of long-lived assets to fair value (in most cases, market value). If a company wishes to revalue an asset it must revalue all assets in the same class on the grounds of consistency. The surplus arising on the revaluation is not accounted for as a gain in the income statement, but as a revaluation surplus (reserve) in stockholder's equity.

Example

Azul S.A. acquired a property on 1 January Year 1 at a cost of €1,250,000. The property was being depreciated on a straight-line basis over 50 years. On 1 January Year 6, the property was revalued to fair value of €1,750,000

Required

Calculate the revaluation surplus and the new depreciation charge.

Solution

$$\frac{1{,}250{,}000}{50} = €25{,}000 \text{ annual depreciation charge}$$

	€
Revaluation on 1/1/Year 6	1,750,000
Net Book Value 1/1/Year 6	(1,125,000)
(1,250,000 – 125,000)	
Surplus arising on revaluation	625,000

The new depreciation charge:

$$\frac{€1{,}750{,}000}{45 \text{ remaining years}} = €38{,}889 \text{ per annum}$$

Points to Note

- Extract from the Balance Sheet 1 January Year 6.

	€
Long-lived assets	
Property	1,750,000
Stockholders' equity	
Revaluation surplus	625,000

- It is possible, under IAS 16, to release the revaluation surplus during the life of the asset to retained earnings **not** through the income statement. This allows the ultimate matching of the increase in value of the asset over its useful life. The income statement will account for the higher depreciation charge of €38,889 so earnings are €13,889 lower due to the revaluation. Each year, €13,889 will however be transferred from revaluation surplus to retained earnings, so the net effect on *retained earnings* is zero.

$$\frac{625{,}000}{45 \text{ years}} = €13{,}889$$

19.2 Impairments

Just as the value of long-lived assets may increase, so too can it decrease. The issue of accounting for decreases is very topical. This is mainly due to the fact that prior to the introduction of IAS 36 Impairment of Assets, there was no definitive standard on the issue.

The issues that need to be addressed when looking at falls in value are:

- Has an impairment occurred?
- How can the fall be measured?

An impairment has arisen when:

Carrying value > Net recoverable amount

In this case, a write down in value of the asset is required. In essence, an asset is impaired if the recoverability of the existing carrying value is in doubt.

The carrying value is basically the value at which the asset is held in the balance sheet (net book value). Recoverable amount is the greater of the selling price net of disposal costs or value in use. The latter term is defined by looking at the net present value of future cash flows associated with the asset in question. In practice, the calculation of value in use can be extremely subjective and challenging.

Identifying an Impairment

IAS 36 provides guidance on both external and internal factors that are likely to give rise to impairments:

- Market decline beyond expectations due to ageing or use of the asset.
- Technological advances
- Evidence of physical damage to an asset.
- Product discontinuation rendering assets used in process worthless.

Accounting for Impairments

Below is a summary of the key provisions of IAS 36.

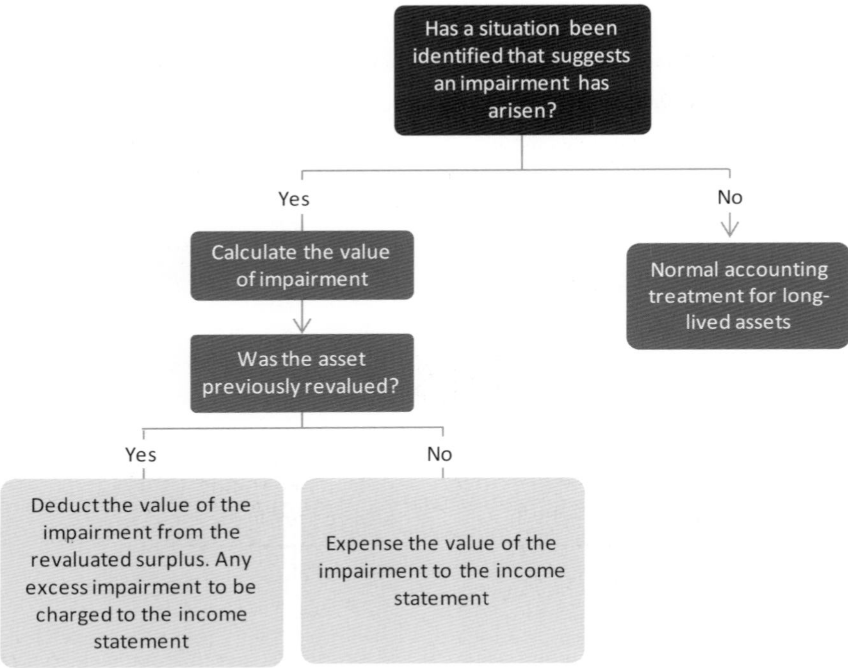

Example

Using the information from the previous example, assume that a year after the revaluation, due to an unexpected fall in the property market, the property now has a net recoverable amount of €985,000.

Required

Account for the impairment.

Solution

	€
Net book value a year after revaluation (1,750,000 – 38,889)	1,711,111
Net recoverable amount	(985,000)
Value of Impairment	726,111

This can be treated as follows:

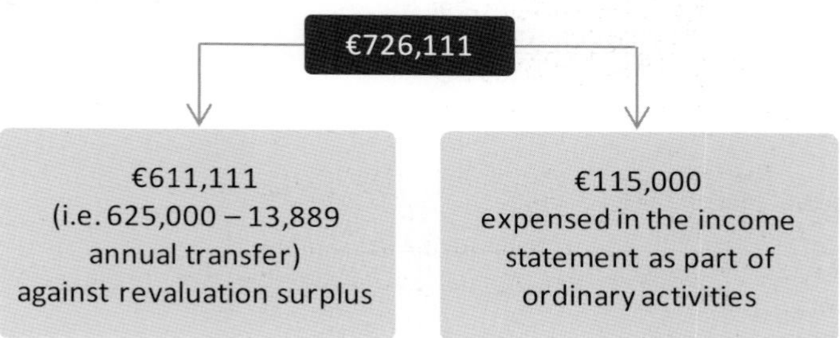

Points to Note

- If the property had not been revalued the full impairment would be expensed in the income statement.
- Assuming no change in useful life, the new depreciation charge will be:

$$\frac{€985{,}000}{44 \text{ years}} = €22{,}386 \text{ per annum}$$

19.3 Accounts Commentary

Turn to page 104 and 105 of the Lufthansa financials. The balance sheet is in a pretty standard format for a Continental European company. It shows total assets first and equity plus liabilities after. Most of the account captions are relatively straightforward but it is useful to mention a few interesting points.

The accounting and valuation policies employed by Lufthansa to prepare the financials are disclosed on page 111. Most of the policies are standard. It is always worthwhile to examine these policies to ensure they are comparable with other companies that are a part of the analysis set. For example, explore the notes to confirm that:

- Goodwill is tested every year for impairment
- Tangible fixed assets are not revalued

The notes to the financial statements are an important part of the information set when exploring accounting information. For example, turn to note 19 on page 131 of the financials. This disaggregates fixed assets into the detail of cost and depreciation as well as setting out the additions and disposals.

Chapter 4: Balance Sheet – Liabilities, Capital Instruments and Provisions

"Over the years, old hacks like me have discovered more reliable indicators that mark out finance leases. Among the soundest: 'if a figure of 89% is mentioned anywhere in the documentation the lease is a finance lease.' My own favourite, which I have found to be almost infallible in practice, is 'if a lease is headed "operating lease", it is a finance lease." [4]

[4] Ron Paterson Accountancy, December 2000. Again, an older quote but so on point. My particular favourite is the idea that what a document is called is prima facie evidence of what it is not!

Accounting for Liabilities

1 Introduction

This chapter addresses the last key element of the balance sheet – liabilities. First, the chapter addresses the major categories of liability and the classification of debt and equity instruments. After this the key areas of equities, bonds, leases, deferred taxation and provisions are covered. Finally, the chapter covers the crucial issue of calculating net debt, a key input into valuation models.

2 Definitions and Categories of Liability

A liability is defined as:

> *"A present obligation of the reporting enterprise arising from past events, the settlement of which is expected to result in an outflow from the enterprise of resources embodying economic benefits."*

In other words, at its most basic level a liability denotes a future cash outflow and hence is of great interest to users of financial statements.

2.1 Classification

Liabilities are often classified according to maturity profile:

Whilst there is no formal need to categorise assets and liabilities as current or long term, this is done as a result of accounting convention. This allows users to differentiate between the short-term financing (working capital cycle) and long-term financing of the entity. The working capital cycle is examined in more detail in Chapter 6.

This chapter focuses on understanding the accounting treatment of the more complex liability captions:

- Debt
- Leases
- Deferred taxation
- Contingencies and provisions

Current liabilities are due for repayment within one year. The major items are:

- Trade and operating liabilities: these represent amounts owed by the company to suppliers.
- Advances from customers: if a customer pays in advance, then the firm has an obligation to supply the goods and services to that value.
- Short-term debt and the current portion of long-term debt.

In general, long-term liabilities will consist of financing items. In particular, it will consist of various forms of debt finance. Each of the major sources of finance is considered below.

2.2 Classification of Debt and Equity

A key issue is whether a particular financial instrument should be classified as debt or equity. It is important for an analyst to understand how financial instruments are classified. However, analysts will often make their own decision on whether an instrument is debt or equity as this will directly impact on valuation issues associated with calculating enterprise value. A framework for calculating an appropriate net debt figure for analysts is included towards the end of this chapter.

IAS 32 *Financial Instruments: Presentation* and 39 *Financial Instruments: Recognition and Measurement* provides detailed definitions of financial liabilities. In essence the following decision chart summarises the appropriate classification issues:

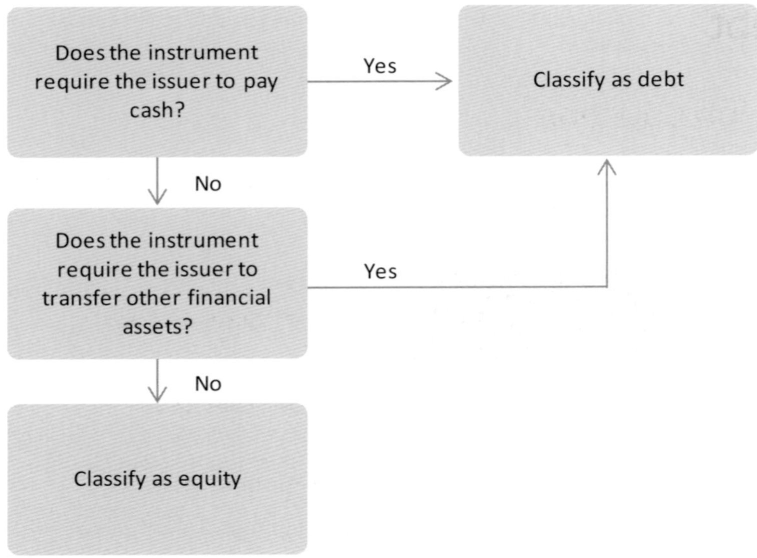

The most important implication of this is that certain preference shares may be classified as debt even though, legally, such instruments are equity. For example, redeemable preference shares which have a mandatory redemption clause are treated as debt. If there is no legal obligation to redeem (e.g. the decision to redeem is at the discretion of the issuer), then such instruments would be classified as equity up until any decision is made to redeem.

Debt

3 Introduction

Long-term debt takes the form of either notes or bonds. The key difference between the two is illustrated below:

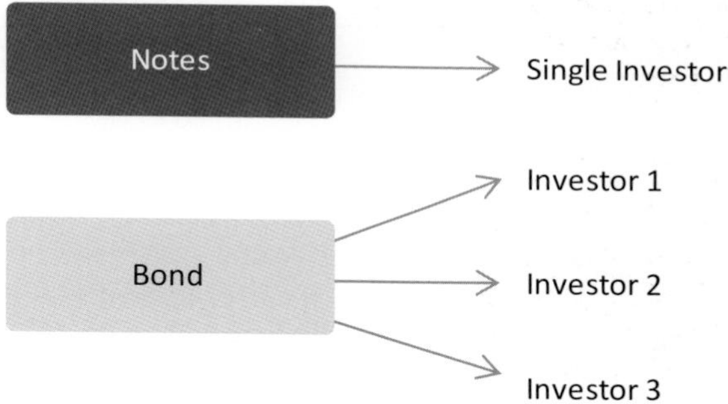

Both notes and bonds involve the issuance of a written agreement between entity and investor which states the principal sum (amount of loan excluding interest), the interest rate, when the interest and principal sum are to be paid and any restrictive covenants.

IFRSs are neither prescriptive nor all-encompassing in their accounting treatment of these forms of debt finance. The following is based on accepted GAAP.

4 Basic Accounting Treatment

The general principle, whether for notes or bonds or other similar forms of debt finance, is as follows:

	€
Total amount repayable	x
Present value of future net cash outflows	(x)
Total cost of finance	x

The cost of finance is then charged on a systematic basis to the income statement during the life of the note or bond.

The reason for this treatment is that the investor rate (sometimes referred to as the coupon rate) often bears little resemblance to the market rate for such borrowing. As far as the financial statements are concerned, they must reflect the true underlying cost of borrowing. The effective rate of interest is generally taken to be the market rate of interest at the date of issuance and it is this rate which is used to calculate the amount of interest expensed to the income statement.

5 Example of Accounting Treatment

On 1 January year 1, Son Inc. issues a six-year €40 million bond with an annual coupon of 6%. Assume market interest rates are 9%.

(i) The cash flow profile for the holder of such a bond would look as follows:

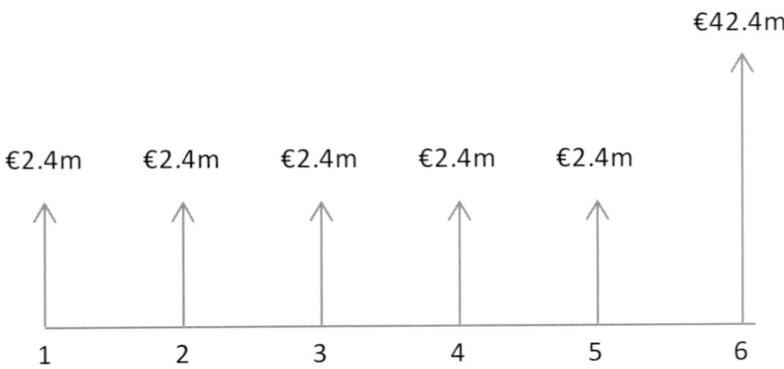

(ii) Bonds are valued at the present value of future cash flows using the market rate of interest.

What is the market value of this bond?

Period	Cash Flow (€m)	Discount Rate		Present Value (€m)
1	2.4	$1/(1.09)^1$	=	2.202
2	2.4	$1/(1.09)^2$	=	2.020
3	2.4	$1/(1.09)^3$	=	1.853
4	2.4	$1/(1.09)^4$	=	1.700
5	2.4	$1/(1.09)^5$	=	1.560
6	42.4	$1/(1.09)^6$	=	25.282
		Price	=	34.617

Price of the bond = €34.617m

(iii) Total Expense

Amount Son Inc. paid out		Less	Amount Son Inc. received on issue
↓			↓
	€		
Coupon = 2.4 × 6=	14.4		
Principal =	40.0		
Total =	€54.4m	Verses	€34.62m

The difference of €19.78m represents the total cost of borrowing that needs to be amortised in the financial statements, i.e. the difference between the amount paid to the lender and the amount received upfront.

Accounting Treatment

- Entry on Issue

↑ Cash	€34.62m
↑ Debt (long term)	€34.62m

Essentially, the discount on the bond (€40m – €34.62m) has been set off against the €40m bringing the loan down to €34.62m.

Annual Interest Expense and Liability

Year	Opening Loan Balance	Interest*	Payment	Closing Loan Balance
	€m	**€m**	**€m**	**€m**
1	34.62	3.12	(2.4)	35.34
2	35.34	3.18	(2.4)	36.12
3	36.12	3.25	(2.4)	36.97
4	36.97	3.33	(2.4)	37.90
5	37.90	3.41	(2.4)	38.91
6	38.91	3.49**	(42.4)	-

*use the market rate of 9% (IRR) **rounded to clear debt exactly

Points to Note

- This bond was issued at a discount. The present value of the cash received is less than the principal sum. If the situation had been the reverse, the bond would have been issued at a premium, but the same concept would have been applied to the accounting treatment, i.e. the premium would be amortised over the life of the bond.
- The interest figure is the amount which is reflected in the income statement of each year. The total across the six years comes to €19.78m.
- The balance sheet includes the loan balance at the end of each year.
- The cash payments are the amounts that would be reflected in the cash flow statement. The cash flow statement would reflect the inflow of €34.62m in year 1.

6 Summary of Accounting Treatment

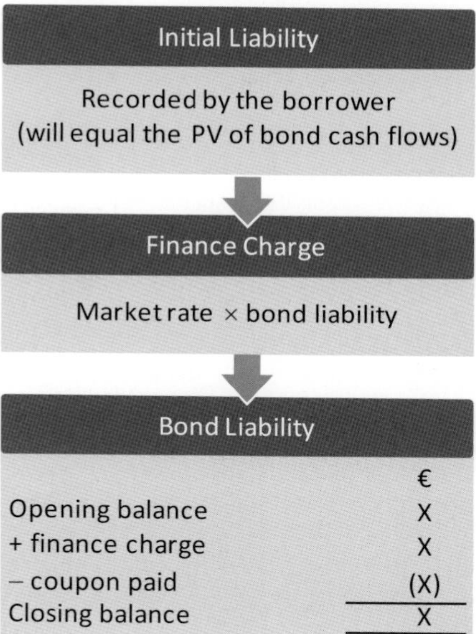

7 Other Issues

7.1 Zero-Coupon Bonds

- Issued at a discount.
- No annual interest is paid so no impact on cash flow.
- An effective discount rate is charged in the income statement in order to reflect the underlying cost of finance (the discount).

This underlying cost of finance is generally tax deductible for the company.

7.2 Variable Rate Debt

These bonds are generally issued at or around par. Hence, the effective interest rate will match the coupon and thus be automatically reflected in the income statement.

7.3 Debt Retirement/Extinguishment

Repurchasing debt involves paying off existing loans or bonds prior to maturity. This may arise due to the availability of cheaper sources of finance. The accounting issue that arises from this type of transaction is illustrated below:

	€m
Amount to be paid	X
Book value of amount outstanding	(x)
Difference	x/(x)

IFRS does not provide specific guidance on the treatment of the difference. In the US, the difference is required to be treated as an "extraordinary" term.

8 Debt with Equity Features

In order to obtain a more attractive cost of debt, companies often attach conversion rights or warrants to debt. The holder then has the opportunity to participate in any equity growth of the issuer if he so chooses. The issue arises as to how to treat the bond itself and the conversion/warrant element.

Convertible Bonds

Under IFRS, the accounting treatment is to account for each component separately.

Residual Allocation Method

	€
Total market value of convertible debt	x
Market value of debt without conversion rights	(x)
Residual balance	x

The residual balance is then allocated to the "paid-in capital" account. It is then reallocated to common stock on conversion of the debt to stock.

Bonds Issued with Warrants

A warrant entitles the holder to purchase a stated number of shares or stock at a certain price within a specific period. As with conversion rights, warrants are issued with debt as incentives and can result in a lower interest rate for the borrower.

The accounting treatment is similar to that of convertible debt. The process is facilitated by the fact that warrants are often traded on the market and so have their own market value. It is therefore more likely that the relative market approach should be adopted in this scenario.

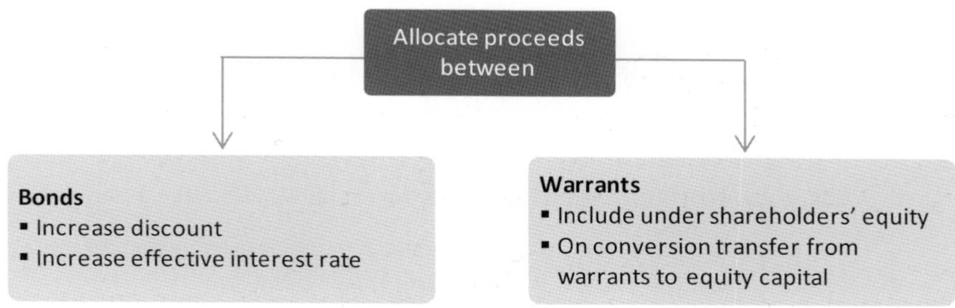

Leasing

9 Introduction

The accounting treatment for leases is about to change with the introduction of IFRS 16 *Leasing* in 2019. However, before addressing the changes we need to understand the existing GAAP for leases to appreciate the rationale for the forthcoming changes.

Leases are needed because not all entities want to or can afford to purchase plant or equipment outright. As a means of financing the use of these assets, entities enter into lease agreements whereby the entity can use the asset in return for rental payments. The terms of lease agreements can vary significantly and it is essential to understand the implications of the agreement to adopt an appropriate accounting treatment in the financial statements of the lessee. It is the substance of the lease agreement that is accounted for rather than its legal form.

10 Types of Lease

Under existing GAAP there are two types of lease agreement:

- Finance (or capital) lease
- Operating lease

Under a finance lease, substantially all of the risks and rewards of ownership are transferred from the lessor (the party with legal title) to the lessee (the party using the asset). IAS 17 *Leases* specifies criteria to help identify this situation:

1. The lease transfers ownership to the lessee by the end of the lease term.
2. The lease contains an option to purchase the leased asset at a price that is substantially lower than fair value at the date the option becomes exercisable (often referred to as a bargain purchase option).
3. The lease term is for the major part of the economic life of the asset.
4. The present value of the minimum lease payments is greater than or equal to substantially all of the fair value of the leased asset.
5. The leased assets are of a specialised nature that only the leasee can use.
6. If the lessee cancels the lease, then they bear the lessor's losses.
7. Gains or losses resulting from fluctuations in fair value accrue to the lessee.
8. The lessee can continue to lease the asset for a supplemental term at a rent which is substantially lower than market value.

In principle, if at least one of the above is met then the lease should be treated as a finance lease. There have been a number of practical problems applying IAS 17. Criteria 4 and 5 are vague as to what constitutes "major part" and "greater than or equal to substantially all of". Convention would imply that 80-90% would be an appropriate interpretation of "major part" and 95% of "greater than".

The most difficult part of accounting for leases is the identification of the nature of the lease. Once this has been done, the accounting treatment of the lease is itself relatively straightforward.

Finance Lease Operating Lease

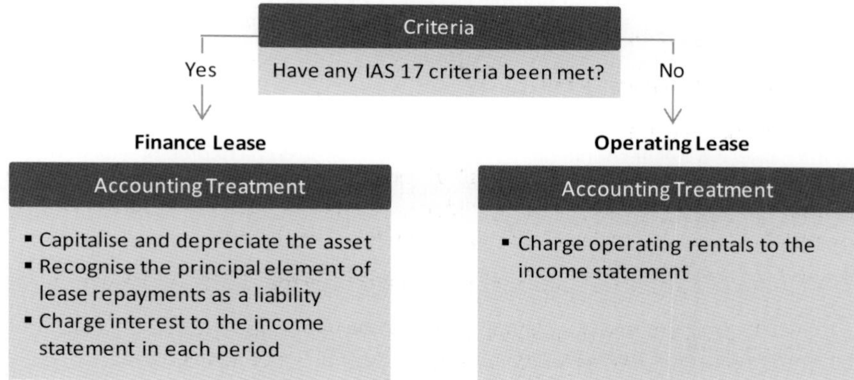

Finance Leases

In essence, the accounting treatment is similar to that if the asset had been purchased by means of a loan, i.e. as if there was an explicit loan and asset purchase. It should be noted that the asset is capitalised at the lesser of the fair value of the asset and of the present value of the minimum lease payments (MLP).

The MLP are calculated as:

	€
Minimum rental payments	x
Guaranteed residual value by lessee to lessor	x
Bargain purchase option*	x
	x

* If reasonably certain lessee will exercise this option.

The present value of the above is calculated using the incremental rate of borrowing of the lessee. The lease term for the purpose of calculating the present value of these cash flows is:

Fixed lease term + Any further optional terms

The asset is depreciated over the shorter of the lease term and the asset's useful life. If it is, however, reasonably certain that title will pass to lessee at the end of the term, then the useful life should be used.

Operating Leases

This is simply a rental agreement, neither an asset nor a liability to repay are recognised on the balance sheet. It should be noted that rentals should be charged on a systematic basis over the rental period. This includes allocating the benefit of any rent-free periods over the lease term.

Example

Lechateau S.A. enters into an operating lease for the use of photocopiers. The terms of the agreement are as follows:

Lease term:	2 years
Monthly rental:	€500
Rent-free period:	3 months

Required

Calculate the annual charge that will appear in the income statement of Lechateau S.A.

Solution

$$\frac{\text{Total return}}{\text{Lease term}} = \frac{21 \times €500}{24\text{ months}} = \frac{€10{,}500}{24}$$

∴ monthly rental charge = €437.5

∴ annual charge = €5,250

Points to Note

- The benefit of the three-month rent-free period is spread over the lease term.
- Total payments made in Year 1 are €4,500 but the expense charged is €5,250. The difference is recognised in the balance sheet as a liability of €750. In Year 2, total payments will be €6,000 but the expense charged will only be €5,250.

11 Comprehensive Example

Example – Finance Lease

Shortcut Inc. needs to acquire an asset with a value of €560,200.

The firm decided to finance the asset with a lease. The document was signed at the company's solicitors on the 1 January year 1. The details of the lease are as follows:

Lease term	:	5 years
Rentals	:	€144,000 payable in arrears
Depreciation Policy	:	Straight line

(i) What type of lease is it assuming the company's incremental borrowing rate is 9%?

Using 9%:

PV of paying €144,000 for 5 years @ 9%

$$= €144{,}000 \times \left(\frac{1}{r}\right)\left\{1 - \left[\frac{1}{(1+r)^N}\right]\right\} = ((1.09)^5 - 1)/.09$$

= €144,000 × 3.89 = €560,110

Fair value of asset = €560,200 ∴ **finance lease** as €560,110 substantially equal to €560,200, (i.e. >90%).

(ii) Calculate the amounts that would appear in the balance sheet and income statement.

Annual Finance Charge

Year	Opening Loan Balance	Interest at 9%	Lease Rental	Capital Repayment	Closing Loan Balance
	€	€	€	€	€
1	560,110	50,410	(144,000)	93,590	466,520
2	466,520	41,987	(144,000)	102,013	364,507
3	364,507	32,806	(144,000)	111,194	253,313
4	253,313	22,798	(144,000)	121,202	132,111
5	132,111	11,889*	(144,000)	132,111	-

*Adjusted for rounding errors of approximately €78

Obligations Under Finance Leases

	1	2	3	4	5
	€	€	€	€	€
Current liability	102,013	111,194	121,202	132,111	-
Non-current liability	364,507	253,313	132,111	-	-
Total obligation	466,520	364,507	253,313	132,111	-

Long-Lived Assets – Leased Equipment

	1	2	3	4	5
	€	€	€	€	€
Cost	560,110	560,110	560,110	560,110	560,110
Accumulated depreciation	(112,022)	(224,044)	(336,066)	(448,088)	(560,110)
Net book value	448,088	336,066	224,044	112,022	

Points to Note

- As an alternative to using the incremental rate of borrowing, the lessee could use the lessor's implicit rate in the lease if practicable (unfortunately, this rate is not disclosed in the lessee's financials)

- At inception of the lease

    ↑ Equipment €560,110

    ↑ Obligations under finance leases €560,110

- The equipment is depreciated over five years, assuming that this is the shorter period between lease term and useful life of the asset.
- The amount of borrowing increases each year by the finance charge which accrues at 9% and decreases each year by the rental payments of €144,000. The table splits the €144,000 between interest and capital payments.
- The income statement will reflect the interest charge each year.
- The closing balance of the obligation is recognised on the balance sheet and is classified between current and non-current liabilities. As the interest accrues during each year, the obligations are shown net of finance charge (i.e. capital element only) as illustrated below:

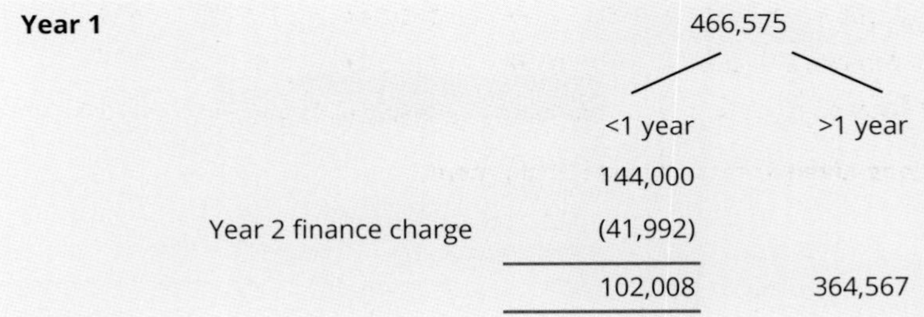

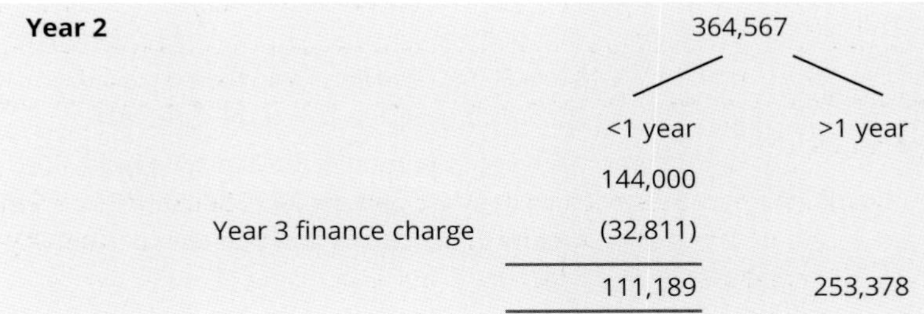

11.1 Illustrating the Linkages

The key linkages can be seen as follows:

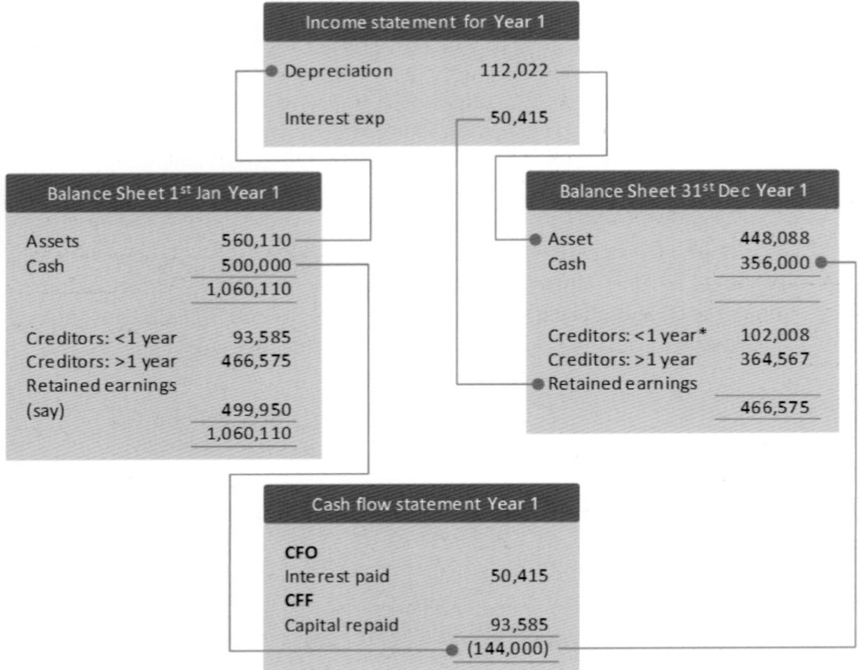

* Creditors: < 1yr	-	The €93,585 is paid off and then replaced with the new amount of principal due within one year.
Creditors: > 1yr	-	Each year a portion of the loan gets reclassified as current and is paid off. Of the €466,575 on 1 January Year 1, €102,008 has now been reclassified as 'current'.

Analysis Focus

When is a Debt not a Debt? When it is an Operating Lease

Some companies go to enormous lengths to ensure that they maximise the use of operating leases. The result is that the fixed assets and the debts in their balance sheets are reduced, which makes them look as if they are earning higher returns on capital, and are less indebted, than they really are.

The equity market is not usually fooled. The ratings of these companies often look insurmountably low. The analyst should try to calculate an NPV for these operating leases (many analysts use the rule of thumb of 7x annual lease payment for capitalisation) and add this to net debt. The rent should be added back to EBIT, to be replaced by a depreciation charge, and the interest on the outstanding amount should be treated as a finance item.

11.2 Lease Accounting Change

New Lease Accounting Standard from 2019

We have already addressed the rules on leasing that have existed for many years. However, as mentioned at the beginning of this leasing section, after years of deliberating and debating, the IASB and FASB have now finalised their new lease accounting standards. These will apply to accounting periods beginning on/after January 2019. Although the two standards are similar there is an important divergence in the income statement approach which we shall address below.

What are the Key Changes in IFRS 16 *Leasing*?

The most significant change is that after the application of the new standard all leases will be '*on balance sheet*'. This will be achieved by requiring companies to recognise a 'lease asset' and a 'lease liability' on the balance sheet. The amounts to be capitalised will be based on the present value of the rental payments. Under IFRS 16, the new accounting will also result in a different cost recognition profile for leases and is likely to have a negative effect on net income for companies which are expanding, as they have more 'newer' leases. Importantly, the US GAAP income statement treatment of leases will not change.

Operating Versus Financial Lease Classification Gone

Central to the conceptual shift in the new accounting is the elimination of the current classification of leases as either 'operating leases' or 'finance leases'. Instead all leases (with a lease term greater than 12 months) will be treated in a similar way to finance leases and be 'capitalised' by recording the present value of the lease as part of their Property, Plant & Equipment. The capitalised value will reflect the company's estimate of value of the right to use the asset and the term of the lease. In addition, companies will recognise an opposite financial liability to reflect the obligation to pay future lease rentals. The period used for the present value calculation is the contractual lease term of the lease.

In effect, once the present value calculation is completed, the mechanics of this operate consistently with the finance lease examples already covered in this chapter.

Income Statement Treatment

Under IFRS, the income statement cost of the capitalised lease will differ to the current 'straight-line' recognition of operating lease rentals. Instead, the rental cost will be replaced with a depreciation charge from the lease asset (included within EBIT) and an interest cost on the lease liability (included within finance costs). Although the depreciation charge would be a straight-line cost, the interest cost would reduce over the life of the lease, resulting in a reducing overall lease cost as the lease contract matures. The reduction in interest cost is intuitive. The lease rentals pay down the principal of the "obligation" over the life of the lease. Therefore, in the early years interest is higher as the loan is higher. The situation reverses in later years.

This difference in cost profile is illustrated in the chart below:

Lease capitalization results in lower net income in the early years of the lease contract, but higher net income in the later years

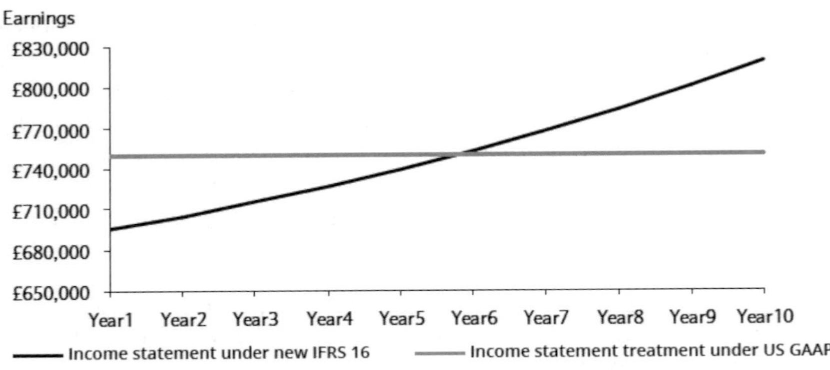

This negative impact on earnings will be particularly acute for companies which have been expanding in recent years, as a greater proportion of their leases will be less than halfway through their lease term. However, where a company holds a portfolio of leases where the start/end dates are evenly distributed, the earnings impact should be more neutral, as the expense profiles of all the leases would result in a broadly stable expense each year.

None of this applies to the new FASB model which will determine US GAAP. It is designed to ensure that the lease cost in the income statement remains on a straight-line basis and is all included within EBIT.

What Will the Impact of the Changes be?

The new standards will eliminate one of the key benefits of using operating leasing, namely that liabilities were 'off balance sheet'. However, many other reasons for leasing may remain. These reasons include taxation, costs relating to operation and maintenance, and the cost of borrowing. The accounting standard setters recognise that there is a risk that companies might seek to circumvent the new accounting rules by negotiating shorter leases with frequent renewal options. Therefore, the new standards contain anti-avoidance provisions which require lease terms to include:

- Periods covered by an extension/renewal option where there is a 'significant economic inducement' to exercise that option.
- Periods covered by an early termination option (e.g. a 'break clause') where there is a significant economic inducement not to exercise that option.

How Will the Market Interpret the Adjustments?

- ***Net income (and EPS)***

  Companies will be required to replace operating lease rentals (currently reported as a cost in EBIT) with amortisation on the leased asset and interest on lease liability. For companies with large individual leases, this will translate into lower net income in early periods which is then offset by higher reported profits towards the end of the lease term. However, for companies with a portfolio of leases, with differing lease start/end dates, this impact should be reduced as the expense profiles of all the leases would result in a broadly stable expense each year. Note under US GAAP no changes would take place as the income statement charge is not being changed.

- ***EBITDA***

  Given that the new approach substitutes rental payments for interest and amortisation and EBITDA is clearly before amortisation and interest, the new rules will lead to higher EBITDA.

- ***Multiples***

  Price should remain relatively unchanged, unless in those cases where the new accounting rules changes perceptions of risk or reveals new information. However, if there are changes to EPS or EBITDA (as discussed above) which are not accompanied by a change in price, multiples may be distorted. Companies where the impact of the changes is significant could experience a material distortion to multiples such as P/E or EV/EBITDA. It will not be straightforward to 'unwind' the new accounting treatments, so it is likely that the market will take the new earnings as the starting point going forward.

How Should the Changes be Handled for Modelling and Valuation Purposes?

The best way to handle operating leases has always been to restate numbers as if they were finance leases. This entails using EBITDAR (as opposed to EBITDA) in sectors that make extensive use of leases and use an 8x multiple (or similar) to derive financial leverage. The figure obtained should be included:

- In the operating capital employed when thinking about capital turns and the return on operating capital.
- In the debt figure when calculating weighted average cost of capital and when deriving a value for the equity from an enterprise value perspective.
- As part of capital expenditure in discounted cash flow models. Possibly because increases in obligations under finance leases are not recorded as investments on reported cash flows, the third point is often ignored. However, increases in rental obligation should be treated as a cash outflow in forecasting free cash flows. In practice, this can be done for each forecast year by deriving free cash flow as forecast net operating profit after tax minus the forecast growth in operating capital employed between the beginning and the end of the year.

12 Sale and Leaseback Transactions

As a means of improving cash flow or sourcing finance, an entity may sell the asset and then immediately lease it back. Therefore, there is no physical transfer of property. From an accounting perspective, there are two separate transactions that require recognition in the financial statements:

- The sale of the asset (is it really a sale?)
- The leaseback (operating or finance?)

IAS 17 states the following:

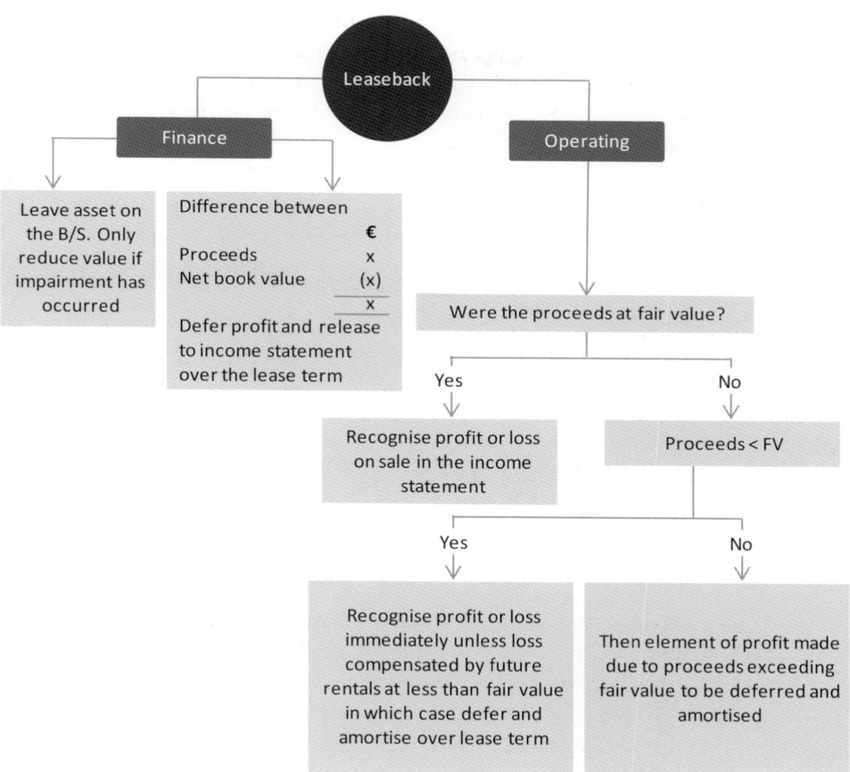

The real issues lie in determining the nature of the leaseback arrangement, i.e. whether the risks and rewards of ownership have really been passed to the new owner of the asset. The accounting treatment is straightforward once these issues have been resolved. Importantly, given the forthcoming changes to lease accounting in IFRS 16 *Leasing*, the motives to enter into sales and leaseback transactions will change. All leaseback agreements will become capitalised and so the off-balance sheet treatment, which is a major attraction of sale and leaseback transactions, will disappear.

13 Equity Instruments

The fundamentals of accounting for equity instruments was covered in Chapter 1. This section addresses some residual aspects.

Net Proceeds

IAS 32 requires that equity transactions are recorded at their net proceeds, i.e. net of costs directly attributable to the specific issues.

Example

An enterprise issues 1,000,000 €10 shares. The nominal value of the shares is €1. The enterprise used an investment bank to underwrite the issue at a cost of €500,000.

Accounting entries:

		€
↑	Cash (10,000,000 – 500,000)	9,500,000
↑	Share capital	1,000,000
↑	Additional paid in capital (9,000,000 – 500,000)	8,500,000

Deferred Taxation

14 Introduction

Deferred taxation is one of the less straightforward areas of accounting. The exact calculation of deferred taxation will vary due to local taxation rules. However, the concepts involved are shared internationally.

Before looking at deferred taxation in detail, it is important to have a basic grasp of income tax and how it is accounted for.

Regardless of location, the general principle for the calculation of income tax for an entity is as follows:

	€
Profit before taxation	X
add back	
Disallowable items for tax purposes	X
Items taxed on a different basis (e.g. depreciation)	X
Less	
Items eligible for taxation relief (e.g. capital allowances)	(x)
Profits chargeable to taxation	X

The local tax rate is then applied to calculate the expense:

Profits chargeable × Local tax rate = Income tax expense

The income tax expense is then:

- Charged as a deduction from profits in the income statement.
- A corresponding liability is set up in the balance sheet recognising the need to pay it.

15 Basic Entries for Income Taxes

Example

Ruler Inc. has calculated its income taxes for 2007 as €475,500. This calculation has been based on taxable income as calculated by the IRS under the modified cash basis approach.

Required

What are the basic entries for this income tax figure?

Solution

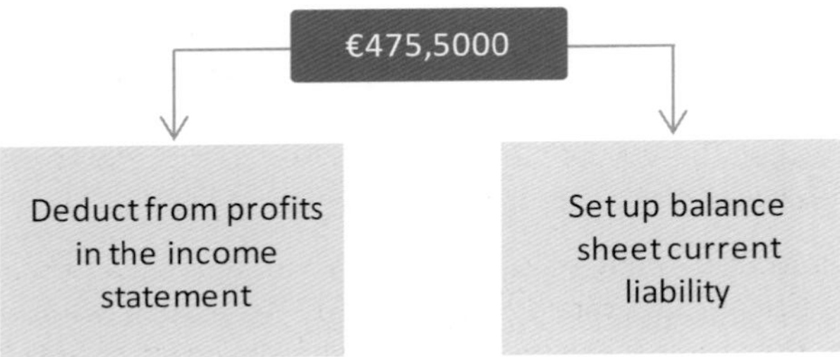

16 The Need for Deferred Taxation

16.1 What Causes Deferred Taxation?

The genesis is the difference between the tax and the accounting treatment of transactions. For example, some transactions are taxed on a cash basis (i.e. when received/paid) whereas accounts are prepared on an accruals basis (earned/incurred). In addition, non-current tangible assets are depreciated but under income tax rules they are given capital allowances (or tax depreciation) at a specified rate. A difference then arises between the amount of depreciation expense deducted from income and the rate of capital allowances. Deferred tax attempts to bridge the gap between these differences to minimise the distortion to the financial statements.

The differences can be split as follows:

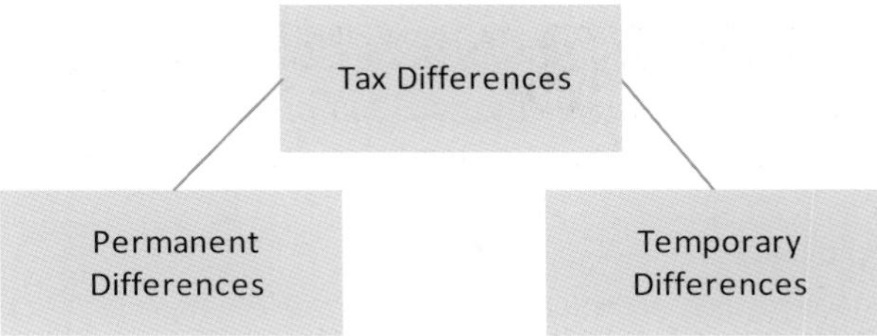

Permanent differences arise when the tax treatment of transactions differs from the accounting treatment. For example, in the UK, entertainment expenditure (such as client dinners) is not allowed as a deduction when calculating taxable profit. This means the transactions will never have a tax effect in the future and companies (and users) must live with this. There is no 'solution' to make the financial more meaningful. Permanent differences, therefore, do not require deferred tax recognition.

Deferred tax is an accounting tool that helps minimise distortions caused by these temporary differences. Temporary differences arise when there is a difference in the **timing** of the tax and accounting treatment but no ultimate treatment difference.

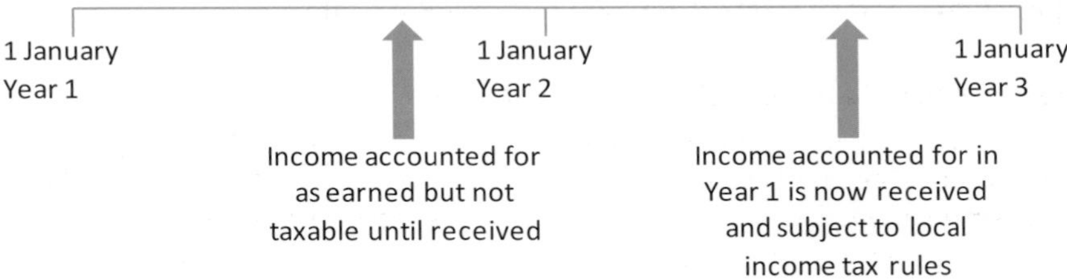

Examples of such differences may include:

- Income recognised in the accounts prior to being recognised for tax purposes (e.g. income recognised on a completed contract method for the tax purposes yet accounted for on a percentage completion basis in the financial statements).
- Income recognised for tax purposes prior to recognition in the accounts (e.g. rental income in advance).

- Expenses that are deductible for tax purposes prior to recognition in the accounts (e.g., straight-line method of depreciation used in the accounts but for tax purposes given immediate tax relief on capital expenditure).
- Expenses that are deductible in the financial statements prior to becoming deductible for tax purposes (e.g. provisions for warranty costs, contingent losses).

16.2 Illustration

Hopeless Inc. has a royalty agreement with several small companies. The royalty results in a one-off payment of €100,000 in January of Year 2. However, the royalty relates to Year 1. Assume the tax rate is 40%.

The income statement summary is as follows:

	YR 1 €	YR 2 €
Income before taxes	500,000	500,000
Royalty income (accruals basis)	100,000	-
	600,000	500,000
Income taxes (see below)	(200,000)	(240,000)
Net income	400,000	260,000

The income tax calculation would be as follows:

	YR 1 €	YR 2 €
Income before taxes	500,000	500,000
Royalties (cash basis)	-	100,000
	500,000	600,000
Tax @ 40%	200,000	240,000

From the illustration, it can be seen that income tax expense in Year 2 is higher than expected, given that the profits are lower. The reason for this distortion is the treatment of the royalty income. It is taxable income and is taxed on a receipts basis but has been accounted for on an accounts basis. As such, a temporary timing difference has arisen. The royalties will be subject to income tax not when they are accounted for but when they are received in cash.

Deferred taxation aims to address this mismatch by providing for the future tax liability in the same period as the accounting treatment.

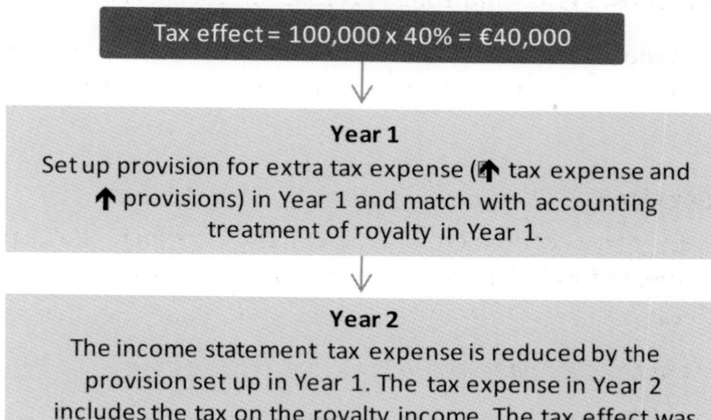

This is summarised below as follows:

Income Statement

	YR 1	YR 2
	€	€
Income before taxes	500,000	500,000
Royalty Income	100,000	-
	600,000	500,000
Income tax expense	200,000	240,000
Deferred tax	40,000	(40,000)
Adjusted tax expense	240,000	200,000
Income after tax	360,000	300,000

Balance Sheet

	YR 1	YR 2
	€	€
Deferred tax liability	40,000	-

Double-Entry Journals

Entry	Year 1	Year 2
Debit	Tax charge	Deferred taxation
Credit	Deferred taxation	Tax charge

Points to Note

- The tax expense in YR 1 is now in proportion to the profits
- For the purpose of the example, it is assumed that all profits are subject to income tax. In practice, this is unlikely to be the case

Example

FMZ Inc. a high technology manufacturer, has recently purchased a new digital laser for €20,000. The local taxation authority has agreed that the recovery (capital) allowance percentages are:

Year	1	2	3	4
Allowance	35%	43%	16%	6%

Further Information

- The depreciation policy of FMZ Inc. reflects the high technology nature of the asset. Due to anticipated developments in technology, it will have a zero-residual value after four years. FMZ Inc. uses the straight-line method of depreciation
- Tax rate is 40%
- The laser should generate income of €15,000 per annum

Required

Calculate the deferred tax implications of the above transaction. All figures in €.

Income statement extracts – (pre tax)

	Year 1	Year 2	Year 3	Year 4	Total
Revenue	15,000	15,000	15,000	15,000	60,000
Depreciation	(5,000)	(5,000)	(5,000)	(5,000)	(20,000)
Income before tax	10,000	10,000	10,000	10,000	40,000

Calculation of income taxes

	Year 1	Year 2	Year 3	Year 4	Total
Revenue	15,000	15,000	15,000	15,000	60,000
Tax allowance for depreciation	(7,000)	(8,600)	(3,200)	(1,200)	(20,000)
Taxable income	8,000	6,400	11,800	13,800	40,000
Tax @ 40%	3,200	2,560	4,720	5,520	16,000

Calculation of timing differences and deferred tax

	Year 1	Year 2	Year 3	Year 4	Total
Depreciation (Accounting)	5,000	5,000	5,000	5,000	20,000
Depreciation (Tax)	(7,000)	(8,600)	(3,200)	(1,200)	(20,000)
Timing differences	(2,000)	(3,600)	1,800	3,800	-
Deferred tax @ 40%	(800)	(1,440)	720	1,520	-

Income statement – (post tax)

	Year 1	Year 2	Year 3	Year 4	Total
Pre-tax income					
Income taxes:	10,000	10,000	10,000	10,000	40,000
Current	(3,200)	(2,560)	(4,720)	(5,520)	(16,000)
Deferred	(800)	(1,440)	720	1,520	-
Income after tax	6,000	6,000	6,000	6,000	24,000

Balance sheet – deferred tax liability

	Year 1	Year 2	Year 3	Year 4
Opening balance	0	800	2,240	1,520
Change in year	800	1,440	(720)	(1,520)
Closing balance	800	2,240	1,520	-

Points to Note

- In terms of overview, the key issue that we are addressing is that in the long run FM2 Inc. charges depreciation of €20,000 and receives tax allowances of €20,000 on the digital laser. The relief for the expenditure is simply managed at a different rate in the accounts to that for tax purposes. Overall, total depreciation = total capital allowances.
- The calculation of the timing differences clearly illustrates how the differences arise. In Year 1 and 2, tax allowances are given at a rate higher than depreciation. Consequently, this reduces taxable income, hence the reduced tax charges in these years. The situation, however, reverses in Year 3 and 4. Depreciation exceeds the tax depreciation. Consequently, this increases taxable income and the tax expense. Deferred tax aims to manage these fluctuations.
- In Year 1, a provision of €800 is required on a timing difference of €2,000. In Year 2, this provision increases to €2,240 due to additional timing differences of €3,600. In Year 3 and 4, the situation reverses and so does the provision. In Year 3, cumulative timing difference is €3,800 and so the level of provision required is only €1,520 (€3,800 at 40%). The reduction in the provision of €2,240 – €1,520 = €720 is released back to the income statement. By Year 4, the cumulative timing difference is nil and hence a provision is not required. The €1,520 is released to the income statement.

17 Advanced Issues in Deferred Taxes

17.1 Assets and Liabilities

The examples used so far have considered deferred tax liabilities. It is also possible that deferred tax assets could arise. What are the recognition criteria for these assets? It would not be prudent to recognise assets unless the entity were certain of the future economic benefits.

In summary:

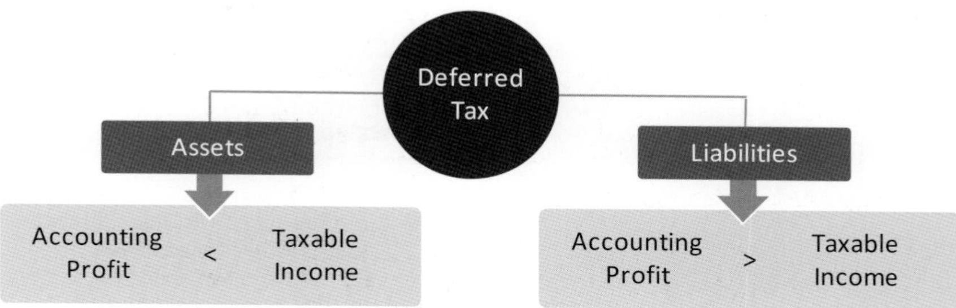

An asset will arise when taxable income exceeds accounting income. This means that currently, the income tax expense is artificially high due to a temporary timing difference. As a result, in the future it is expected that the situation will reverse, i.e. the income tax expense will be reduced. The future reduction (benefit) should be recognised.

IAS 12 *Income Taxes* permits that deferred tax assets be carried on the balance sheet to the extent that the benefits are probable, i.e. there will be future taxable profits against which a deferred tax asset can be utilised. If the benefits are not probable, then the asset is not recognised. However, if the judgment changes later and it now seems likely that the asset will be realisable, then it can be recognised.

17.2 Level of Provision

In practice, there are two methods of determining how much deferred tax should be provided for. The method used is disclosed in the explanatory notes to the financial statements.

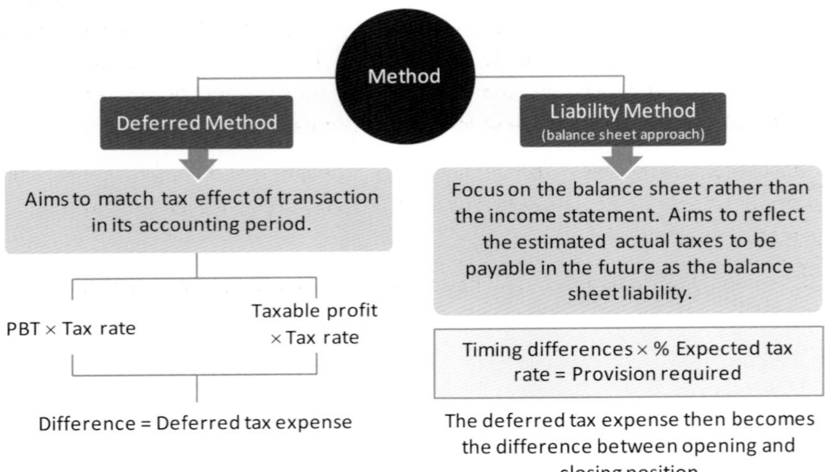

There is a technical difference between an approach to deferred tax based on timing differences, as we have focused on here, and one based on temporary differences. Temporary differences look at asset and liability values instead of income statement versus tax computation. Deferred tax will arise due to differences between the tax base of an asset and its accounting (book) value. Often, this will result in the same answer. For example, consider the following based on numbers above:

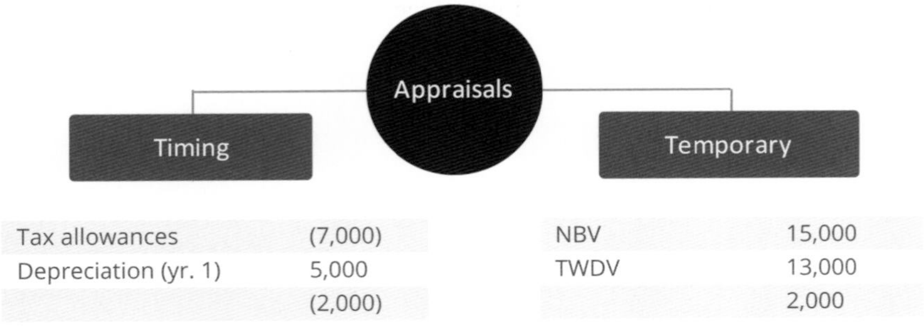

Timing	
Tax allowances	(7,000)
Depreciation (yr. 1)	5,000
	(2,000)

Temporary	
NBV	15,000
TWDV	13,000
	2,000

Therefore, the difference is largely academic from a practical perspective.

Analysis Focus

Do We Grow It or Does It Reverse?

Analysts try to model cash flows when they value companies. Deferred tax is a source of cash (because it has been charged to the profit and loss account, but it has not been paid). There are two options: that it represents a real liability, so the annual contribution will stop and the balance sheet provision will be paid out; or that it will continue to increase so long as the company keeps growing.

Most Valuation models automatically assume the latter, and analysts assume: "It does not matter, it's only a non-cash item". If that were true then there would be no need to account for it!

Therefore, deferred taxes should be analysed to establish whether they represent a material liability.

18 Contingencies and Provisions

18.1 Introduction

The balance sheet provides information about the net asset position of a company at a given point in time. In order to provide additional information about the short- and long-term financing of the entity, both assets and liabilities are analysed into current and non-current. Our review of liabilities has so far concerned itself with transactions that they have occurred which have given rise to known liabilities (e.g. bonds and leasing). What about events that have happened or are ongoing during the current accounting period and the outcome is yet unknown (litigation)? How should these uncertainties be dealt with in financial statements?

18.2 Contingencies

Under IAS 37 *Provisions, Contingent Liabilities and Contingent Assets,* the accounting treatment can be summarised as follows:

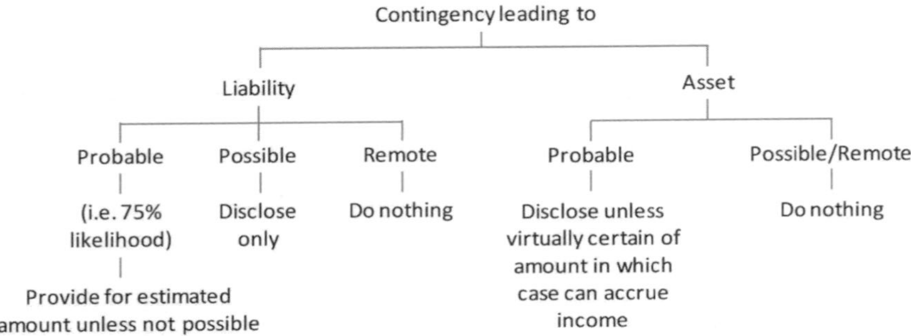

Given the above, the accounting treatment of contingencies is subjective and requires expert judgment. The latter may have to be sourced from third parties.

18.3 Provisions

Introduction

IAS 37 governs provisions which it defines as liabilities of uncertain timing or amount. Under IAS 37 provisions should be recognised when:

- There is a present obligation as a result of a past event.
- There is a probable future out flow of economic benefits.
- A reliable estimate can be made of the amount of the obligation.

All of the conditions must be met for a provision to be recognised.

Accounting Entries

The accounting entries for establishing and amending provisions are important. In particular, as provisions are subjective they can be used as a profit smoothing technique. Furthermore, provisions are a reconciling item between profit and cash as they are a non-cash expense or income item.

Example

1 Jan X0 — Newco, a recently formed entity, is sued by a customer. The lawyers estimate that there is a probable chance of losing €50m.

↑ Provisions	€50m
↑ Expenses	€50m

1 Jan X1 — the case has not yet been settled. The lawyers estimate that the customer may get €55m.

↑ Provisions	€5m
↑ Expenses	€5m

1 Jan X2 — the case has still not been settled. However, due to the outcome of a recent similar case, the lawyers now think the customer is highly unlikely to gain more than €45m.

↓ Provisions	€10m
↓ Expenses*	€10m

* this is effectively income

1 Jan X3 — the case is settled for €44m

↓ Provisions	€45m
↓ Cash	€44m
↓ Expenses	€1m

An alternative set of entries, which achieve the same result would be:

Entry I		Entry II	
↓ Cash	€44m	↓ Provision	€45m
↑ Expenses	€44m	↓ Expense	€45m

Application of Recognition Criteria

- Restructuring provisions

  To provide for restructuring costs an entity must have:

  - A detailed formal plan for the restructuring
  - Raised a valid expectation in those affected that the plan will be implemented

- Future operating losses

  These cannot be recognised by IAS 37 since, in effect, they do not represent a liability.

- Environmental provisions

  Provisions would be required for any environmental damage an enterprise has already done for which there is a constructive or legal obligation to make good.

- Warranty provisions

  These provisions are required to achieve complete matching. For example, a car manufacturer puts an estimate of the cost of offering a warranty for the sales made that year. Naturally, it is an uncertain liability as most of the warranty costs will not arrive until future years. IAS 37 identities the past event as being the sale rather than the claim made under the warranty policy.

Analysis Focus

Are They Really Equity or Really Debt?

Sometimes, it is quite obvious what to do with a provision. If, for example, a company does not have a funded pension scheme, and the liability appears as a provision in its balance sheet, then this should be treated by an analyst as debt. Equally, if the provision covers an eventuality that is quite unlikely to arise, then it may be safely treated as equity.

But what about the provision to decommission a nuclear power station in 20 years' time? It will happen, but its NPV may be much smaller than the liability shown in the balance sheet, then it should be discounted. And, in some cases, such as disputed claims, probability should be considered.

19 Calculation of Net Debt

Calculation of the net debt position can be problematic. In principle, what is needed is an estimate of the market value of the company's debt less the value of any "spare cash" balances and liquid short-term investments.

The definition of net debt is as follows:

		€
Short-term debt (including current portion of long-term debt)		x
plus	Long-term debt	x
plus	Finance leases	x
plus	Pension provisions (see note below)	x
plus	Redeemable preference shares (see note below)	x
minus	Cash	(x)
minus	Marketable securities	(x)
=	**Net Debt**	**x**

In practice, this data is hard to obtain/estimate and in a typical analysis the following assumptions would be made:

- Total debt is valued at book value (i.e. as reported in the annual report). This is a fair assumption for bank debt but may be misleading for long-term bonds which may be trading at a discount/premium according to the interest rate environment. Should the company have traded bonds (check on Bloomberg) the market value of bonds can be easily identified. Should the company have convertible bonds outstanding, it is advisable to check if anything has changed since the balance sheet date, such as the conversion of the bonds.
- Finance leases are part of the capitalisation of a company. Instead of borrowing from a bank or a bondholder the company has entered into a leasing contract. Sometimes, finance leases are classified separately, always check the notes to the financials and other liabilities. In addition, certain industries finance a large amount of assets with operating leases. Particularly for comparable company analysis it might make sense to capitalise such operating leases to capture the true net debt position of the company and to make two companies that have different capitalisation structures comparable.

- Continental European companies do not operate separate pension funds but build pension provisions which reflect the potential future liability. This means that no money has physically left the balance sheet and a comparison to non-European (or UK) companies will become impossible. One solution is to include the pension liabilities in net debt as if they were interest-bearing liabilities.
- Redeemable preference shares are assumed to be part of debt since they exhibit strong debt characteristics.
- All cash balances and short-term liquid investments are considered to be "spare cash" and can therefore be deducted from total debt in order to arrive at a net debt position. We are assuming that this spare cash can be used to reduce the actual debt position. In practice, companies will need a certain amount of cash balances just to run the business, but for most businesses, this is a fair approximation. Care has to be taken with companies which are dependent on their cash balances to finance operating cash flow needs, such as young companies that have recently gone public. The notes to a company's accounts will state if short-term securities are marketable or not, so always check the notes since short-term securities might include illiquid investments the company intends to sell within the next 12 months.

For most companies, net debt is not materially seasonal, so that the year-end balance accurately reflects the current average debt for the year. This may not be true for some companies, such as tour operators or retailers who have very large swings in liquidity. To identify whether there are seasonal changes in net debt you can look at the interim balance sheet as well as the year end and consider whether the net interest paid and payable is reasonable in the context of your net debt estimate. The most important factor in any case is to use the most recent balance sheet available. In addition, it is advisable to check news-runs on the companies analysed to ensure that any major capital structure changes have been captured, such as share buybacks/rights issues/secondary issues/debt issues/acquisition finance with debt or equity.

Occasionally, a firm's net debt definition might include minority interest. Please note that a non-controlling interest is not part of net debt but has been included to calculate the enterprise value of a company. For any leverage ratios, non-controlling interests must not be included in the net debt calculation.

20 Statement of Stockholders' Equity and Share Transactions

We have already seen that most gains and losses go through the income statement and are therefore apparent to investors and users. However, certain gains and losses bypass the income statement. These tend to be the more obscure items. In order to clearly show these items (and changes in related captions) there is a separate working of opening and closing equity.

20.1 Transactions Impacting on Equity Accounts

The impact of transactions on equity accounts and balance sheet numbers in general is summarised in the following table:

Transaction	Effect on Account	
1. Issue of shares for cash at nominal value	Cash Share capital	↑ ↑
2. Issue of shares for cash above nominal value	Cash Share capital Share premium*	↑ ↑ ↑
3. Rights Issue (below market price, above nominal value)	Cash Share capital Share premium*	↑ ↑ ↑
4. Bonus (or script) issue	Share capital Reserves (P&L)	↑ ↓
5. Stock split	No effect	

* Often referred to as additional paid in capital

20.2 Treasury Shares

The treatment of share repurchases is governed by IAS 32.

The required treatment is to reflect the share repurchase as a deduction from equity. Any subsequent re-issue of those shares should be accounted for in equity and not in the income statement. Therefore, the appropriate entries for a buyback would be:

↓ Cash

↓ Equity (additional paid in capital and share capital)

20.3 Accounts Commentary

The key liabilities for Lufthansa (and indeed many other companies) are:

Borrowings

These are disclosed in note 34. This splits the long-term borrowings into the three forms, namely corporate bonds, bank loans and other liabilities. This last caption is essentially finance lease agreements. Note 34 provides various extra information and breakdowns.

Deferred Taxation

Normally, we would expect this to be a liability. However, since there is a substantial tax shield on the pension provision the deferred tax asset is much larger than the deferred tax liability. Note 14 on the tax expense provides much background information for understanding deferred tax and indeed taxes generally. Particularly useful is the tax reconciliation. The basic idea is that you take the PBT figure and multiply it by the tax rate and then reconcile it to the actual charge in the financials. We also see in here the breakdown of the sources of the deferred tax assets.

Pension Provisions

This is a very substantial number and is addressed in note 32. This note is addressed in detail at the end of Chapter 15.

Provisions (General)

Other provisions are disclosed in Note 33 It is always worth looking at the provision utilisation line as this is the amount transferred back to the income statement to offset costs incurred or costs that have not transpired. In this way it can be used to enhance earnings. The additions line shows new provision amounts that have been made.

Chapter 5: Analysis of Cash Flows

"As the WorldCom scandal has taught investors, cash flow is as vulnerable to manipulation as net income. So before using it as a measure of financial health, you have to check for the practices that mask weak performance or produce one-time gains." [5]

[5] Source: Bloomberg, Anne Tergesen (2002). The idea that cash is vulnerable to manipulation is such an important idea. There are lots of lazy statements out there suggesting that cash represents the truth in some sense or, even worse, the hackneyed 'cash is king' cliché.

1 Introduction

Chapter 1 provided an overview of the purpose and structure of the cash flow statement. The objective of this chapter is to examine the significance of the cash flow statement to users of financial statements, as well as to examine the content, structure and methods of preparation in greater depth. Key international accounting differences are also highlighted.

2 Purpose of the Cash Flow Statement

As we have already seen in earlier chapters financial statements are prepared using the accruals concept. Transactions are recognised when earned or incurred rather than when cash is received or paid. This means that financial statements are not distorted by cash flow management.

Examples of the application of the accruals concept are:

- Depreciation (non-cash expense)
- Borrowings (finance charges expensed systematically to the income statement rather than amount paid).
- Long-lived assets (not expensed immediately to the income statement).
- Accruals (expenses are charged when incurred not when paid).
- Long-term contracts (revenue not recognised until reasonably certain about completion of contract rather than when cash is received).

Although net income is of vital importance in assessing the trend in performance of a business, it is from cash and not net income that expenses are paid, loans repaid, interest and dividends paid, etc. Therefore, a thorough understanding of cash flow is important for meaningful fundamental analysis.

3 The Cash Flow Statement – Definition

As mentioned above, the cash flow statement is a part of the financial statements of a company. It is the third major component and the information it provides helps in assessing:

Liquidity	**Solvency**	**Flexibility**
Availability of cash to meet short-term obligations	Availability of cash to meet short- and long-term obligations	Ability to generate cash in the future in order to take advantage of opportunities as they arise

The income statement provides information about earnings. The balance sheet is a statement of resources and obligations at a given point in time. The cash flow statement is directed at helping users look to future cash activity. It aims to:

- Provide an insight into the financial structure of an entity, and its ability to affect the amounts and timings of cash flows in order to adapt to changing circumstances.
- Provide useful information to assist with evaluating changes in assets, liabilities and equity.
- Serve to indicate the amount, timing and certainty of future cash flows.

4 The Cash Flow Statement – Classification

The aim of the cash flow statement is to explain the movement in cash (and cash equivalents) over the accounting period.

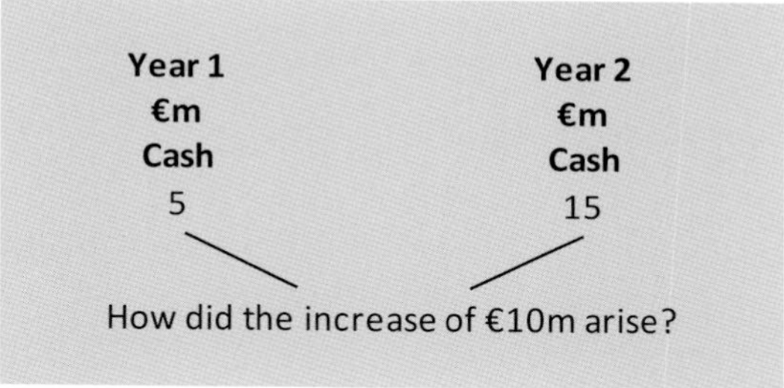

In order to ensure comparability between one enterprise and another, IAS 7 *Statement of Cash Flows* specifies the key headings for analysis of the movement in cash and cash equivalents:

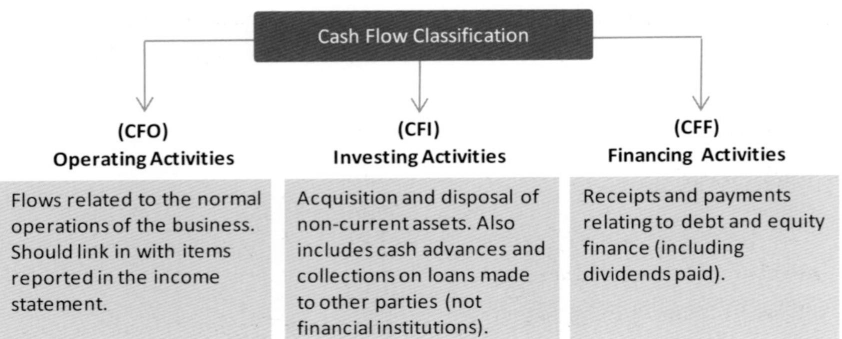

5 Converting Income to Cash

In order to calculate CFO a number of adjustments are required to turn net income into operating cash flow. A basic set of rules underpin these adjustments:

Assets	▪ An increase in an asset is a **USE** of cash ▪ A decrease in an asset is a **SOURCE** of cash
Liabilities	▪ An increase in a liability is a **SOURCE** of cash ▪ A decrease in a liability is a **USE** of cash
Revenues and expenses	▪ Revenues are a **SOURCE** of cash ▪ Expenses are a **USE** of cash

- Cash inflows are positive (a source of funds)
- Cash outflows are negative (a use of funds)

6 Direct and Indirect Approaches

There are two methods of calculating the CFO figure: indirect and direct.

6.1 The Indirect Method (or Reconciliation Method)

This involves starting at the bottom of the income statement and working up from net income.

The approach can be summarised in a single working as follows:

Indirect Method

	€m
Cash flows from operating activities:	
Net income before income taxes	x
Adjustments for:	
Depreciation	x
Interest expense	x
Operating profit before working capital changes	x
+/− Dec./Inc. accounts receivable	x/(x)
+/− Dec./Inc. inventories	x/(x)
+/− Inc./Dec. accounts payable	x/(x)
Cash generated from operations	x
Interest paid	(x)
Income taxes paid	(x)
Net cash flows from operating activities	x

Basically, net income is adjusted for revenue and expense items by addition or deduction to arrive at net cash from operating activities. This is best illustrated by an example.

6.2 Comprehensive Example

The following information relates to Hopeless Inc.

	€
Increase in inventory	680
Net income before taxes	800
Depreciation	300
Interest expense	150
Other expenses	1,600
Issue of debt	1,000
Increase in receivables	840
Increase in payables	200
Interest paid	100
Dividends paid	50
Acquisition of plant	700

Use the indirect method to calculate:

- CFO
- CFI
- CFF

Solution

CFO		CFI		CFF	
Net income before taxes	800	Acquisition of plant	(700)	Issue of debt	1,000
– Inc. in inventory	(680)			Dividends paid	(50)
+ Depreciation	300				
– Inc. in receivables	(840)				
+ Inc. in payables	200				
+ Interest expense	150				
– Interest paid	(100)				
Total	**(170)**	**Total**	**(700)**	**Total**	**950**

Net change in cash and cash equivalents = 80

Points to Note

- The increase in inventory is a deduction from net income because if inventory is rising, it is an increase in an asset and hence an outflow.
- Depreciation is added back to net income as it was deducted in arriving at that figure. It is not a cash expense. However, the purchase of the non-current asset gives rise to a cash outflow and this would have been reflected under investing activities in the year of purchase.
- The increase in receivables is a deduction because if receivables have gone up then this is an increase in an asset and hence a cash outflow.
- The increase in payables is an addition because if payables are not being paid then cash has increased. In other words a liability has increased which is an inflow.
- Under IAS 7, interest paid could be classified as either an operating or a financing cash flow.
- There is no taxation in this particular example.

6.3 Direct Method

This involves starting at the sales figure in the income statement and then addressing the individual components of net income such as sales and cost of sales. It is presented as follows:

Direct Method	**€m**	**€m**
Cash flows from operating activities:		
Cash received from sale of goods	x	
Cash dividends received	x	
Cash provided by operating activities		x
Cash paid to suppliers	(x)	
Cash paid for operating expenses	(x)	
Cash paid for income taxes	(x)	
Cash paid for interest	(x)	
Cash disbursed for operating activities		(x)
Net cash flows from operating activities		x

The above calculation can also be visualised as:

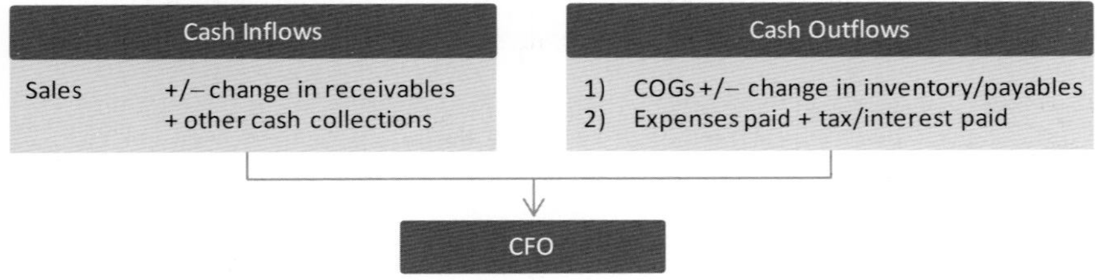

The direct method provides more information to users as it includes information about specific cash flows from operating activities as opposed to a series of adjustments to net income.

Obviously, both approaches are attempting to calculate the same figure, but it is the direct method which is preferred by IAS 7. Having said that, most companies use the indirect method. These methods exist outside IFRS (e.g. UK and US GAAP). In these countries, the indirect method also dominates.

Example

Let us now put together the above information in a more comprehensive example. The following information relates to Pluck Inc.

	€
Sales	1,250
Cost of goods sold	625
Increase in inventory	170
Increase in payables	50
Increase in receivables	210
Issue of debt	250
Interest expense	30
Interest paid	25
Payment of dividends	12.50
Purchase of plant	350
Depreciation	75
Other expenses	400

Requirement

Using the direct approach, calculate cash flow from operating, cash flow from investment and cash flow from financing activities.

Solution

CFO	€	CFI	€	CFF	€
Cash inflows Sales	1,250				
− Increase in receivables	(210)	Purchase of plant	(350)	Issue of debt	250
	1,040				
Cash outflows					
COGS	625			Payment of dividend	(12.5)
+ Increase in inventory	170				
− Inc. in payables	(50)				
	(745)				
Expenses	(400)				
Interest paid	(25)				
Total	**(130)**	**Total**	**(350)**	**Total**	**237.5**

Net change in cash and cash equivalents = (242.50)

7 Preparing a Cash Flow Statement: Comprehensive Example

The following information relates to Hermes Inc.

Balance Sheet	**Year 1 €**	**Year 2 €**
Cash	750.00	752.50
Accounts receivable	375.00	250.00
Inventories	187.50	250.00
Accrued income	37.50	62.50
Total current assets	1,350.00	1,315.00
Plant and equipment	562.50	625.00
Patents and royalties	25.00	437.50
Total assets	1,937.50	2,377.50
Accounts payable	225.00	351.25
Deferred income	37.50	12.50
Tax due	500.00	250.00
Long-term debt	375.00	250.00
Share capital	10.00	12.50
Retained earnings	790.00	1,501.25
Total liabilities and equity	1,937.50	2,377.50

Year 2

Income Statement	**€**
Sales	6,250.00
COGS	3,750.00
Depreciation	100.00
Other expenses	500.00
loss (gain) on sale of equipment (zero net book value)	(62.50)
Interest expense	62.50
Interest received	25.00
Income tax expense	588.75
Dividends	625.00
Retained earnings	711.25

Requirement

Prepare the cash flow statement for Hermes Inc. for Year 2.

Solution

	€	€
Net cash flows from operating activities (Note 1)		1,262.50
Cash flows from investing activities		
Purchase of plant and equipment (W3)	(162.50)	
Purchase of patents (437.50 – 25.00)	(412.50)	
Sale of equipment	62.50	
Net cash used in investing activities		(512.50)
Cash flows from financing activities		
Payment of debt (375 – 250)	(125.00)	
Proceeds from issue of share capital	2.50	
Payment of dividend	(625.00)	
Net cash used in financing activities		(747.50)
Net increase in cash and cash equivalents during the year		2.50
Cash and cash equivalents at beginning of the year		750.00
Cash and cash equivalents at the end of the year		752.50

Note	€
1. Cash flows from operating activities	
Net income before income taxes (W1)	1,925.00
Adjustments for:	
Depreciation	100.00
Gain on sale of equipment	(62.50)
Operating profit before working capital	1,962.50
Decrease in receivables	125.00
Increase in inventories	(62.50)
Increase in accrued income	(25.00)
Increase in payables	126.25
Decrease in deferred income	(25.00)
Cash generated from operations	2,101.25
Tax paid (W2)	(838.75)
Net cash flows from operating activities	1,262.50

Workings

1. Net Income Before Income Taxes	€
Net income	711.25
Dividends	625.00
Income tax expense	588.75
	1,925.00

2. Tax Paid	€
Opening liability	500.00
Tax expense	588.75
	1,088.75
Tax paid	?
Closing tax liability	250.00
∴ Tax paid	838.75

3. Plant and Equipment	€
Opening balance	562.50
Depreciation	(100.00)
	462.50
Additions	?
Disposals	-
Closing balance	625.00
∴ Additions	62.50

Points to Note

- No separate disclosure is made about interest expense and interest received as it is assumed that these amounts are the same as the cash flows. This is a reasonable assumption in the absence of assets/liabilities on the balance sheet.
- The gain on sale is deducted from net income as the proceeds themselves are reflected under investing activities.
- Accrued income is essentially income earned not yet received. Movements are treated in the same way as movements in receivables. Increases are reductions of cash and decreases are a source of cash.

- Deferred income is income which has been received in cash but not yet accounted for in the income statement. Increases are sources of cash, but decreases are reductions in cash.

8 Further Issues Relating to Cash Flow Statements

Further points of consideration when examining cash flow statements are:

- There should be no netting off between receipts and payments of similar items. For example, separate disclosure is made of acquisitions and disposals of non-current assets.
- There should be an accompanying note to the cash flow statement which reconciles cash and cash equivalents to amounts disclosed in the balance sheet.
- Where further calculations are required, such as depreciation (below), we can use a standardised layout to our workings. This is often represented by 'BASE', standing for beginning balance, additions, subtractions, leaving the user with the ending balance. In the context of non-current assets this would be the assets at the start plus the additional assets purchases less depreciation and disposals leaving the ending balance.

From the point of view of calculations to be made, note the following examples:

Example 1 – Calculations of Proceeds on Disposal of Assets

The following is a balance sheet extract from Cash is King Inc.'s financial statements:

Long-Lived Assets	Year 2	Year 1
PP&E	€150,000	€200,000

Further information:

- Depreciation for year 2 was €22,000.
- Some PP&E was sold for €120,000 giving rise to a profit on disposal of €25,000.

What is the cash expended/received on long-lived assets in Year 2?

Solution

PP&E

	€
Opening balance (net book value)	200,000
Depreciation	(22,000)
Disposals*	(95,000)
Cash expended (balancing number)	67,000
Closing balance	150,000

*Profit on disposal is calculated as:

	€
Proceeds	X
-Net book value	X
Profit or (loss)	x/(x)

Substituting in numbers

	€
Proceeds	120,000
-Net book value	?
Profit or (loss)	25,000

∴ Net book value must be = €95,000

Example 2

In some occasions, assets are not always bought for cash alone. Take this scenario: The following extract relates to long-lived assets.

	Year 2	**Year 1**
PP&E	€150,000	€80,000

Depreciation for Year 2 was €28,000. €20,000 of PP&E was acquired by direct exchange for a bond.

What is the cash expended on PP&E acquisitions?

Solution

PP&E	**€**	
Opening balance	80,000	
– Depreciation	(28,000)	
+ Acquisition (bond)	20,000	
+ Other (cash) acquisitions	78,000	(balancing figure)
Closing balance	150,000	

This calculation is a good example of the BASE structure discussed before.

9 Analysing Cash Flow Information

From our examination of cash flow statements, we can see that these are useful sources of information about an entity's performance. An entity may be profitable, but does it generate enough cash to meet short and long-term obligations?

Analysis Focus

Free Cash Flow, a Definition

When an analyst constructs a DCF valuation model to ascertain the value of a company or an asset, what they discount is the cash that it would generate if it were financed entirely by equity, i.e. we ignore the company's capital structure. Free cash flow is:

EBIT × (1 – Tax rate) + Depreciation, amortisation and provisions +/– Changes in Working capital – Capital expenditure

What this means in practice is that the tax rate is notional rather than actual. If there are fiscal benefits from the use of debt finance, then these are picked up in the discount rate: the Weighted Average Cost of Capital (WACC).

The WACC calculation is used extensively in company valuation. It is not an accounting concept so we do not address it further here. However, you will find comprehensive coverage in almost any finance related textbook or online source.

The diagram below summarises the key analytical uses.

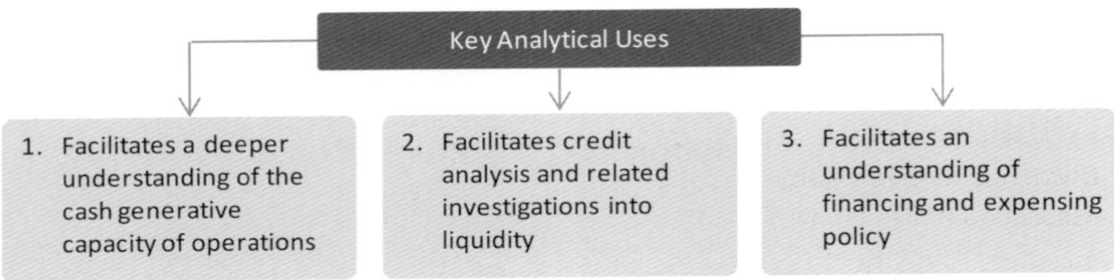

Use 1 – Cash Generative Capacity

This can be illustrated by reference to Hermes Inc. in section 7 of this chapter. By highlighting cash from operations and the link with the income statement, it is possible to predict ongoing cash generation. If surplus cash is generated the question that arises is what happens to this surplus? For example, in the case of Hermes, the surplus has been used to finance investment in plant and equipment, acquire patents and pay off debt and dividends. If companies have negative cash flow from operations, they may require significant financing in the future to survive.

Use 2 – Credit Analysis

This area focuses on the cash generated from operations and management of current assets and current liabilities (working capital). In the example of Hermes, working capital generated a net increase of €138.75. This indicates a favourable position but would also need to be compared to previous years cash flow statements as well as to those of other entities in the same industry. Coverage ratios such as operating cash flow to interest and total debt to operating cash flow can now easily be calculated.

Use 3 – Financing and Expensing Policy

The cash flow statement can provide information about how companies generate cash (operations, sale of assets, issuance of share capital etc.) and how cash is expended (acquisition of long-term assets, dividends, interest payments). In the example of Hermes, the investment in plant and equipment could be indicative of future cash flows. In addition, there has not been a need to source any major finance during the year. Repayment of long-term debt should be indicative of lower interest expense in the income statement in future years.

Statement of Group Cash Flow for the Year Ending 31 March Year 3

	Notes	Year 3 €m	Year 2 €m	Year 1 €m
Net cash inflow from operating activities	26	586	582	856
Dividends received from associated undertakings		5	4	5
Returns on investments and servicing of finance	27	(230)	(307)	(350)
Taxation		(104)	(65)	(220)
		257	214	291
Capital expenditure and financial investment	28	(226)	(356)	(520)
		31	(142)	(229)
Acquisitions and disposals				
Acquisitions	29	(13)	(12)	(860)
Disposals	31	(125)	2,040	902
		(138)	2,028	42
Equity dividends paid		(231)	(232)	(232)
Cash inflow (outflow) before use of liquid resources and financing		(338)	1,654	(419)
Management of liquid resources	30	(12)	215	529
Financing				
Issues of shares		1	1	8
Increase (Decrease) in debt		335	(1,910)	(143)
	32	336	(1,909)	(135)
(Decrease) in cash	34	(14)	(40)	(25)

Accounts Commentary

The cash flow statement is provided on page 107 of the financials, available here: bit.ly/lufthansa2017. The first thing to note is that Lufthansa is cash generative at the operating level. This is no surprise for a mature company. In the CFO calculation the largest item is depreciation. The results from investments under the equity method is merely the dividend stream from the equity investments held.

The CFI section is again pretty standard. The main positions are capital expenditures for Fixed Assets (mostly new planes and parts).

The CFF items are also very much typical for a reasonably large industrial company. It is interesting to note that the substantial investments appear to have been funded by a small amount of financing cash flows and a significant level of operating cash flow.

Chapter 6: Analysis of Financial Statements Using Ratios

"As all good golfers know, less is often more. Might the same be true when it comes to financial reporting? The page count inflation of company reporting over the past two decades has been staggering. Back in the mid-1990s the typical report and account was fewer than 100 pages; this spring's annual report season saw most major companies publish weighty tomes, often more than 250 pages. Putting aside the environmental damage from tree felling or the resulting back conditions afflicting an army of postal workers, has all this extra disclosure actually helped stakeholders better understand the businesses? Does more disclosure reflect a genuinely more complicated world, does it merely reveal the complexities that were always there, or is it simply the regulatory and accounting world gone mad?" [6]

[6] Source: Simon Samuels, partner of Veritum Partners, writing in the Financial Times. Simon makes a great point here about the sheer volume of financial information available that can sometimes overwhelm. That is why interpretation using ratios is so important – it allows the user to spot interesting areas for further analysis even if it does not give any answers in itself.

1 Introduction

Ratios are an essential tool of analysis. Analysts use a wide range of ratios in their work and definitions can differ widely. Unfortunately, there is no established standard format for ratio analysis.

This chapter explains the uses and limitations of analysing accounts using ratios, to demonstrate the significance of the principal ratios used by investors, and to indicate the principles of calculating and interpreting operating and financial ratios as a means of assessing management's effectiveness.

Ratios must be used with care. On their own, they never provide answers. They are relevant as a systematic method of analysing accounts to enable a user to ask intelligent questions.

Ratio analysis should always provide a list of points which require further thought and research.

2 Benchmarks

If ratios are to be of any value they must be related to other information benchmarks such as:

- Previous performance – trends
- Other companies – competitors
- Forecasts or budgets

2.1 Internal Comparisons

Company managers are often interested in measuring performance against those of their competitors and for internal purposes usually monitor actual results compared with budget on a monthly basis.

2.2 External Comparisons

External users have difficulty in comparing actual performance with budgets or forecasts unless they have access to more information than is publicly available. One of the functions of the investment analyst is to forecast future performance in terms of profits and financing requirements.

Considerable care is required when attempting to make ratio comparisons using financial information for different companies. Firstly, are the companies truly comparable in terms of their business activities? Secondly, the choice of accounting policies in relation to certain transactions can have a significant impact on ratios. One essential element of valid inter-company comparisons is to compare in detail the notes on accounting policies.

Statistical data services such as Datastream make some adjustments to published numbers to achieve greater consistency but often do not have access to sufficient information to do a comprehensive job.

Where ratios are used to analyse historic performance, it is important to appreciate that the ultimate objective is to assess future prospects. While past performance is not a definitive guide to the future, it can be helpful to understand the factors which have influenced a company in the past.

3 Common Size Statements

Firms of different sizes are difficult to compare. Common size statements are an attempt to deal with this problem. Such statements are based on expressing financial statement components as a percentage of a relevant base.

Common size statements are also useful for developing insights into the economic characteristics of different industries. An example of a common size income statement is given in paragraph 7.1 below. Such statements are very straightforward to prepare using spreadsheets.

4 Classification

There are various approaches to classifying ratios. This is one such approach:

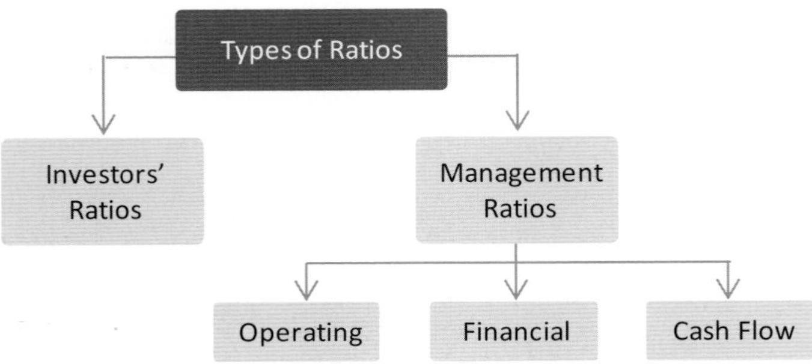

Investors Ratios

These ratios are primarily concerned with establishing individual per share statistics on profits, dividends, assets and cash flow for the equity shareholders, and relating these measures of performance to the market price of equity shares.

Management Ratios

These ratios look more carefully at the ways in which the company is organised and managed, at the 'fundamentals' of the business, namely operating performance, and financial structure.

5 Management Ratios

5.1 Introduction

Accounts provide information about profits, assets and cash flows and users try to assess the magic ingredient, the quality of management. Management is responsible for overall strategy and for raising capital from both shareholders and lenders, and for investing that capital within and outside the business.

Ratios are frequently used to highlight particular aspects of management performance:

Operating Ratios

These ratios measure the rate of return earned on the assets/capital employed in the business and are usually sub-analysed into profit margins and asset use/turnover.

Financial Ratios

Financial ratios can be divided into two categories:

- Gearing ratios examine the financing structure of the business in terms of the relative levels of capital raised from shareholders and lenders (i.e. debt finance). They are significant to shareholders in measuring the degree of risk attached to the company and the sensitivity of profits and dividends to changes in the level of activity. Lenders are also concerned about gearing.
- Liquidity and coverage ratios are used to examine the ability of the company to raise cash to meet payments when due. In practice, information contained in the cash flow statement is often more useful when analysing liquidity.

Cash Flow Ratios

Cash flow ratios are increasingly used to analyse both operating and financial efficiency. Cash flow ratios are discussed towards the end of this chapter.

6 Operating Ratios

6.1 Introduction

Return on assets/capital employed expresses profits as a percentage of the assets in use/capital employed in the business and can be subdivided into profit margins and asset turnover.

It is important to appreciate that the ratios are inter-related, and the interlocking relationship should be borne in mind when explaining the reasons for changes:

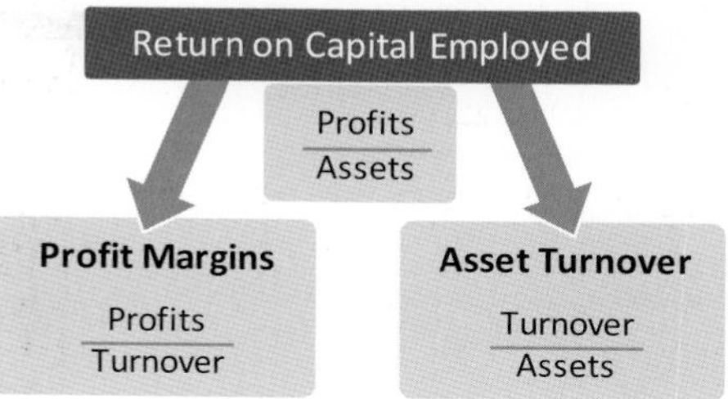

If the ratios are calculated in this way it should be possible to prove the return on capital employed by multiplying profit margin by asset turnover:

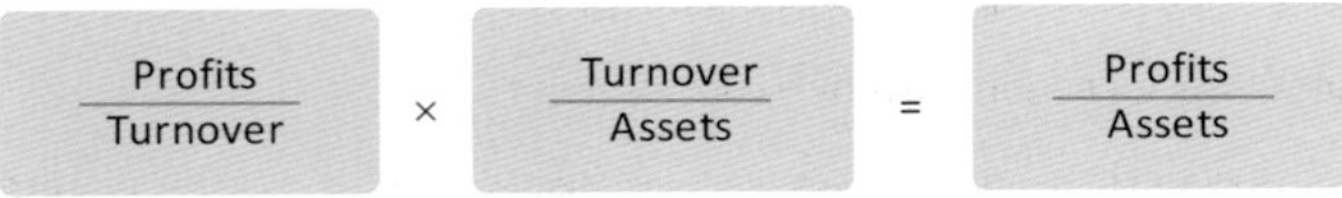

$$\frac{\text{Profits}}{\text{Turnover}} \times \frac{\text{Turnover}}{\text{Assets}} = \frac{\text{Profits}}{\text{Assets}}$$

This is often referred to as DuPont analysis. Note that a more detailed section on DuPont analysis is included later in the chapter. In practice, analysts pay more attention to profit margins than to the other two ratios. This reflects not only the fact that they are primarily interested in profits and earnings but also that they lack confidence in balance sheets as comprehensive statements of resources under management's control.

Analysts are not generally concerned about establishing the symmetry of the interlocking relationship and therefore tend to analyse the ratios as individual items.

Analysis Focus

The Heart of Forecasts and Values

The DuPont system mentioned above, shows how a firm's return on capital is a product of its margins and its capital turn. These, usually broken out further, are the building blocks of an analyst's forecasts. Given a growth in sales, sales margins and a capital turn, all the required ingredients for a valuation model are in place. Since free cash flow can be defined as profit minus net investment, it is the amount of profit that is left over after the company has made the required investment to expand its balance sheet.

6.2 Which Assets? How is Capital Employed Measured?

There is no correct answer to this question, it is largely a matter of individual preference. A number of options exist including:

- Total assets, i.e. non-current + current assets

  This approach argues that we want to measure the return on the total resources (assets) management have available to generate profits. The ratio, if we divide this into EBIT, would be return on total assets (ROTA).

- Total assets less current liabilities

  For this approach think about the accounting equation. The other side of total assets less current liabilities is equity plus long term liabilities. Assuming long-term liabilities are mostly debt then this is effectively calculating 'debt plus equity'.

- Total assets less 'adjusted' current liabilities

  This approach adjusts for the fact that some debt is in current liabilities, so we only deduct the non-financing current liabilities. This leaves us with equity plus long-term liabilities and debt like short-term liabilities.

Example

These different approaches are applied to Ransomes SA, using its consolidated balance sheet.

Assets	**€'000**	**€'000**
Non-current assets		
Property, plant and equipment		34,877
Current assets		
Property availability for disposal	25,247	
Inventories	42,199	
Receivables	56,499	
Cash	3,013	
		126,958
Total assets		**161,835**

Liabilities and Stockholders' Equity	€'000	€'000
Current liabilities		
Borrowings, finance leases and dealer finance schemes ('interest-bearing)	101,725	
Other creditors	34,789	
Total current liabilities		136,514
Non-current liabilities		
Borrowings and finance leases	1,098	
Other creditors	2,917	
		4,015
Provisions for liabilities and charges		5,206
Stockholder's equity		16,100
Total liabilities and stockholder's equity		**161,835**

The various approaches to calculating Return on Capital employed are considered below.

Total Assets	€'000
Non-current assets	34,877
Current assets	126,958
	161,835
Total assets less current liabilities	**25,321**

Total Assets Less 'Adjusted' Current Liabilities	€'000	€'000
Non-current assets		34,877
Current assets	126,958	
Current liabilities - other than interest bearing:		
Other creditors	(34,789)	
		92,169
		127,046

NB. An alternative method of arriving at this last version would be:

	€'000
Total assets less total liabilities	25,321
Add: interest bearing creditors included in current liabilities	101,725
	127,046

Which Profit Should be Treated as the Return?

A logical figure of profit to relate to capital employed should include all types of return on the assets (including investments) which are included in the capital employed. This should therefore be before charging interest on any type of financing included in capital employed. If year-end capital employed includes loans, overdrafts and finance lease obligations the return should be the profit before all interest charges including interest on bank loans, overdrafts and finance lease obligations.

Thus, the relevant profit would be profit for the year before deducting interest payable and taxation.

This approach does not distinguish between different methods of financing and relates profits before all financing costs to the assets/capital employed. Financial ratios, such as gearing and interest cover, examine the relationship between different methods of financing as a separate exercise.

Illustration

The consolidated profit and loss account of Ransomes S.A. shows a profit before taxation of €9.2 million:

	€'000
Revenue	180,184
Cost of sales	(127,587)
Gross profit	52,597
Distribution costs	(3,545)
Administrative expenses	(29,730)
Other operating income	1,928
Operating profit	21,250
US loan notes early redemption premium	(1,666)
Interest	(10,368)
Profit on ordinary activities before taxation	**9,216**

The notes to the accounts show that, in arriving at the interest charge of €10,368,000, interest receivable of €257,000 has been set off against interest payable of €10,625,000. In principle, interest receivable should be included in profit before interest payable and tax when calculating return on capital employed, if capital employed includes the cash on which the interest receivable represents a return. In practice, many analysts would ignore it and relate operating profit to capital employed.

In this illustration, the profit before interest payable and tax includes interest receivable:

	€'000
Operating profit	21,250
Add: interest receivable	257
	21,507

The one-off cost (€1,666,000) of early redemption of US dollar loan notes has not been charged in computing profit before interest payable and tax as it is non-recurring and of financing in nature.

Return on capital employed for this year might therefore be calculated as any of the following:

$$\frac{\text{Profit before interest payable and tax}}{\text{Total assets}} \times 100 = \frac{€21.5\text{m}}{€161.8\text{m}} \times 100 = 13.29\%$$

$$\frac{\text{Profit before interest payable and tax}}{\text{Total assets less current liabilities}} \times 100 = \frac{€21.5\text{m}}{€25.3\text{m}} \times 100 = 84.98\%$$

$$\frac{\text{Profit before interest payable and tax}}{\text{Total assets less 'adjusted' current liabilities}} \times 100 = \frac{€21.5\text{m}}{€127\text{m}} \times 100 = 16.93\%$$

In this illustration, the third approach will be used. If the interlocking relationship between return on capital employed, profit margin and asset turnover is to be established, the last two ratios must be calculated using profits of €21.5 million and assets/capital employed of €127 million.

Profit Margin

$$\frac{\text{Profit before interest payable and tax}}{\text{Turnover}} \times 100 = \frac{€21.5\text{m}}{€180.2\text{m}} \times 100 = 11.93\%$$

Asset Turnover

$$\frac{\text{Turnover}}{\text{Asset Capital Employed}} \times 100 = \frac{€180.2\text{m}}{€127\text{m}} \times 100 = 1.42 \text{ times}$$

Profit margin (11.93%) × Asset turnover (1.42) = Return on capital employed (16.9%)

6.3 Average or Year End Capital Employed?

Due to the artificial cut-off point when preparing financial statements, the use of year-end figures can be problematic. Ideally the profits for the year should be related to the assets in use/capital employed during the year (average capital employed). In practice, the ratio is usually computed using the assets/capital employed at the year-end (year-end capital employed). Year-end figures of capital employed can distort trends and inter-company comparisons:

- Acquisition of a subsidiary during the year: Profits are likely to be included in the group accounts only from the date of acquisition, whereas the balance sheet at the year-end contains all the assets of the new subsidiary. This is discussed in more detail in Chapter 7.
- Funds raised near year end: If cash has been raised three months before the year end, profits will only reflect a return for three months whereas all the cash will be part of year end assets/capital employed. Similar considerations apply to any ratios which relate figures from the profit and loss account with items in the balance sheet, such as asset turnover.

Impact of Revaluations

The revaluation of fixed assets under the alternative accounting rules will have the immediate effect of depressing the return on capital employed of a company, thus affecting both trends and inter-company comparisons with companies that do not revalue assets. Non-current assets are increased without any increase in profits and thus the return on assets must fall. This will also reduce asset turnover ratios.

Segmental Analysis

IFRS 8 *Operating Segments* requires that certain numbers are broken down between geographical segments and between segments representing different classes of business activity:

- Revenue
- Profit before taxation
- Interest and dividend income and interest expense
- Total assets at carrying value
- Liabilities
- Contingencies
- Extraordinary items
- Depreciation and amortisation
- Capital expenditure

The requirements of IFRS 8 enable users to calculate return on capital, profit margins and asset turnover both by geographical segment and by class of business. Such information is potentially of crucial use to an investment analyst.

7 Profit Margins

7.1 Different Margins

Two different measures of profit margin on sales are illustrated here, using the information of Ransomes SA:

Gross Profit Margin

$$\frac{\text{Gross profit}}{\text{Turnover}} \times 100 = \frac{€52.6\text{m}}{€180.2\text{m}} \times 100 = 29.19\%$$

Operating Profit Margin

$$\frac{\text{Operating profit}}{\text{Turnover}} \times 100 = \frac{€21.3\text{m}}{€180.2\text{m}} \times 100 = 11.82\%$$

If the objective of analysing margins is to understand relationships between turnover, costs and profits, the net margin is the least logical because it includes income in the form of interest receivable (€257,000) which bears no relationship to turnover. If Ransomes had significant dividend income from investments and/or share of profits of associates included under equity accounting these would also form part of profit before interest payable and tax but do not represent profits earned on turnover, recognised in the profit and loss account.

For these reasons, the operating profit margin is more logical. If the company adopts the typical income statement format which analyses operating costs into cost of sales, distribution and administrative expenses, then not only can the gross profit margin be calculated but also the relationships between turnover and distribution and administrative costs can be established. One useful method is to use a so-called 'common-size' approach where turnover is expressed as 100% and other costs and profits are listed as percentages of turnover.

	12 Months to 30.9.95		12 Months to 30.9.94	
Ransomes SA	**€'000**	**%**	**€'000**	**%**
Revenue	180,184	100.0	131,603	100.0
Cost of sales	(127,587)	(70.8)	(93,173)	(70.8)
Gross profit	52,597	29.2	38,430	29.2
Distribution costs	(3,545)	(1.9)	(3,002)	(2.3)
Administrative expenses	(29,730)	(16.5)	(22,054)	(16.8)
Other operating income	1,928	1.0	1,027	0.8
Operating profit	21,250	11.8	14,401	10.9

This approach focuses on the different elements of cost classified by function and more work can be undertaken to establish which are the significant elements of costs, e.g. staff costs, and see how they have altered. Employee numbers are also disclosed, and this should help to distinguish between price and volume changes in employment costs.

7.2 Difference Between Sectors and Class of Business

Different margins can be expected depending on the nature of the business. Low margins within a sector may arise from a policy designed to increase market share by cutting selling prices or may be due to high development costs associated with new products, both of which may be positive factors for the future. However, low margins are often associated with inefficiency and poor-quality management.

Conversely high margins relative to competitors or improving margins are usually taken as indicators of efficiency and good management. High margins through dominance in a particular market may however attract competitors into that market and imply lower margins in the longer term.

Analysis of profit margins is usually based on consolidated accounts (see Chapter 7) which aggregate profits and losses of individual companies. The segmental analysis of profits and turnover by class of business (and by geographical area) may be extremely useful for calculating which are high and low margin activities, and in which category of business significant changes in margins have arisen.

Clearly, the acquisition of new subsidiaries and disposal or termination of other activities will change the structure of the group and this change in mix will inevitably affect overall profit margins.

7.3 Factors to Consider When Analysing Changes in Profit Margins

Turnover	*Cost of Sales*	*Other Costs*
• Are sales increasing or decreasing – growth rate? • Which products/ activities – the more profitable (higher margin) or less profitable? • Export or domestic sales – impact of exchange rate movements/currency factors? • Price and volume changes. • Competition • Who are the customers – how are they faring? • Relationship with main customers – economic dependence/arm's length?	• Manufacturing costs – mix of materials/labour/ overheads. • If manufacturing, what is the effect on margins of changes in raw material prices? • If raw materials are imported, how have costs been affected by exchange rates? • Are the supply sources of materials and components secure? Who are the suppliers? • Labour costs – changes split into price and volume. • Stocks written down from cost to net realisable value produce lower gross and operating margins	• Which are the most important "other expenses"? • How sensitive are they to changes in activity? • Research and development as a percentage of turnover? • Experience with bad and doubtful debts.

7.4 Operational Gearing

Businesses whose fixed operating costs are high, relative to their variable operating costs, are said to have high operational gearing. Examples would be sectors such as airlines and hotels. Their profits are likely to rise disproportionately from a given increase in activity and conversely to fall disproportionately when activity declines.

It is not possible to measure precisely which operating costs are fixed. 'Fixed' and 'variable' are expressions which attempt to classify how costs behave when the volume of activity rises or falls. Costs are only 'fixed' for certain periods and for certain levels of activity.

If manufacturing costs are taken as an example, significant elements of labour and production overheads, such as rent of premises and depreciation of plant are likely to be fixed costs. If a company is operating at 80% of production capacity, it should be able to cope with a 10% increase in sales volume without incurring additional labour, rent or depreciation costs. Raw material costs would be expected to increase more or less in line with a 10% increase in production and are an obvious variable cost. If some of the additional demand could be met by selling existing stocks (destocking), there would be no increase in raw materials.

The good news is that operating profits will rise by more than the 10% increase in sales volume, thus increasing operating profit margins. Conversely a 10% fall in sales volume would be reflected in considerably reduced operating profits and margins. Both are illustrated below:

Illustration	**Existing Position**		**Sales Increase by 10%**		**Sales Decrease by 10%**	
	€'000	€'000	€'000	€'000	€'000	€'000
Revenue		1,000		1,100		900
Less:						
Operating costs						
Fixed	700		700		700	
Variable	200		220		180	
		900		920		880
Operating profit		100		180		20
% change in operating profit				+80%		–80%
Operating profit margin		10%		16.4%		2.2%

Operating Profit Margin

High operational gearing makes operating profits extremely sensitive to changes in the level of activity. In the illustration a 10% change in sales resulted in an 80% change in operating profits. This is extremely important both for shareholders, because of the impact on earnings per share, and for lenders who look to operating profits as the main source of cover for interest payments.

It is always helpful to establish at what level of capacity a business is currently operating. If it is operating near to or at the limit of its capacity and sales are expected to rise, fixed costs may have to increase substantially to provide sufficient labour, premises and machinery. Conversely, if sales are expected to fall the company will have to reduce its fixed cost base rapidly if it wishes to protect operating profit margins. This implies redundancies and disposals or subletting of property, etc.

The financial ratios deal with other aspects of gearing both in the profit and loss account and in the balance sheet structure.

7.5 Asset Turnover and Utilisation

Another aspect of efficient management is to 'make the assets work'. This may well involve disposing of those 'underperforming' assets which cannot be made to generate sales as well as developing and marketing the company's products or services.

Use of assets can be measured by relating assets in use to turnover. Logically, this is only relevant for those assets such as intangibles, tangible fixed assets, stocks and debtors, which are known as 'operating' assets, and which are owned with a view to generating sales. No useful relationships can be established between turnover and 'investment' assets such as trade investments, investments in associates and interest-earning deposits.

Depending on which operating assets are the most important to the business, asset turnover can be broken down into a number of sub-analyses:

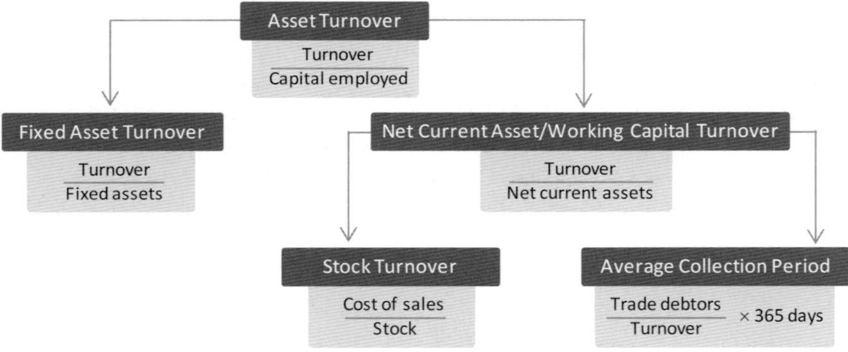

7.6 Further Issues on Asset Utilisation

Non-Financial Measures

Partly because balance sheets do not always adequately disclose resources at management's disposal, especially in terms of intangibles including staff, and partly because they are easier to understand, analysts also use non-financial methods of asset utilisation:

- Retailers – sales per square foot
- Hotels – occupancy rates
- Airlines – load factors
- Service industries – turnover per employee

Distortions in Asset Turnover Ratios

- **Revaluations:** Asset revaluations will reduce both asset turnover and fixed asset turnover ratios because fixed assets are increased by the surplus on revaluation, but turnover is not affected.
- **Changes in the composition of a group:** Where acquisition accounting is used the assets of the group are increased by the fair values of the separable net assets of the new subsidiary and profits are consolidated from the effective date of acquisition.

Disposals can also have a distorting effect on these ratios. If a subsidiary was sold two months before the end of the accounting period its turnover and profits would be included in consolidated accounts for the ten months up to the date of the disposal. If it owned substantial tangible fixed assets and stocks, these would not be in the balance sheet at the end of the year, having been replaced with the proceeds of disposal. Consequently, return on capital and asset turnover ratios may be distorted when comparing the year of disposal both with the previous and subsequent periods.

Differences Between Sectors

Asset turnover will tend to be lower in capital-intensive manufacturing industries which carry substantial fixed assets, stocks and trade debtors than in service industries where the principal resource is people. For example, manufacturers' asset turnover might be 2.5 whereas the ratio for a management consultancy might be 4.6.

There are often trade-offs between asset turnover and profit margins in different sectors. For example, food retailers have relatively low profit margins compared to electronic equipment manufacturers, but asset turnover is higher:

	Profit Margin	×	Asset Turnover	=	Return on Capital Employed
Food retailer	3.7%	×	6.7	=	24.8%
Electronic equipment manufacturer	10.3%	×	2.3	=	23.7%

7.7 Working Capital Cycle

In addition to considering the long-term financing of an entity, attention must also be given to the short-term financing, often referred to as the working capital cycle. This is the financing derived from the operations of the entity through purchase or sale of goods. The respective balance sheet items are receivables, payables and inventories. The key question is whether or not the entity has sufficient current assets to meet its current liabilities. If not, then longer term finance would need to be sourced in the form of equity or debt. This would not be an ideal situation. There are three key ratios to calculate when examining liquidity:

- Current ratio
- Quick ratio
- Cash ratio

7.8 Comparing Current Assets and Liabilities

$$\text{Current ratio} = \frac{\text{Current assets}}{\text{Current liabilities}}$$

The current ratio lets the user know if there are sufficient current assets to meet short-term financing obligations. Care needs to be taken when looking at this ratio in order to establish historic trends and sector norms. A more conservative measure of liquidity is the quick ratio.

$$\text{Quick ratio} = \frac{\text{Cash} + \text{Marketable securities} + \text{Receivables}}{\text{Current liabilities}}$$

As can be seen from the calculation, the quick ratio essentially involves deducting inventories from current assets. This is done in order to recognise that inventory needs to be sold before it can generate cash. The quick ratio looks at the cash or cash equivalent assets compared to current liabilities. An even more conservative ratio is sometimes called the cash ratio.

$$\text{Cash ratio} = \frac{\text{Cash} + \text{Marketable securities}}{\text{Current liabilities}}$$

This calculation is obviously extremely prudent. It gives a worst-case scenario by focusing on readily available cash. Receivables are ignored as they can take too long to pay and, in some cases, may not even pay.

7.9 More Detailed Measures

More detailed analysis of the results of these ratios can be achieved by examining the following current asset and liability component ratios.

Ratio	Meaning
Receivables Turnover $\frac{\text{Sales}}{\text{Average receivables}}$	• Relates sales to accounts receivable
Average Collection $\frac{365}{\text{Receivable turnover}}$	• Establishes an approximate overall customer payment period
Inventory Turnover $\frac{\text{Cost of goods sold}}{\text{Average inventories}}$	• Estimates how often inventories are replaced
or $\frac{\text{Average inventories}}{\text{Cost of goods sold}} \times 365$	• Estimates how long it takes to sell the average inventory

Payables Turnover Cost of goods sold ――――――― Average trade payables	• Relates purchases to amounts owed to suppliers
Payables Payment Period 365 ――――――― Payable turnover	• Estimates an approximate measure of payment period for suppliers

Use of the above ratios can provide an insight into why there may be liquidity problems:

- Is the entity not selling its stock quickly enough? There may be problems with warehousing or demand.
- Is the entity paying its suppliers too soon and hence is out of pocket?

7.10 Cash Cycle

Given that there may be issues in managing working capital, the calculation of the cash cycle is a useful analytical tool. The calculation is illustrated below.

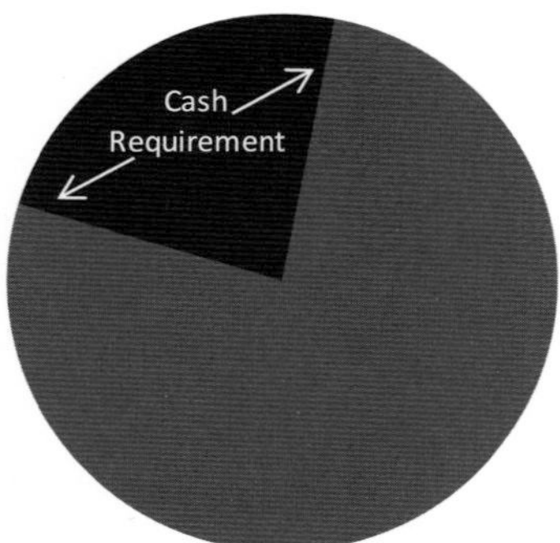

Cash cycle = Inventory days + Receivable days − Payable payment period

The cash cycle looks at how many days the company may have to provide funding to manage its operations. It is a measure of efficiency. The company's objective should be to minimise the cash cycle by maximising the efficiency of its working capital and this is reflected in the calculation.

8 DuPont Analysis and Return on Equity

8.1 Introduction

Analysts often find it extremely useful to link various ratios together in order to attain a better appreciation of the drivers behind various ratios and results. This disaggregation is commonly referred to as DuPont analysis. The key ratio broken down is return on equity. In general terms, this is defined as:

$$\frac{\text{Net income}}{\text{Average equity}}$$

This ratio shows the profit generated for the equity shareholders after all other providers of finance have been serviced. As such, it is a measure of efficiency - how efficient has management been in turning investments (equity) into earnings?

8.2 Basic DuPont Analysis

The basic form of DuPont analysis has three components as follows:

$$\text{ROE} = \underbrace{\frac{\text{Net income}}{\text{Sales}}}_{\text{Net income margin}} \times \underbrace{\frac{\text{Sales}}{\text{Assets}}}_{\text{Asset turnover}} \times \underbrace{\frac{\text{Assets}}{\text{Equity}}}_{\text{Leverage}}$$

Note that if cross-multiplication is carried out, the sales cancel as do the assets. This merely leaves net income/equity which is, of course, the definition of return on equity. This disaggregation shows that ROE is a function of how profitable a business is, how active it is and how it is financed.

8.3 Extended DuPont

A more powerful representation of return on equity can be achieved by further disaggregation of the elements of the basic DuPont formula above.

$$\text{ROE} = \left[\underbrace{\left(\frac{\text{EBIT}}{\text{Sales}}\right)}_{\substack{\text{Operating}\\\text{profit}\\\text{margin}}} \times \underbrace{\left(\frac{\text{Sales}}{\text{Assets}}\right)}_{\substack{\text{Total}\\\text{assets}\\\text{turnover}}} - \underbrace{\left(\frac{\text{Interest expense}}{\text{Assets}}\right)}_{\substack{\text{Interest}\\\text{expense}\\\text{rate}}}\right] \times \underbrace{\left(\frac{\text{Assets}}{\text{Equity}}\right)}_{\substack{\text{Financial}\\\text{leverage}\\\text{multiplier}}} \times \underbrace{1 - \text{t}}_{\substack{\text{Tax}\\\text{retention}\\\text{rate}}}$$

9 Financial Ratios

9.1 Balance Sheet Gearing Ratios Used by Lenders in Financial Covenants

Historically, lenders have used balance sheet gearing ratios to control risk in relation to loan agreements. Rather than restrict a company's scope for increasing borrowings by fixing monetary limits on levels of debt, borrowings are allowed to rise when stockholders' equity/net worth increases, provided that borrowings never exceed a permitted multiple or percentage of stockholders' equity:

$$\frac{\text{Borrowings}}{\text{Equity}} \times 100$$

Borrowings and stockholders' equity will be defined in detail in the loan agreement. Although based on numbers in the audited accounts, the financial covenants frequently require adjustments to remove intangible assets from stockholders' equity, and to ignore the effects of revaluing non-current assets after the date of the loan agreement. Borrowings might be defined to include redeemable share capital if it is repayable before the loan.

Equity shareholders have long used balance sheet gearing as a yardstick of a company's financial structure. In principle borrowings are repayable in priority to share capital and from the lender's point of view it is logical to relate borrowings to total shareholders' funds.

Equity shareholders will normally want to establish the relationship between their interests in capital and reserves (equity interest) and the claims of others with a prior entitlement (borrowings and non-equity interests). This is often referred to as the debt/equity ratio:

$$\frac{\text{Debt (Borrowings + Non-equity interests)}}{\text{Equity interests}} \times 100$$

Example

The balance sheet of Ransomes S.A. analyses capital and reserves as follows:

	€'000
Equity interests	6,793
Non-equity interests– 8.25c cumulative	
convertible preference shares	9,307
	16,100

Taking borrowings from the balance sheet in the paragraph above:

	€'000
Current liabilities	101,725
Non-current liabilities	1,098
	102,823

The balance sheet gearing ratios from a lender's and equity stockholder's point of view are therefore:

Lender

$$\frac{\text{Borrowings}}{\text{Stockholder's equity}} \times 100 = \frac{€102.8\text{m}}{€16.1\text{m}} \times 100 = 638.5\%$$

Equity Shareholder

$$\frac{\text{Debt (Borrowings + Non-equity Interests)}}{\text{Equity interests}} \times 100$$

$$= \frac{€102.8\text{m} + €9.3\text{m}}{€6.8\text{m}} \times 100 = 1{,}648.5\%$$

9.2 Net Debt/Equity

As discussed in Chapter 4, investment analysts, and companies themselves, often prefer to calculate balance sheet gearing by deducting surplus cash and highly liquid investments from the borrowings/debt figure. In its balance sheet, Ransomes current assets included cash at bank and in hand of €3 million. It makes an insignificant difference to the ratios in this case, given the high levels of borrowing (€102.8m) and debt (€112.1m).

In most cases, companies would quote net borrowings (€99.8 million) simply because it is a lower figure. Investment analysts have to be careful if they emphasise net debt to equity for the following reasons:

- Companies can manipulate the amount of cash held at the year end, a form of window dressing.
- Cash held at the year-end is not necessarily freely available to repay borrowings, it may be required for some other purpose.
- If short-term investments are deducted from borrowings, it is essential that they are highly liquid/easily convertible into cash.
- In a group, if borrowings are in one country/currency but cash is held in another country/currency, there may be problems of remitting cash to repay debt.

9.3 Impact of Financial Gearing

From the point of view of equity shareholders, the impact of financial gearing on earnings is important. The effect of gearing is that for a given change in the level of profit before interest and tax there is a disproportionate effect on earnings. If profits before interest and tax are expected to rise by 20%, any financial gearing will lead to an increase in earnings of more than 20%; the higher the financial gearing the greater will be the increase in earnings. This may be particularly significant for shareholders in a company which has come through a period of low profits but expects a substantial recovery in the near future. In this instance, the gearing effect will be highly beneficial.

Conversely, if profits before interest and tax are expected to fall and borrowings are rising, earnings for equity shareholders in a highly geared company may be eroded rapidly. This would have serious implications for dividends and the share price.

High gearing implies high risk/high reward. An advantage of low financial gearing is that it provides scope to increase borrowings when potentially profitable projects are available to the company; not only will companies with low gearing find it easier to borrow but also it should be possible to borrow more cheaply than if gearing is already high.

Example

Two companies have assets in use of €20 million, financed in different proportions by debt and equity:

	Company A		Company B	
	€m		€m	
Stockholders' equity	16		8	
Debt – interest payable at 12%	4		12	
	20		20	
Debt/equity ratio	$\frac{4}{16}$	x 100	$\frac{12}{8}$	x 100
	= 25%		= 150%	

The table below shows the comparative impact on earnings of a 33% fall in the level of profit before interest payable and tax:

	Company A		Company B	
	Before	After	Before	After
	€'000	€'000	€'000	€'000
Profit before interest payable and tax	3,000	2,000	3,000	2,000
Interest payable	(480)	(480)	(1,440)	(1,440)
Profit before tax	2,520	1,520	1,560	560
Income taxes	(832)	(502)	(515)	(185)
Profit after tax/earnings	1,688	1,018	1,045	375

% change in profit before interest and tax	–33%
	–33%
% change in profit after tax/earnings	–40%
	–64%

Conversely, if profit before interest payable and tax increased by 33%, A's earnings would increase by 40% and B's by 64%. If companies have high levels both of operational and financial gearing, their earnings will be extremely sensitive to quite small changes in the level of activity.

9.4 Factors Which Affect Gearing Ratios

The following factors have an impact on gearing levels based on balance sheet numbers:

Reduce Gearing	Increase Gearing
• Issues of shares for cash – rights issues and placings. • Conversion of loan stocks/bonds into equity shares. • Upward revaluation of tangible fixed assets. • Recognition of intangibles not previously reported. • Increased retained profits from profitable trading. • Repayment of debt.	• Increase in debt – bond issues/bank borrowing, etc. • Purchase of own share. • Retained losses incurred. • Acquisitions of subsidiaries involving the immediate write off of purchased goodwill direct to reserves. • Deficits on revaluation of fixed assets.

9.5 Drawbacks of Balance Sheet Gearing Ratios

As the economy has moved from manufacturing to services, balance sheets have ceased to be a relevant measure of a company's worth. Companies like Apple, Google, Microsoft and Coca-Cola derive their worth from intellectual property, media creations and brands. Unlike physical assets such as land and machinery, these intangibles are not adequately reflected in balance sheets.

Even in the manufacturing sector inflation and choice of methods of depreciating assets mean that balance sheets are a poor guide to value. Therefore, a ratio of borrowings to shareholders' funds in the balance sheet may not represent a helpful measure of debt relative to equity.

NB: This ratio may be relatively reliable for property investment companies and for investment trusts.

One response from investment analysts is to measure gearing as follows:

$$\frac{\text{Debt}}{\text{Market capitalisation}}$$

Market capitalisation is the number of shares multiplied by their current market price and clearly does not suffer from the defects of accounting in the balance sheet.

Another response is to assess risk and volatility by reference to the returns generated by all the business' assets relative to interest costs. Returns can be measured as profits or as cash flows and the ratios used are:

- Interest cover

$$\frac{\text{Operating profit}}{\text{Interest payable}}$$

- Cash flow cover

$$\frac{\text{Operating cash flow}}{\text{Interest payments}}$$

9.6 Interest Cover

Interest cover measures how easily companies can service their borrowings. Clearly, different levels of cover are appropriate for different sectors. For example, companies in cyclical industries and those with high operational gearing need higher levels of cover than utilities, such as electricity or water companies.

Interest cover is a standard financial covenant in loan agreements. Lenders often define the operating profit component as operating profit before exceptional items and loan agreements have to define interest payable in detail.

Like all profit-based yardsticks, the ratio is affected by the directors' selection and implementation of accounting policies. Judgement has to be exercised about costs such as depreciation charges, provisions for doubtful debts and valuation of stocks at the lower of cost and net realisable value. Consequently, there are attractions in using operating cash flows, especially as the company needs cash to service its debt.

If a company pays interest of €2 million and records an operating loss of €1 million, after making a non-cash charge of €4 million for depreciation of plant property and equipment, it has positive operating cash flow of €3 million. Arguably, cash flow cover is a more reliable guide as to the company's ability to service its debt.

10 Ratio Analysis and Cash Flows

Cash flow ratios are increasingly used by lenders, investors and management. The following ratios have been selected to give an insight into two main areas:

- Operating performance
- Financial analysis

10.1 Operating Performance

- Operating cash flow/sales

$$\frac{\text{Net operating cash flow}}{\text{Turnover}} \times 100$$

This ratio looks at the cash generated as a percentage of sales.

It is the cash flow equivalent of operating profit to sales. It is a useful ratio to compare with other direct competitors of the business concerned and sector norms.

- Operating cash flow/total assets

$$\frac{\text{Net operating cash flow}}{\text{Total assets}} \times 100$$

This ratio compares the cash generated from operations with the total investment in the business.

Again, this is the cash flow equivalent of operating profit to total assets but should be higher as operating profit is stated after depreciation, whereas net operating cash flow ignores depreciation. Again, this is a ratio to compare with competitors and sector norms.

- Net operating cash flow/CAPEX

$$\frac{\text{Net operating cash flow}}{\text{Payments to purchase tangible non-current assets}}$$

This is a capital expenditure cover ratio. It shows us the number of times the capex could be covered from operating cash flow. In a capital intensive business, a low value would be expected as the business has to continually invest substantial amounts of capital each year in order to remain competitive. In a low capital business, higher values would be expected.

10.2 Financial Analysis

- Debt repayments in years

$$\frac{\text{Total debt}}{\text{Cash flow available to service debt}}$$

This ratio can be a good indicator of whether a business is exceeding its debt capacity.

- Interest cover

$$\frac{\text{Cash flow available to service debt}}{\text{Interest expense}}$$

- Debt servicing

$$\frac{\text{Cash flow available to service debt}}{\text{Interest expense and principal}}$$

The last two ratios are likely to be the most useful ratios for a lender. They measure the level of cash flow generated by a company which is available to service debt. The level of cover which is acceptable will vary from company to company, industry to industry. It is essentially dictated by the volatility and predictability of the company's cash flow. If the cash flow is steady and predictable (for example a supermarket or utility company) bankers may well be willing to tolerate a lower coverage level than, say, for a computer software design company.

Because cash flow is not readily manipulated through accounting practices, it is held by many lenders as a better measure of the company's real ability to service debt, particularly since, in reality, interest is serviced through cash and not profits. The difficulty with this measure, however, is that for anything other than mature, stable companies, the cash figure is more volatile than the profits figure, because it is after capital expenditure and additional investment in net working assets which may be high and/or variable for companies' growth and/or dynamic industries.

11 Investor Ratios

11.1 Introduction

This section considers the ratios most commonly used by equity investors/ analysts. The ratios considered are:

Earnings Per Share	$\dfrac{\text{Earnings}}{\text{Weighted average shares outstanding}}$
Price-Earnings Ratio	$\dfrac{\text{Market price}}{\text{Earnings per share}}$
Dividend Yield	$\dfrac{\text{Dividend per share}}{\text{Market price}} \times 100$
Dividend Cover	$\dfrac{\text{Earnings per share}}{\text{Dividend per share}}$
Net Assets per Equity Share (NAV)	$\dfrac{\text{Equity shareholders funds}}{\text{Number of equity shares in issue}} \times 100$
Cash Flow per Share	$\dfrac{\text{Free cash flow}}{\text{Weighted average shares outstanding}} \times 100$
Enterprise Value Ratios	$\dfrac{\text{Enterprise value}}{\text{EBIT}}$ $\dfrac{\text{Enterprise value}}{\text{EBITDA}}$ $\dfrac{\text{Enterprise value}}{\text{Sales}}$

Each of these ratios and their applications are described below.

Historic or Forecast Figures?

Ideally, investor ratios should be based on forecast earnings, dividends, asset values and cash flows; since these figures are often related to current market prices of shares which are anticipating future earnings, dividends, assets and cash flows, it is logical to use forecast figures.

12 Earnings per Share (EPS)

The P/E multiple is probably one of the most extensively quoted ratios used in the markets and is one of the key valuation tools for analysis. It is examined in more detail later in this chapter.

The purpose is essentially to assess how effective an entity has been in generating earnings from the resources provided by the equity stockholders. This is a measure of return for these stockholders as, unlike preference stockholders, dividend income is not certain. Complications arise in the calculation when there is potential additional equity by virtue of convertible debt or stock options. Let us now examine the types of EPS.

13 Types of EPS

Essentially, there are two types of EPS calculation:

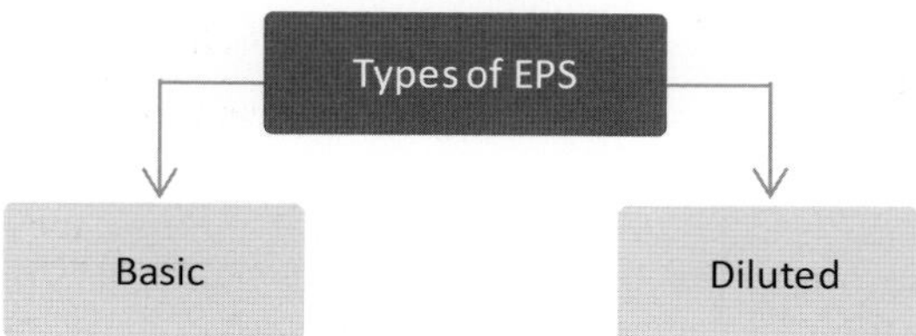

14 Basic EPS

$$\text{Basic EPS} = \frac{\text{Net income} - \text{Preference dividends}}{\text{Weighted average number of common shares outstanding}}$$

This is the simplest form of EPS.

Points to Note

- The earnings figure reflects earnings available to common stockholders regardless of dividend policy and is after minority interest. Preference dividends are deducted as the claims of senior securities must be deducted before any income is available to the common stockholder. The amount deducted is the value of the dividend declared in the year on the preference shares. If the share is cumulative, the dividend will always occur whether or not preference dividend has been declared. If the shares are not cumulative, and no dividend declared then a deduction from net income is not necessary
- The weighted average number of common shares in the issue reflects the change in the number of shares in issue during the accounting period. The assumption being that these changes may also impact earnings. There are a number of potential complications that need to be considered

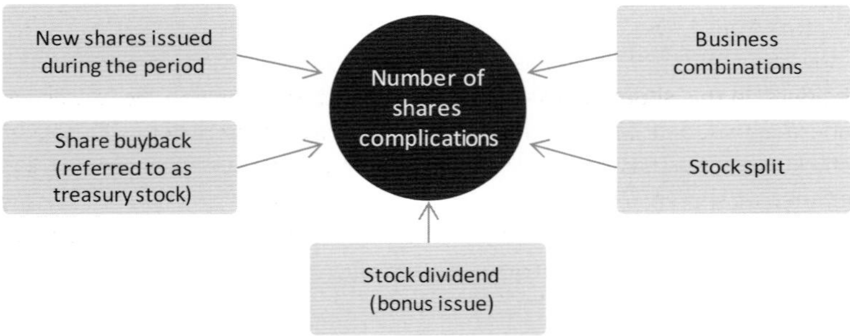

Let us look at each in turn:

New Shares Issued

If there has been an issuance of new shares in the period, then the number should be time apportioned from the date of issuance. The theory being that the cash generated from the issue can only have contributed to any increase in earnings from that date. The same also applies to any shares that have come into existence as a result of a conversion into common stock. Consideration should also be given to the effect of a rights issue during the period. This kind of issue entitles the shareholder to purchase additional stock at a specified price. The rights are taken up if market conditions are favourable, i.e. that shares can be acquired at below market price.

In essence, part of the shares acquired are for free and this is similar to a scrip/bonus issue. It is often referred to as the bonus element and is calculated as follows:

$$\frac{\text{Fair value prior to the exercise of the rights}}{\text{Theoretical ex-rights fair value}}$$

This fraction is applied retrospectively to shares in issuance as if the free shares had always existed.

Share Buyback

The entity reacquires its own shares if legally permissible to do so. As a result, the amount reacquired is deducted in the calculation of the weighted average number of shares. The logic of this exclusion is that the funds used to buy back shares are no longer available to generate earnings from the date of buyback. This is basically the opposite treatment to that of new issuance of shares.

Stock Dividend and Stock Split

These items both have the same impact on the calculation. A stock dividend is an alternative term for a bonus issue, i.e. the issuance of free shares to existing equity stockholders. In this situation, cash is not generated from the variance and so it does not generate additional earnings, neither does a stock split (for every €2 equity shares each stockholder now has 2 €1 equity shares). Both transactions do, however, increase the number of shares. The effect of these transactions is to apply a retrospective adjustment as if the stock dividend or split had occurred for the entire period. The reason being that there has been no change in ownership of the individual equity stockholder – they have all benefited from the change.

Example

Durable Inc. had the following stock related transactions during the year.

Jan 1	Year 1	Shares in issue and outstanding	20,000
Apr 1	Year 1	Shares issued at full market price	8,000
Jul 1	Year 1	Stock dividend declared of 10% (i.e. 1 for every 10 held)	
Sep 1	Year 1	Stock buyback	6,000

Calculate the number of shares to be used in the EPS calculations.

Solution

Step 1

Adjust all shares in issue at 7.1 Year 1 for stock dividend:

Shares outstanding at beginning	20,000 × 1.1	=	22,000
Shares issued on 4.1 Year 1	8,000 × 1.1	=	8,800

Step 2

Weighted average computation:

Shares outstanding at beginning 22,000 × 12/12	=	22,000
Shares issued on 1.4 Year 1 8,800 × 9/12	=	6,600
Share buyback on 1.9 Year 1 6,000 × 4/12	=	(2,000)
Shares to be used in EPS calculations	=	26,600

Prior Year EPS Restatement

As we have noted, there are a number of scenarios whereby shares are issued without impacting ownership and earnings namely:

- Stock dividends
- Rights issues (bonus element)

In order to ensure comparability, the prior year's EPS should be restated to account for these changes.

This is summarised by the diagram below.

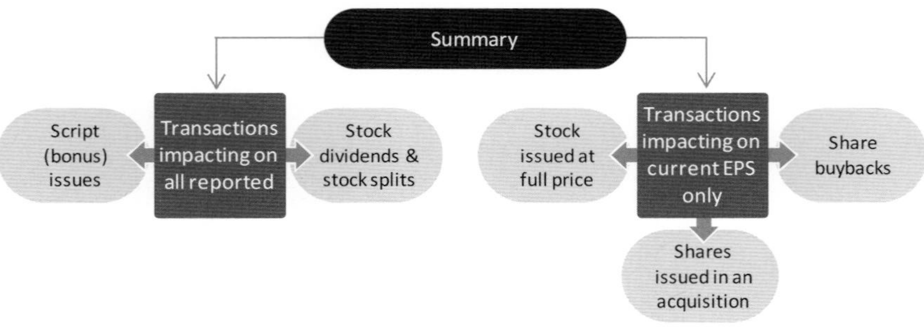

In most cases, we do not have to calculate the weighted number of shares outstanding, companies report the figures in the note to EPS in their financial statements.

Analysis Focus

EPS, Does it Matter?

Despite all the attention given to EPS measurement, there is little correlation between EPS growth and share price performance, or between price / earnings ratios and subsequent share price performance.

Apart from the problems of measurement and issues regarding dilution (see below), there are two more basic reasons why EPS alone is unhelpful. The figure alone gives us no indication of how much capital had to be invested to generate it. And it gives no idea of what the risks were that the provider of capital undertook. If you do not know either, then how can you assess the value?

15 Diluted EPS

15.1 Introduction

Diluted EPS only arises if a firm has a complex capital structure, i.e. a capital structure that includes dilutive securities. Dilutive securities are any financing instrument that can be converted or exchanged into common stock thereby potentially reducing EPS in the future. Examples would include convertible debt, options and warrants. The purpose of this calculation is to pre-warn stockholders of any potential decline in EPS.

15.2 Technical Issues

Dilutive Investment	Impact on Earnings	Impact on Number of Shares
Convertible debt	Save after tax interest	Increases number of shares in issue if converted
Options and Warrants	None	▪ Increases number of shares. ▪ Amount of dilutive shares are those issued at less than full market price as would only exercise option/warrant if conditions were favourable.
Convertible preferred stock	Save gross dividend (no tax implications as paid from after tax profits)	Increases on conversion

Example 1

Justin Inc. has 8,000,000 common stock in issue and outstanding. Its income statement looked as follows:

Justin Inc. Income statement for Year Ended 31.12. Year 1 (extract)

	€
Net income	60,000,000
Preferred dividends	(10,000,000)
	50,000,000

Justin Inc. has an 8% €200,000,000 convertible bond which offers holders one unit of common stock for every €120 of debt (@ par value). It also has 200,000,000 units of 5% preferred stock. These convert into 3,000,000 shares. Taxes are charged at 30%.

Calculate the basic and diluted EPS for Year 1. Ignore the anti-dilutive rule.

Solution

$$\text{Basic EPS } \frac{50{,}000{,}000}{8{,}000{,}000} = €6.25$$

Diluted

Adjustment to Number of Shares

$$\text{Convertible bond } = \frac{200{,}000{,}000}{120} = 1{,}666{,}667$$

$$\text{Preference stock } = \frac{3{,}000{,}000}{1} = 3{,}000{,}000$$

Total shares = 8,000,000 + 4,666,667 = 12,666,667

Adjustment to Earnings

	€
As before	50,000,000
+ preferred dividend (saved if converted)	10,000,000
+ after-tax interest saving	
200,000,000 × (1 − 0.3) × 8% =	11,200,000
	71,200,000

$$\text{Diluted EPS } \frac{71{,}200{,}000}{12{,}666{,}667} = €5.62$$

Points to Note

- The adjustment to number of shares assumes the conversion took place at the beginning of the period. If the convertible bonds and preferred stock were issued during the period, then the number would be time apportioned.
- Both basic and diluted EPS should be disclosed on the face of the income statement.

Example 2

Felix Inc. common stock has traded at an average market price of €40 per share during Year 1. Its capital structure can be summarised as follows:

- 4,000 shares of common stock.
- 2,000 shares of 10% preferred stock with a par value of €100. They are convertible into 20 shares each.
- 2,000 stock options each of which gives the holder the right to buy ten shares in Felix Inc. stock at €30 per share.

All of these elements of capital structure were in issue for the entire year.

Calculate the diluted EPS if net income before preference dividends is €23,120.

Solution

$$\textbf{Step 1}\text{: Basic EPS } = \frac{€23{,}120 \; - \; €20{,}000}{4{,}000} = €0.78$$

Step 2:

Check whether the preferred stock is anti-dilutive.

Preference shares = 2,000 × 20 = 40,000 shares

Earnings saving = €20,000 so overall EPS would be

$$\frac{3{,}120 \; + \; 20{,}000}{44{,}000} = €0.525$$

As basic EPS is above this calculation, preferred stock is dilutive.

Step 3:

Calculate impact of options.

The market price is €6.40 but the option price is €5.80. Therefore, the gain to employees is €0.60 per share. Employees are getting some shares free. In terms of number, it works out that they are getting 5,000 more shares than an arm's length buyer would get. See the points to note below for a detailed calculation.

Step 4:

$$\text{Diluted EPS} = \frac{23{,}120}{40{,}000 + 5{,}000 + 4{,}000} = €0.47$$

Points to Note

- Items that do not have a dilutive effect are ignored when calculating diluted EPS. In this case each item is dilutive. However, re-examine Example 1 – is the convertible bond dilutive?
- The ultimate aim is to calculate the worst possible (i.e. most diluted) EPS.
- The method used to calculate the impact of the exercise of the options is known as the "Treasury Stock Method". The following is a more detailed explanation of the calculations above.

Step 1:

Calculate the proceeds that would be received if options were exercised, i.e. €600,000.

Step 2:

Calculate how much stock at average market price could be purchased from these proceeds: i.e. €600,000 / €40 = 15,000

Step 3:

=	Number of shares issued if exercised	20,000
	Number of shares that could be bought at average price	15,000
	Shares issued at below market price	5,000

Given there is a bargain element to an option, it is this element that has a dilutive effect because no proceeds are generated (and hence, no impact on income) yet more shares are in issuance.

16 Price-Earnings Ratios

16.1 Introduction

Price-earnings ratios are used to help to decide whether a company's equity shares are 'cheap' or 'dear' relative to earnings. This can only be considered in the context of the relationship between the earnings and share prices of comparable companies.

For the comparison to be reliable certain assumptions have to be made:

- Methods of measuring earnings per share are comparable – questionable.
- The share prices of the companies concerned are influenced greatly by earnings and that other factors are insignificant.

It is more useful to compare price-earnings ratios calculated using forecast rather than historic earnings per share because, to the extent that prices are driven by earnings, it is future profits which are critical. Nevertheless, both 'historic' and 'prospective' price-earnings ratios are used in practice.

Illustration

Two companies in the same line of business prepare accounts each year to 31 March:

	Company A	Company B
Market price at 30 June YR 1	€1.50	€1.32
Earnings per share for year ended 31 March YR 1	€0.10	€0.12
Historic price-earnings ratio	15×	11×

Company A is said to have a 'higher rating' than company B because A's share price represents a higher multiple of earnings per share (15) than B's (11). A number of possible explanations could account for this difference in ratings:

- Better growth prospects for A's earnings per share.
- Higher quality/less risky earnings.
- Recovery prospects.
- Other factors affecting the share price – for example, prospects of a takeover.
- A's shares are overpriced, or B's are undervalued.

If A's earnings per share for the year ended 31 March YR 2 were expected to grow by 25% to €0.125 per share whereas B's earnings were only anticipated to grow by 10% to €0.132, it can be seen that the prospect of faster earnings growth accounts for a significant part of the difference in the historic price-earnings ratios. This is made clearer by looking at the prospective price-earnings ratios based on forecast earnings per share:

	Company A	**Company B**
Market price at 30 June YR 1	€1.50	€1.32
Forecast earnings per share	€0.125	€0.132
	12×	10×

The differences in prospective ratings could still be explained by the above factors. Investors are generally prepared to pay higher prices relative to profits where they perceive that a company's profits are more secure. This depends on a combination of factors, including the record of management, position in the market relative to competitors and whether growth is achieved organically or by acquisition.

A company whose shares are highly rated has significant advantages. It is in a good defensive position in that any takeover attempt might prove to be too expensive for some potential predators.

It also enables a company with highly rated shares to make potentially many more acquisitions, or at least to have a wider choice of targets. Given that one of the primary objectives of management is to achieve consistent growth in earnings per share, it may be vital for a company to grow by acquisition as well as organically.

Growth by Acquisition

A general principle can be established that any acquisition financed by an issue of equity shares will have the automatic effect of increasing earnings per share of the combined businesses if the target company is taken over at a P/E multiple lower than that of the bidder.

Illustration

	Bidder	Target
Forecast earnings	€10 million	€4 million
Equity shares in issue	100 million	
Forecast earnings per share	€0.10	
Market price	€1.60	
Prospective price-earnings ratio	16×	

Bidder wishes to acquire Target and to finance the acquisition by issuing equity shares. Bidder's own price-earnings ratio, here 16, is crucial in determining what price it can afford to pay for the shares of Target while ensuring that the earnings per share of the combined businesses will be greater than its own prospective figure of €0.10 per share. The cut-off point is a total consideration which represents 16 times the earnings of target (16 × €4 million = €64 million).

Total Consideration Less Than €64 Million – Growth in EPS

If Target's shareholders could be persuaded to accept a price of €48 million for their business, earnings per share of the combined businesses will be greater than €0.10 because Target has been acquired on a lower rating than Bidder's price-earnings ratio of 16.

€48 million paid for €4 million earnings represents a rating of 12 (€48 million/€4 million). This is known as the 'exit' price-earnings ratio. A price of €48 million would involve Bidder issuing 30 million shares at €1.60. Prospective earnings per share for the combined businesses would therefore rise to €0.108:

$$\text{Earnings}(€10\text{m} + €4\text{m})\ €14\text{m}(+40\%)$$

$$\text{Equity shares in issue}\ (100\text{m} + 30\text{m})\ 130\text{m}(+30\%)$$

$$\text{Earnings per share} \qquad \frac{€14\text{m}}{130\text{m}} \times 100 \qquad €0.108(+8\%)$$

Total consideration more than €64 million – dilution of eps

If Bidder has to offer a price of more than €64 million, valuing Target on a higher price-earnings ratio than its own 16, earnings per share will be diluted below €0.10 if the consideration is financed by issuing new equity shares in Bidder. A price of €72 million for earnings of €4 million represents an exit price-earnings ratio of 18 (€72 million/€4 million). 45 million shares must be issued at €1.60 to satisfy the consideration. Earnings per share of the combined businesses will fall to €0.097:

$$\text{Earnings} \quad (€10\text{m} + €4\text{m}) \;\; €14\text{m} \;\; (+40\%)$$

$$\text{Equity shares in issue} \quad (100\text{m} + 45\text{m}) \;\; 145\text{m} \;\; (+45\%)$$

$$\text{Earnings per share} \quad \frac{€14\text{m} \times 100}{145\text{m}} \times 100 \;\; €0.97 \;\; (-3\%)$$

Avoidance or Postponement of Dilution of Earnings Per Share

If an immediate reduction of 3% in earnings per share is considered to be undesirable/unacceptable it would be possible to avoid the problem if the consideration of €72 million could be paid in the form of some other security whose net of corporation tax cost is not more than €4 million. This could be achieved by some form of convertible:

- Convertible preference shares with a maximum dividend rate of 5.5% or
- Convertible bonds/loan stock with a maximum coupon of 8%

Issue €72 million 5.5% convertible preference stock of €1 each:

Earnings:	**€m**
Bidder	10.00
Target	4.00
	14.00
Less preference dividends (5.5% × €72m)	(3.96)
	10.04

$$\text{Earnings per share} = \frac{€10.4\text{m} \times 100}{100\text{m}} \times 100 = €0.10$$

Issue €72 million 8% convertible loan stock:

Earnings:		**€m**	**€m**
Bidder			10.00
Target			4.00
Less:	interest on loan stock (8% × €72m)	5.76	
	income tax at 31%	(1.79)	
			(3.97)
			10.03
			€0.10

$$\text{Earnings per share} = \frac{€10.3 \times 100}{100\text{m}} \times 100$$

In both cases, it is likely that the terms of conversion would set out the conversion price at more than the existing market price of €1.60, thus not merely postponing but actually avoiding dilution of earnings per share in future. For example, if holders of convertible preference shares or loan stock could convert at a price of €2 per ordinary share, prospectively only 36 million shares (72 million/€2) would be issued. The availability of such arrangements depends on finding investors prepared to accept the convertible securities.

It is clear from the illustration that a high price-earnings ratio is very important if companies are to be able to grow by acquisition. The recent fall in market prices halted a number of acquisitive companies in their tracks because it not only reduced their own share ratings, but also meant that target company shareholders and other investors were often no longer prepared to accept a bidding company's shares as consideration. Subsequently finance for acquisitions had to come from increased borrowings or surplus cash. Leveraged acquisitions financed by borrowings entail considerable risks if interest rates rise and underlying economic activity and profits decline.

17 Dividend Yield

As with earnings per share, the historic dividend is clearly less important than the prospective amount payable in the future. If the historic dividend yield is used, it is often considered in conjunction with the dividend cover ratio to assess the ability of the company to maintain the payment of dividends at the existing level.

Illustration

Company C pays a net dividend of €0.08 per share for the year ended 31 December 1999. Earnings per share for the period were €0.12. The market price of the ordinary shares at 30 June 2000 is €1.25 per share. The historic dividend yield is 8% calculated as follows:

$$\frac{\text{Dividend per Share}}{\text{Market price}} \times 100$$

$$\frac{€0.08}{€1.25} \times 100 = \ 6.4\%$$

If the average dividend yield on the share of other listed companies at 30 June 2000 is 5%, at first sight a return of 6.4% looks attractive to a shareholder interested in receiving dividend income.

18 Dividend Cover

The problem with the higher than average dividend yield of 6.4% may be that the yield is higher because the share price has fallen due to doubts about the company's capacity to increase or even maintain the current level of €0.08 per share.

As stated above, dividend cover may help to assess the safety of the historic payment. The simplest method of calculation produces cover of 1.5 times:

$$\frac{\text{Earnings per share}}{\text{Dividend per share}}$$

$$\frac{€0.12}{€0.08} = \ 1.5 \text{ times}$$

If the average dividend cover is 2.5 times, the yield and cover can usefully be considered together:

	Company C	Market average
Dividend yield	6.4%	5%
Dividend cover	1.5	2.5

The impression is that C's dividend payment is less secure than average because profits earned are a lower multiple of the dividend payment. This is not definitive because companies with adequate cash can pay dividends out of the retained profits of previous years.

19 Market Capitalisation: Net Assets

$$\frac{\text{Market capitalisation}}{\text{Net assets}}$$

Net asset values based on balance sheet amounts must be interpreted with care. Firstly, the amounts at which assets are included in a balance sheet do not necessarily represent a realistic current market value but are more likely to reflect the purchase price paid. Secondly, they are likely to be of little relevance in certain industries; in a 'people' business such as public relations or advertising, the tangible asset base is likely to be negligible and the company should be considered from the point of view of earnings generated by its staff who are not reported as assets in the balance sheet. In addition, net asset value might be affected by accounting treatments such as revaluations and goodwill write-offs. In research or marketing intensive companies such as GSK or Coca-Cola, the net asset value does not take such expenditure into account even though both types of expenses are expected to generate future returns.

Ideally therefore, net asset values are most relevant when up to date information is disclosed about the market values of assets and where the assets in the balance sheet are the basis upon which current and future profits are generated.

Property investment companies in the UK are required to revalue their investment properties each year and look to increases in asset values as the basis upon which growth in rental income can be anticipated when periodic rent reviews take place. The relationship between net asset values and the market price of the shares represents for these companies the equivalent of the price-earnings ratio for other types of business.

If the market price of a company's shares falls significantly below net asset value there may be a possibility that the company might be vulnerable to shareholder pressure to sell off its assets or to install new management which could use the assets more effectively within the business.

The amount of the 'discount' to net asset value at which a property company's or investment trust's shares stand is frequently used in these sectors as an indicator of 'cheapness' or 'dearness'.

In sectors such as manufacturing, distribution and services the share price will normally exceed net asset value, i.e. stand at a 'premium' to net assets.

Asset backing per share may be calculated using the following ratio:

$$\frac{\text{Net assets}}{\text{Number of shares in issue}}$$

20 Cash Flow Per Share

Because of the problems of earnings as an investment performance measure, cash flow is increasingly being used. Cash flow is less easily manipulated by accounting policies and is therefore felt by many investors to give a superior indicator of a company's investment performance. The typical measure used is:

$$\frac{\text{Free cash flow}}{\text{Weighted average shares outstanding}}$$

Free cash flow is defined as net operating profits less interest paid, less cash taxes paid, plus depreciation, plus or minus the decrease (increase) in working capital, less capital expenditure. As such it represents the cash flow available to the equity shareholder before dividends are paid.

The problem with cash flow as a measure is that cash flow may be low or negative for start-up and rapidly growing companies and even for more mature companies will typically be subject to greater volatility than with earnings measures.

21 An Introduction to Enterprise Value Ratios

21.1 Introduction

Corporate financiers tend to calculate company values by reference to a range of values for quoted comparable companies. An indicative valuation multiple can then be set by reference to these comparable companies. This multiple is applied to the company in question to arrive at a likely value. This process may be used both in company flotation and acquisition situations.

Although corporate financiers may use P/E and Market Capitalisation/Net Asset ratios for this type of analysis, it is more usual to use a combination of EBIT, EBITDA or Sales to Enterprise Value ratios because of the fact that:

- Enterprise Value ratios reduce the distorting effects of different capital structures
- EBIT, EBITDA and Sales are 'higher up' the profit and loss account and there is therefore less of a distorting effect as a result of differences in accounting policies between the comparable company group

21.2 Definition of Enterprise Value

The Enterprise Value (EV) of the company is the current market value of the business on a de-geared basis. As such it is a measure of the underlying value of the business after having allowed for the debt/cash position of the company and represents the aggregate value of a company to all its providers of capital.

EV	=	Market capitalisation of equity + Non-controlling interests + Net debt
Market Capitalisation (of Equity)	=	Share price(s) times number of shares outstanding for each class of share, including: ▪ Ordinary shares ▪ Preference shares ▪ Other classes of shares
Net Debt	=	Total short-term debt + Total long-term debt + Finance leases and other interest bearing liabilities − Cash and cash equivalents

21.3 Multiples Based on EV

EBIT Multiple

$$= \frac{\text{EV}}{\text{EBIT}}$$

EBIT = Earnings before interest and tax

EBITDA Multiple

$$= \frac{\text{EV}}{\text{EBITDA}}$$

EBITDA = EBIT + Depreciation + Amortisation

Both of these valuation metrics are used extensively by finance professionals. If depreciation and amortisation are especially important then the difference between the two measures is unlikely to be significant. In asset intensive industries depreciation and amortisation can be highly distortive as companies adopt different accounting policies which do not necessarily better represent their economics. Hence using an EBITDA measure can minimise the challenges for users.

Sales Multiple

$$= \frac{\text{EV}}{\text{Total sales}}$$

The sales multiple is not always a helpful valuation multiple because it can vary dramatically according to the type of company. It is however useful for:

- Comparing companies within the same industry where one would usually expect broadly similar profit margins.
- Companies whose profits have collapsed so that profit multiples are not relevant (on the implicit assumption that profitability can be retained).
- Companies in sectors where market share can be as important as financial profitability (e.g., food retailing, airlines).

Applications

The main application of these ratios is valuation for flotation and acquisition purposes. The aim is to derive a set of Enterprise Value multiples for a range of comparable quoted companies. These multiples are then applied to the company to be floated.

Comparable company EV/EBIT	×	Company to be floated EBIT	=	Indication of EV of company to be floated
Comparable company EV/EBITDA	×	Company to be floated EBITDA	=	Indication of EV of company to be floated
Comparable company EV/Sales	×	Company to be floated SALES	=	Indication of EV of company to be floated

To derive shareholder value from the enterprise value calculated, it is necessary to deduct net debt, minority interests and any preference shares, if applicable.

Chapter 7: An Introduction to Consolidation

"Accountants Will Save the World" [7]

[7] Peter Bakker, Harvard Business Review, March As reported in Accountancy Magazine, March 2013. Clearly, I love this quote and I promise you it is accurate. Go and have a look!

1 An Introduction to Consolidation

So far, we have only concerned ourselves with the preparation of the financial statements of individual entities. The remaining chapters focus on the preparation and interpretation of financial statements for groups of entities.

If an entity wishes to expand into new markets, new products or increase market share it could achieve this by organic growth. However, this could be a very long process and in many cases growth is achieved by the acquisition of another entity. This is achieved by acquiring the stock of the desired target. From an accounting perspective, it is important to achieve best presentation of performance and net assets of the combined entities.

This chapter examines the accounting treatment of investments in the financial statements of the parent entity and provides an introduction to basic methods of consolidation.

2 Treatment of Investments

2.1 Introduction

The accounting treatment of equity investments in the financial statements of the investing company is determined by the intention of the company at acquisition and the extent of ownership. Accounting rules require the initial equity investment to be recorded in the balance sheet of the investor at the purchase price (cost). However, the subsequent accounting will differ based on whether the company intends to hold the investment as a long term or short-term investment.

The accounting guidance for equity investments is generally addressed by IFRS 9 'Financial Instruments'. It requires equity investments to be fair valued at each balance sheet date. However, since this will result in the company needing to recognise fair value gains and losses each period, there is some choice over how these gains and losses are presented.

For shorter term investments (and the default treatment under IFRS 9) fair value gains and losses are recognised in earnings. In general, these investments are classified as 'fair value through profit and losses' (FVPL). For longer term investments, companies generally prefer to avoid recognising fair value gains and losses in earnings. IFRS 9 has specific provisions for this situation and allows companies to recognise fair value gains and losses in equity, instead of earnings, by classifying the investments at 'fair value through other comprehensive income' (FVOCI).

The following example illustrates the basic accounting treatment of investments under IFRS 9.

Duplex S.A. has acquired Simplex S.A. for €25m. The consideration was financed as follows:

	€
Issue of €10,000,000 shares at par (€1)	10,000,000
Issue of a 6% bond	10,000,000
Cash	5,000,000
	25,000,000

Required

What is the accounting impact of such a transaction?

Solution

The accounting impact of this transaction in the accounts of Duplex S.A. is:

Non-Current Investment €'000

Investments 25,000

Points to Note

- The initial carrying value of this investment is at cost with subsequent changes to fair value being accounted for as per paragraph 2.1 above.
- The carrying value does not necessarily reflect the underlying relationship between the two companies nor provide users with useful information about this relationship. It is out of this issue that the need for consolidated financial statements has arisen.
- Obviously, the financing will also be reflected:

↓ Cash	5,000,000
↑ Bonds	10,000,000
↑ Common Stock	10,000,000

Consolidated or group financial statements are prepared to provide more detailed and meaningful information to users about the activities of companies. The need for consolidated accounts comes from the unsatisfactory results of treating acquisitions and takeovers as single line fixed asset investments.

3 Forms of Investment

It is therefore vital to understand the true relationship between investor and investee and to what extent there has been any influence or control exercised over the assets and liabilities of the investee company for the benefit of the investor.

The table below summaries the three levels of investment and the corresponding accounting treatment. The percentages given are only indicative of the nature of the relationship.

	Holding 0 < 20%	**Holding 20% < 50%**	**Holding >50%**
Extent of influence over investment	None	Significant	Control
Accounting term	Investment	Associated undertaking	Subsidiary undertaking
Accounting treatment	Financial asset[8]	Equity method	Purchase method in consolidated financial statements

From the above table, it should be noted that fully consolidated financial statements are only prepared if the parent entity has at least one subsidiary undertaking. The fact that the holding company has control over another entity means that regardless of legal form, the holding company controls the resources (assets and liabilities) as well as performance (earnings). The nature of such a relationship requires more meaningful information for the holding company investors.

The equity method must be used, even if consolidated financial statements are not prepared (see later). As noted earlier, the pooling of interest method is now prohibited (under both IFRS and US GAAP).

[8] As these are likely to be long-term investments, they are likely to be classified as "FVOCI".

4 The Meaning of Group Accounts

Group accounting generally refers to full consolidation where control has been attained. The fundamental idea behind group accounting is that separate legal entities (i.e. companies) within the group are treated as a single economic unit as illustrated below.

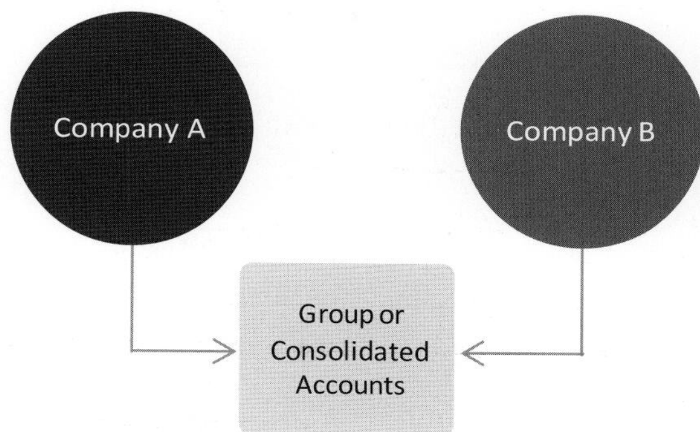

It should be noted that the assumption of single entity has its own implications. Transactions, such as intragroup trading and loans, all need to be eliminated in order to present the group's transactions with third parties only. The format of a typical consolidated balance sheet is given in Section 6 with a summary of theory points to note.

5 Techniques of Consolidation

IFRS 3 *Business Combinations* requires that purchase accounting is used. Purchase accounting is summarised below.

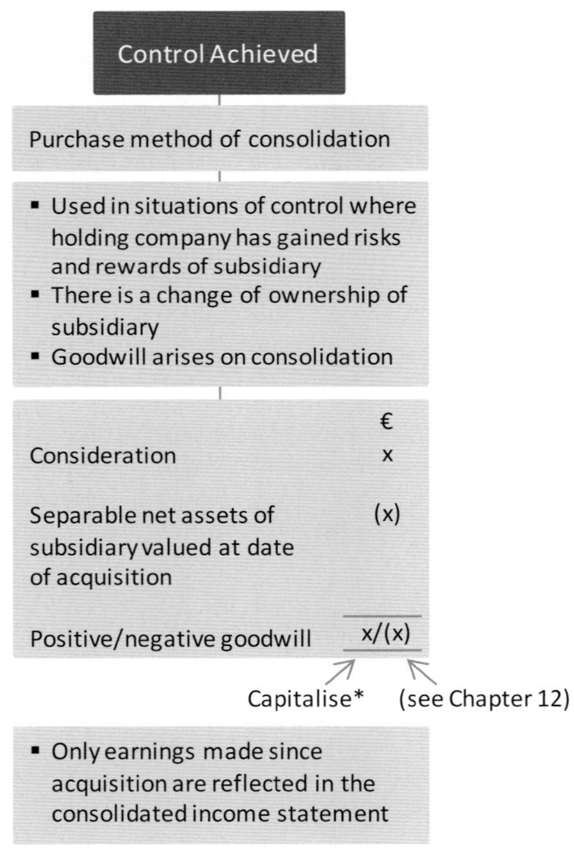

* Up to the IFRS transition in 2005, goodwill was amortised to the income statement.

The next example and Chapters 8 to 10 focus on the purchase method of consolidation. This is the method most widely used.

6 The Anatomy of a Consolidated Balance Sheet

December 31	**Year 2**	**Year 1**
	€	**€**
Assets		
Current assets:		
Cash and cash equivalents	239.0	258.6
Accounts and notes receivable	1,770.7	1,733.6
Inventories	2,164.5	1,835.2
Prepaid expenses and other current assets	354.9	336.5
Total Current Assets	**4,529.1**	**4,163.9**
Long-term accounts and notes receivable	173.5	201.9
Investments in equity securities	111.4	124.6
Intangible assets	1,317.3	1,143.2
Properties and plants	4,358.5	4,149.7
Other assets	99.5	134.1
Total Assets	**10,589.3**	**9,917.4**
Liabilities		
Current liabilities		
Accounts payable – trade	1,113.7	1,383.4
Salaries, wages and commission	651.0	682.7
Other current liabilities	276.9	321.8
Deferred tax	252.6	287.0
Obligations under capital leases	723.3	365.2
Long-term debt due within one year	259.0	210.9
Total Current Liabilities	**3,276.5**	**3,251.0**
Obligations under capital leases	1,945.9	1,945.7
Long-term debt (Note 9)	1,186.5	844.5
Other long-term liabilities	175.6	224.5
Non-controlling interest	259.0	256.2
Total Liabilities	**6,843.5**	**6,521.9**

	Year 2	Year 1
Shareholders' Equity		
Preferred stock, no par value:		
Authorised, 50,000,000 shares, unissued	-	-
Common stock, no par value:		
Authorised, 300,000,000 shares		
Outstanding shares, 155,943,535	155.9	156.6
Capital surplus	1,015.9	1,061.6
Retained earnings	3,477.8	2,983.4
Accumulated other comprehensive income	(903.8)	(806.1)
Total Shareholders' Equity	**3,745.8**	**3,395.5**
Total Liabilities and Shareholders' Equity	**10,589.3**	**9,917.4**

Points to Note

- There are no investments in subsidiaries in consolidated accounts. This is because the carrying value of the investments has been replaced by the underlying net assets of the subsidiary. The investment balance is then used in the calculation of goodwill.
- The net assets represent the amalgamated net assets of each of the subsidiaries. Users are then provided with information to review short- and long-term financing of the group.
- Non-controlling interests (also referred to as minority interests) reflect the outside interest in the net assets of the subsidiary that have been consolidated by the holding company, i.e. 100% of the net assets of the subsidiary will have been added to the group's net assets to reflect control, but the holding company may only own 75% so a 25% non-controlling interest must be reflected. Note that although reasonably unusual non-controlling interest can be negative – it means that the subsidiary has accumulated losses which result in negative shareholders' equity.
- Common stock and preferred stock relate to the holding company only. Under the acquisition method, consolidated financial statements are prepared from the holding company's perspective. Interest in the stock of the subsidiary is replaced by interest in the underlying net assets.
- The retained earnings equal the holding company's retained earnings plus a share of the subsidiary's post-acquisition retained earnings. This is to reflect the change in ownership of the subsidiary and the ownership of earnings.

Accounts Commentary

We can see the operation of the basic consolidation mechanics by looking at the Lufthansa financials and, in particular, the balance sheet on page 104. Note that the balance sheet fixed assets do not contain any 'investment in subsidiaries'. This has been cancelled on consolidation. Instead the individual assets have been aggregated for all of the subsidiaries and allocated to the relevant individual balance sheet category.

'Investments accounted for using the equity method' is included and this refers to those joint ventures and associates in which Lufthansa has made investments.

The Lufthansa financials are available online, just type the following into your browser's address bar to download the PDF:

bit.ly/lufthansa2017

Chapter 8: Consolidation Techniques I – The Balance Sheet

"There is no rationale for not treating stock options as an expense. Except that if you did it would have greater impact than Greenspan resigning, the election and another financial crisis rolled into one" [9]

[9] Unnamed investment banker. Note: stock options are now an expense and we are all still (broadly) fine!

1 Introduction

Consolidation can be viewed as a process involving two major steps:

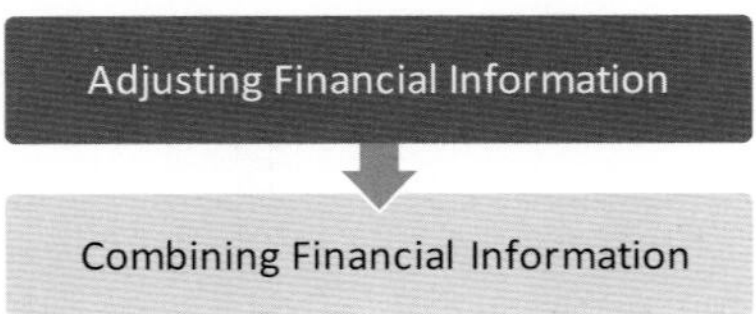

This chapter addresses the fundamental mechanics of consolidation starting with some basic examples before addressing more complex issues.

2 Basic Balance Sheet Example

MD S.A. acquired all of the common stock of Sublime S.A. on 1 January Year 1 for €10,000. The balance sheets immediately after acquisition were as follows:

	MD SA	Sublime SA
	€	€
Investment in Sublime S.A.	10,000	-
Other assets	20,000	10,000
	30,000	10,000
Common stock	16,000	10,000
Retained earnings	14,000	-
	30,000	10,000

Requirement

Prepare the consolidated balance sheet of the MD Group as at 1 January Year 1.

Approach

Solution

MD S.A. Consolidated Balance Sheet 1 January Year 1

	€
Other assets	30,000
Common stock	16,000
Retained earnings	14,000
	30,000

Points to Note

- No non-controlling interest as MD acquired 100% of Sublime.
- Other assets reflect the assets over which MD has control.
- Common stock is only that of MD.
- Common stock of Sublime is cancelled with the cost of investment. No goodwill arises on this cancellation since MD acquired Sublime for book value.

	€	€
Consideration		10,000
Net assets acquired as represented by:		
Stock	10,000	
Earnings	-	
100% x	10,000	(10,000)
		-

- Retained earnings are only those of MD. The next section considers the issue of the subsidiary's reserves/retained earnings at the date of acquisition.

3 Reserves

3.1 Introduction

A fundamental principle of the purchase method is that, in relation to subsidiaries' earnings, only those generated after the acquisition are included in the group accounts. This is based on the fact that the management of the holding company should not get 'credit' for earnings generated by others. In particular, the acquiring company may well have expended significant sums acquiring such earnings – the idea that such reserves become part of retained profits or earnings would be flawed.

Group Reserves

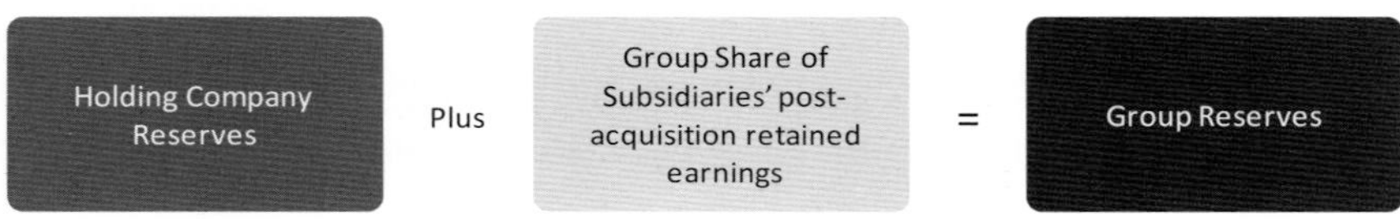

Example

Great S.A. acquired 100% of Notes S.A. on 1 January Year 1 for €40,000. Immediately after the acquisition, the balance sheets looked as follows:

	Great SA	Notes SA
	€	€
Investment in Notes SA	40,000	-
Other assets	130,000	40,000
	170,000	40,000
Common stock	38,000	10,000
Retained earnings	132,000	30,000
	170,000	40,000

Required

Prepare the consolidated balance sheet of Great S.A. Group.

Solution

Consolidated Balance Sheet as at 1 January Year 1

	€
Assets	170,000
Common stock	38,000
Retained earnings	132,000
	170,000

Points to Note

- Assets are those controlled by Great S.A.
- No non-controlling interest due to 100% acquisition.
- Common stock is only that of Great S.A.
- Common stock and earnings of Notes S.A. are cancelled with the cost of investment. No goodwill arises.

	€	€
Cost of investment		40,000
Net assets acquired as represented by:		
Common stock	10,000	
Retained earnings	30,000	
	40,000	
	× 100%	(40,000)
Goodwill		-

- Retained earnings are only those of Great S.A. We cannot consolidate earnings of Notes S.A. as these arise pre-acquisition and as a result were not controlled by the group.

4 Goodwill on Acquisition

4.1 Introduction

The examples used so far have ignored the goodwill issue. We must now turn our attention to goodwill as it is a major feature of the purchase method of consolidation. Most acquisitions involve the acquirer paying a premium. This premium arises because the purchase price is in excess of the net assets acquired. The investing company is prepared to pay in excess for a combination of reasons not reflected in the net assets (market share, product diversity, customer profile, location, management, brand names).

Under IFRS 3 *Business Combinations*, goodwill has to be capitalised and tested annually for impairment. Historically, before the IFRS transition goodwill was capitalised and amortised. The amortisation period would not normally be longer than 20 years, unless a longer life could be demonstrated. Further consideration of the more detailed aspects of goodwill (fair values and impairments) are considered in Chapter 12.

Analysis Focus

Returns on Capital

When calculating return on capital, what do we do with goodwill? Since it does not have to be replaced, it is clearly not a cost. We add back the impairment (if any) into profit. What about the balance sheet? Well, when the company builds a new plant it is not going to build goodwill as well, so when forecasting it is returns on capital excluding goodwill that should drive our valuation. So, is goodwill irrelevant? Is it irrelevant that management spent lots of money and may not get a fair return on it? Clearly, we need both measures, but for different purposes.

Example

MD S.A. acquires 100% of the issued common stock of Sublime S.A. on 1 January Year 1 for €10,000 when Sublime's retained earnings were €1,000.

Balance sheets two years later are as follows:

	MD SA	Sublime SA
	€	€
Investment in Sublime S.A.	10,000	-
Other assets	17,000	10,000
	27,000	10,000
Common stock	24,000	8,000
Retained earnings	3,000	2,000
	27,000	10,000

Requirement

Produce the consolidated balance sheet of the MD S.A. group.

Solution

MD S.A. Consolidated Balance Sheet at 1 January Year 3

	€
Intangible assets	1,000
Goodwill (W1)	
Other assets	27,000
	28,000
Common stock	24,000
Retained earnings (W2)	4,000
	28,000

Workings

(W1) Goodwill	€
Cost of investment	10,000
Net equity (8,000 common stock + 1,000 earnings)	(9,000)
	1,000

(W2) Reserves	€	€
MD SA		3,000
Sublime SA	2,000	
- pre-acquisition	(1,000)	1,000
		4,000

- The goodwill adjustment only happens on consolidation. It does not appear in the individual company financial statements.
- The goodwill is recognised in the group balance sheet as an intangible asset.
- The retained earnings of the group only include the post-acquisition earnings of Sublime.
- No non-controlling interest due to 100% acquisition of Sublime.

5 Non-Controlling Interests

5.1 Introduction

Although it varies from group to group, many subsidiaries are not wholly owned. As established in the previous chapter, it is control that is the key and not ownership of every share.

However, on the 'top' of any group balance sheet all the assets are amalgamated, irrespective of actual ownership once it is sufficient to gain control (i.e. >50%).

The non-controlling interest account caption is used to capture the net assets that have been consolidated on the top of the balance sheet that are not actually owned by the holding company (the outside interest in what has been consolidated by the group). Prior to the introduction of a revised version of IFRS 3 in 2008, these interests were referred to as 'minority interests'.

The revised accounting standard also amended the calculation of goodwill and non-controlling interests to adopt the 'full goodwill' method (the previous approach was referred to as the 'partial goodwill' method). This approach ensures that the parent company includes 100% of the goodwill of the acquired business in the consolidated balance sheet (as is the case for all other assets of the acquired business), even when there is a non-controlling interest. The full goodwill method is as follows:

> Goodwill = Purchase consideration + Value of the non-controlling interest - FV of separable net assets

However, there is a choice as to how the value of the non-controlling interest is assessed; using either the non-controlling interest's proportionate share of net assets or estimating the fair value of the non-controlling interest. Both approaches are demonstrated below.

Example

MD S.A. acquired 75% of the issued common stock of Sublime S.A. on its incorporation on 1 January Year 1 for €7,500. The value of the remaining 25% stake is estimated to be €3,000 on that day.

The balance sheets of the two companies as at that date are as follows:

	MD SA	**Sublime SA**
	€	**€**
Investment in Sublime SA	7,500	
Other assets	20,000	10,000
	27,500	10,000
Common stock	12,000	10,000
Retained earnings	15,500	-
	27,500	10,000

Requirement

Prepare the consolidated balance sheet of MD S.A. Group, assuming that the non-controlling interest is valued:

a) Based on the proportionate share of net assets.

b) Using the fair value of the non-controlling interest.

Solution

a) MD S.A. Consolidated Balance Sheet as at 1 January Year 1

	€
Goodwill	-
Investment in Sublime S.A.	-
Other assets	30,000
	30,000
Non-controlling interest	2,500
Common stock	12,000
Retained earnings	15,500
	30,000

Workings

(W1) Goodwill	**€**	**€**
Cost of investment		7,500
Net assets acquired as represented by:		
Common stock	10,000	
Retained earnings	-	
	10,000	(10,000)
Value of non-controlling interest (W2)		2,500
Goodwill		-

(W2) Non-Controlling Interest	**€**	**€**
Net assets consolidated as represented by:		
Common stock	10,000	
Retained earnings	-	
	10,000	
	x 25%	= 2,500

b)

	€
Goodwill	500
Investment in Sublime SA	-
Other assets	30,000
	30,500-
Non-controlling interest	3,000
Common stock	12,000
Retained earnings	15,500
	30,500-

Workings

(W1) Goodwill	**€**	**€**
Cost of investment		7,500
Net assets acquired:		
Common stock	10,000	
Retained earnings	-	
	10,000	(10,000)
Value of non-controlling interest (fair value)		3,000
Goodwill		500

Points to Note

- Although only 75% holding, this is sufficient to gain control.
- 100% of other assets consolidated because they are controlled by MD S.A.
- The value of goodwill depends on how the non-controlling interest is valued.
- Non-controlling interest reflects third party interest of the net assets consolidated by MD S.A.
- Retained earnings are just those of MD.
- Under IAS 27 *Consolidated Financial Statements,* non-controlling interests should be presented separately within stockholders' equity.

6 Comprehensive Example

The balance sheets of Kane GmbH and Able GmbH immediately before an 80% acquisition by Kane GmbH of Able GmbH were as follows:

Pre-Acquisition Balance Sheets – Dec. 31, Year 1

	Kane GmbH	Able GmbH
	€	€
Current assets	96,000	32,000
Other assets	64,000	16,000
Total	160,000	48,000
Current liabilities	80,000	28,000
Common stock	56,000	12,000
Retained earnings	24,000	8,000
Total	160,000	48,000

Kane GmbH paid €80,000 cash for Able GmbH.

Required: Prepare the consolidated balance sheet immediately after the acquisition, assuming that the non-controlling interest is valued based on the proportionate share of net assets.

Solution: Kane Group Consolidated GmbH Balance Sheet

	€
Assets	
Current assets (96 + 32 – 80)	48,000
Goodwill (W1)	64,000
Other assets	80,000
	192,000
Liabilities	
Current liabilities	108,000
Non-controlling interests (W2)	4,000
Common stock	56,000
Retained earnings	24,000
	192,000

Workings

(W1) Goodwill	€
Cost of Investment	80,000
Value of non-controlling interest (W2)	4,000
Net assets/equity acquired	(20,000)
	64,000

(W2) Non-Controlling Interest	€	
Net assets consolidated as represented by:		
Stock	12,000	
Earnings	8,000	
	20,000	× 20% = €4,000

Points to Note

- Control is obtained via 80% stockholding. Kane GmbH only owns 80%, so there is a 20% non-controlling interest.
- Current assets are reduced to reflect the payment to acquire stock in Able GmbH:

  ↑ investment €80,000

  ↓ cash €80,000
- Cost of investment cancels with net assets acquired to produce goodwill of €64,000. This is reflected as an intangible asset in the consolidated balance sheet.
- Non-controlling interest are allocated their share of net assets of Able GmbH consolidated by the group.
- Common stock is just that of Kane GmbH.
- No post-acquisition reserves of Able GmbH as consolidation takes place at the same date as acquisition.

7 Other Technical Issues

7.1 Preferred Stock

If preferred stock exists, then care must be taken when calculating non-controlling interests if the percentage of preferred stock owned by the holding company is not the same as its share of common stock. This is illustrated by the example below.

Example

Trust S.A. is controlled by Worthy S.A., which owns 80% of Trust's common stock and 46% of its 6% preferred stock. The finance section of the balance sheet of Trust S.A. is as follows:

	€
Common stock	48,000,000
Preferred stock	13,000,000
Retained earnings	22,000,000
	83,000,000

Trust S.A. has just decided to pay a common stock dividend of €1,500,000 which has not yet been adjusted for.

Required

Calculate the non-controlling interest figure to be included in the group balance sheet.

Solution

Split the financing section of the balance sheet into amounts relating to the preference and common stockholders.

	Preferred Stock	Common Stock
	€	€
Common stock		48,000,000
Preference stock	13,000,000	
Retained earnings*		21,220,000
Dividend (preferred stock)	780,000	
Total	13,780,000	69,220,000
Non-controlling interest%	54%	20%
Non-controlling Interest =	**7,441,200**	**13,844,000**
Total non-controlling interest =	21,285,200	

* After dividend to preferred stockholders [22,000 – (6% × 13,000) = 21,220].

Points to Note

- The common stock dividend adjustment has no impact on the calculation of non-controlling interest. For reasons of simplicity, the calculation above uses earnings of €21,220,000. Alternatively, it could have been:

	€	
Earnings	19,720,000	× **20%**
Dividend	1,500,000	
	21,220,000	

The result is the same as the non-controlling interest is entitled to share of dividends and share of retained earnings.

- As the common stock dividend is declared this must mean that the preferred stock dividend is also declared. This is calculated as 6% × €13,000,000 = €780,000. The preferred stock dividend needs to be adjusted for, as the % ownership is different to that of retained earnings (54% vs. 20%).

7.2 Mid-Year Acquisitions

The critical cut-off point for consolidation is the date that control is acquired. Obviously, few acquisitions actually take place on the balance sheet date. The impact of mid-year acquisitions is quite straightforward.

Simply consolidate from the moment control is acquired. The practical impact of this is merely to split the reserves figure between pre and post-acquisition periods. This helps us re-establish the net assets at acquisition and the earnings post-acquisition.

Example

The balance sheet of Got S.A. on 31 December Year 1 is as follows:

	€
Current assets	225
Non-current assets	247
	472
Current liabilities	50
Common stock	100
Retained earnings:	
Opening balance	300
Retained for year	22
	472

Got S.A. was acquired by Substantial S.A. on 31 March Year 1.

Required

Calculate the net assets that would be consolidated into the group accounts of Substantial SA, assuming profits accrue evenly throughout the year.

Solution

Net assets = Common stock + Retained earnings

Net assets at 31 March Year 1

= 100 + (300 + (3/12 × 22))

= 100 + 300 + 5.5

= 405.5

Points to Note

- The amount of €405.5 would be used to calculate goodwill.
- The earnings for the year are time apportioned to arrive at retained earnings for 31 March Year 1.

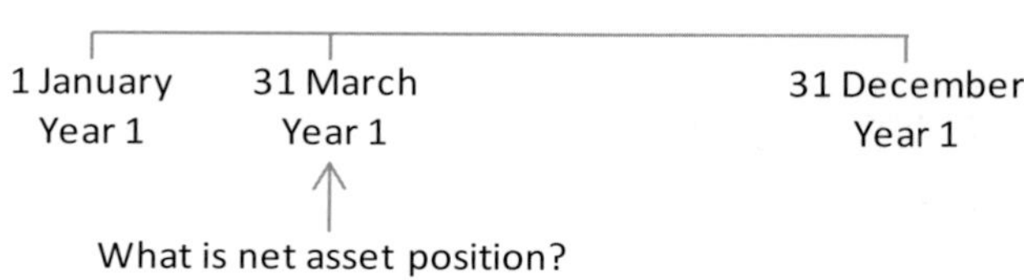

- The earnings made since 31 March Year 1 (9/12 × 22) would then be consolidated in the group income statement. These earnings arise since Got S.A. gained control.
- Earnings are assumed to accrue evenly. In practice, consideration would have to be given to specific items of income or expenditure arising pre- or post-acquisition in the calculation of retained earnings at the date of acquisition.

Chapter 9: Consolidation Techniques II – The Balance Sheet

"Bank audit might as well have been done in the pub" [10]

[10] Brooke Masters, Financial Times, 1 December, 2017. Although the audit remains one of the most reassuring aspects of the reliability of accounting information, it is far from perfect. Bank audits, in particular, are more complex, risky and judgement laden than many other industries. And when they go wrong, it is felt widely through society.

1 Introduction

The process of consolidation involves preparing an additional set of financial statements that reflects the economic position that would exist if the holding and subsidiary companies were a single economic entity. This, quite obviously, does not reflect legal reality. Each entity is typically a separate legal entity. Such companies trade with each other and this is reflected in their financial statements. However, if we are assuming a single economic entity then it no longer makes sense to reflect such transactions in the consolidated accounts. This chapter covers the process whereby such transactions are eliminated from consolidated accounts.

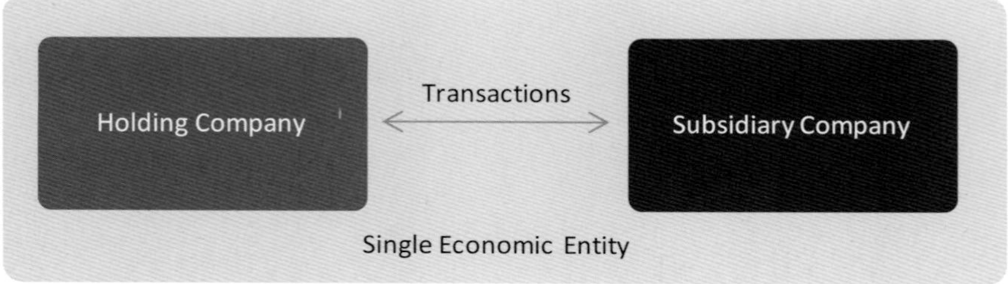

It should be borne in mind that none of these adjustments has tax implications, as tax is levied at the individual company level. Given that dividends are also paid by individual companies, group accounting adjustments have no impact on distributable reserves.

2 Outstanding Inter-company Trading Balances

If a holding company and its subsidiaries trade, then such transactions will normally be on credit. Therefore, in each set of financials there will be the following balances (assuming the holding company is selling and the subsidiary is buying).

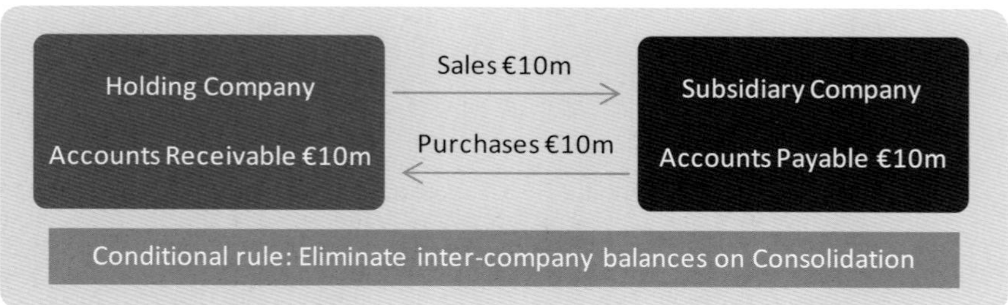

If balances do not agree then appropriate adjustments must be made for cash or goods in transit.

3 Inter-company Trading – Example

Holding S.A. acquired 80% of the common stock of Subsidiary Inc. many years ago when its reserves were €2,000. The balance sheets of the two companies as at 31 December Year 6 are as follows:

		Holding S.A. €'000	Subsidiary S.A. €'000
Current assets			
Inventory		44	36
Accounts receivable–	Subsidiary SA	80	-
	Other	112	78
Cash		8	30
		224	144
Non-current assets			
Tangible		400	100
Investment in Subsidiary S.A.		20	-
Total assets		664	244
Current liabilities			
Accounts payable (other)		162	100
Holding S.A.		-	40
		162	140
Stockholders' equity			
Common stock		200	20
Retained earnings		302	84
		664	224

Additional Information

(i) It has been discovered that cash in transit of €8,000 from Subsidiary S.A. to Holding S.A. existed at the year end.

(ii) Inventory sent by Holding S.A. to Subsidiary S.A. before the year end to the value of €32,000 had not been received by Subsidiary Inc. until January Year 7. The original historic cost of the goods was €32,000.

Requirement: Prepare a consolidated balance sheet, assuming that the non-controlling interest is valued based on the proportionate share of net assets.

Solution: Holding S.A.. Consolidated balance sheet as at 31 December Year 6

		€'000
Current assets		
Inventory (44 + 36 + 32)		112
Accounts receivable –	Subsidiary S.A.	-
	Other	190
Cash (30 +8 + 8)		46
		348
Long-lived assets		
Tangible (400 + 100)		500
Investment in Subsidiary S.A.		-
Intangibles (W1)		2.4
		850.4
Current liabilities		
Accounts payable		262
Holding S.A.		-
		262
Stockholders' equity		
Common stock		200
Retained earnings (W2)		367.6
Non-controlling interest (20% × 104)		20.8
		850.4

W1		
Intangible assets – goodwill	**€'000**	**€'000**
Cost of investment		20
Net equity acquired:		
Common stock	20	
Retained Earnings	2	
	22	(22)
Value of non-controlling interest (20% × 104)		20.8
		2.4

W2	**€'000**
Group reserves	
Holding S.A.	302
Subsidiary S.A. (84 – 2) × 80%	65.6
	367.6

Points to Note

The intercompany balances prior to consolidation do not agree. They must be adjusted for cash and goods in transit:

	Holding S.A. **€'000**	**Subsidiary S.A.** **€'000**
Intercompany balance	80	40
Cash in transit	(8)	-
Goods in transit	-	32
	72	72

The adjustment for cash in transit is to:

↑ Cash balance of Holding S.A.

↓ Reduce amount owed by subsidiary S.A.

The adjustment for goods in transit is to:

↑ Inventory of Subsidiary S.A.

↓ Amount owed to Holding S.A.

- Once the balances agree they are cancelled out (left out) against each other on consolidation. This is to reflect the group as a single economic entity.
- Group stock is increased by the €32,000 in transit as it is still owned by the group.
- Group cash is increased by €8,000 in transit as it still belongs to the group.
- No adjustment is made for any unrealised profit on the intercompany sale as the goods were sold at cost, i.e. no intercompany profit.

- The cost of the investment in subsidiary S.A. does not appear in the consolidated balance sheet. It is used to calculate goodwill on consolidation (W1). The net asset position of Subsidiary S.A. at the date of acquisition is not given. It is calculated on the basis that at any point in time:

Net assets = Stockholders' equity

The balance on retained earnings at the date of acquisition is given. Assume share capital has not changed.

- The full amount of goodwill of €2,400 is shown as an intangible asset on the consolidated balance sheet.
- The group reserves comprise the reserves of Holding plus the group share of the post-acquisition earnings of subsidiary S.A.

4 Provision for Unrealised Profit in Stock

As illustrated by the previous example, all inter-company transactions must be eliminated to maintain the integrity of the single economic entity assumption of consolidated financial statements.

If goods had been sold between the components of a group at a profit then, in addition to eliminating the sale, the profit must also be eliminated. The group should only reflect profit generated on third party transactions.

The objective is to achieve the following:

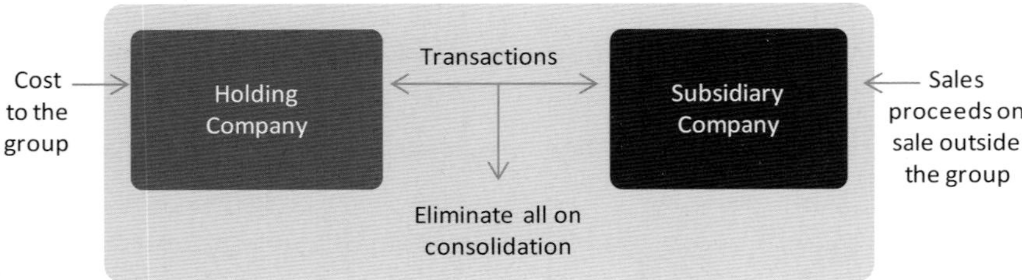

Consolidation Rule

> *Reduce inventory by making a provision for unrealised profit against the selling component of the group. It is the seller that will have recorded the profit in its accounting records.*

Example

Determine S.A. sold €18m of inventory to Fatalist S.A. These goods had originally cost Determine S.A. €18m less a mark-up of 20%.

What adjustments should be made on consolidation under the following three scenarios assuming Fatalist S.A. is a 90% subsidiary of Determine SA?

i) All of the goods have now been sold on by Fatalist S.A. to third parties.

No adjustment necessary as no profit left in inventory.

ii) Half of the goods have been sold by Fatalist with the remaining goods remaining in inventory.

Must eliminate half of the profit.

Profit = 20% Mark-Up

	%	€
Sales	120	18m
Costs	(100)	(15m)
Profit	20	3m

Adjustment: Reduce inventory by 1.5m (half of total profit)
Reduce Determine S.A. profit 1.5m

iii) Fatalist S.A. actually sold the goods to Determine S.A. and all remained in inventory at year end.

Total profit	= €3m recorded by Fatalistic SA	
Adjustment	Inventory	€3m ↓
	Profit (of Fatalist SA)	€3m ↓

5 Inter-Company Dividends

The principles are the same for other inter-company transactions:

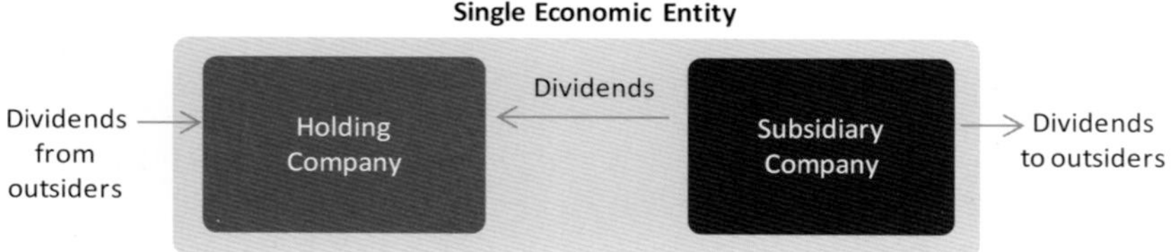

The consolidated financial statements should only reflect dividends paid to and received from third parties. Dividends payable and receivable within the group are therefore cancelled on consolidation. This is illustrated by the next example.

Example

Hild S.A. acquired 80% of Sild S.A. many years ago for €1,000 when Sild's retained earnings were €200.

	Hild SA	**Sild SA**
	€	**€**
Current assets	3,000	2,000
Long-lived assets	2,000	500
Investment in Sild Inc.	1,000	-
Total assets	6,000	2,500
Current liabilities	750	500
Common stock	1,000	200
Retained earnings	4,250	1,800
Total liabilities	**6,000**	**2,500**

Hild S.A. proposes a dividend of €1,000 while Sild S.A. proposes a dividend of €400.

In the five years since the acquisition, goodwill has been impaired by 25% of its original value.

Required: Prepare the consolidated balance sheet.

Solution: Hild Inc. consolidated balance sheet

	€
Current assets	5,000
Long-lived assets	3,010
Investment in Sild Inc.	
Total assets	8,010
Current liabilities	2,330
Common stock	1,000
Retained earnings	4,360
Non-controlling Interests	320
Total liabilities and stockholders' equity	8,010

W1 – Dividend Workings

				€
Receivable	By Hild from Sild	=400 × 80%	=	320
Payable	By Hild to 3rd parties		=	1,000
	By Sild to 3rd parties		=	80
				1,080

W2 – Reserves

		€
Hild	(4,250 + 320 – 1,000)	3,570
Sild	(1,800 – 400 – 200) × 80 %	960
		4,530
Goodwill impairment		(170)
		4,360

W3 – Goodwill

	€	€
Cost of investment		1,000
Net equity acquired:		
Common stock	200	
Retained earnings	200	
	400	(400)
Value of non-controlling interest (20% × 400)		80
Total goodwill		680

Impaired	**1/4 × 680**	**170**
Remaining	3/4 × 680	510
		680

Points to Note

- The key to understanding the dividend adjustments is to remember that the financial statements presented in the example are prior to any adjustments for the proposed dividends.

	Hild	**Sild SA**
	€	**€**
Dividends receivable	+ 320	–
Dividends payable	+ 1,000	+ 400
Retained earnings	– 1,000 + 320	– 200

Dividend adjustments:

To reflect proposed dividend of Hild S.A.

↑ Dividends payable
↓ Retained earnings

To reflect proposed dividend of Sild S.A.

↑ Dividends payable
↓ Retained earnings

To reflect share of dividend receivable from Sild S.A. (80%).

↑ Dividends receivable
↑ Retained earnings

The intercompany dividends then cancel out leaving €80 payable to third parties by Sild S.A. and €1,000 by Hild S.A.

- Current assets are just €3,000 + €2,000 as intercompany dividend receivable is cancelled on consolidation.
- Non-current assets comprise:

	€
Hild	2,000
Sild	500
Remaining goodwill	510
	3,010

- Cost of investment in Sild S.A. forms calculation of goodwill.
- Current liabilities comprise:

	Hild		Sild		
	€		€		
Per example	750		500		
Dividend payable	1,000		80		
	1,750	+	580	=	2,330

- Retained earnings of the group (W2) include group share of post-acquisition reserves of Sild S.A. after adjustment for the dividends which had not previously been accounted for.

Chapter 10: Consolidated Income Statements

"You could cut off R&D, not train people, and piss off your customers for a while and in the short-term cash flow (and profits) would still rise" [11]

[11] Bob Herz, PriceWaterHouseCoopers Reported in the Financial Times, 2000 by Andrew Hill. This is a crucial point – cashflow is not immune to manipulation. Earnings and cashflow numbers should be combined to enhance analytics.

1 Introduction

Consolidated income statements are prepared on a similar basis to balance sheets in that all profits under the control of management are consolidated. In a similar manner to balance sheet consolidations, income statements are consolidated based on the single entity assumption. Therefore, the sales of subsidiaries are aggregated with the sales of the holding company in order to calculate group sales.

Example of Consolidated Income Statement

	€
Revenue	78
Cost of sales	(45)
Operating profit	33
Interest	(4)
Profit before taxes	29
Income taxes	(9)
Profit after taxes	20
Non-controlling interest	(2)
Net profit for the period	18
Dividends	2
Retained profit for the period	16

Points to Note

The consolidated income statement should only reflect transactions with third parties. As we saw in Chapter 9 consolidation adjustments may be required to:

- Eliminate intercompany sales and purchases.
- Eliminate any unrealised profit in closing inventory.

As 100% of the results of the subsidiary are consolidated to reflect the earnings over which the group has control, a deduction must be made for earnings consolidated but not owned by the group, i.e. non-controlling interest.

Dividends will only be those of the holding company, just as the stock in the consolidated balance sheet is only that of the holding company. Dividends receivable from the subsidiary are not consolidated because **earnings** are consolidated instead. Similarly, the minority interest are given their share of **earnings** not dividends.

2 Methodology

- Aggregate all income statements captions
- Omit intercompany dividends

Exclude non-controlling interest share of Net Income as a deduction

3 Basic Consolidated Income Statement Calculation

	Home S.A.	Time S.A.
	€	€
Revenues	49,000	31,200
Cost of goods sold	(28,000)	(20,000)
Operating income	21,000	11,2000
Dividend from Time S.A.	3,000	-
Income from continuing operations before taxes	24,000	11,200
Income taxes	(10,000)	(3,200)
Income from continuing operations	14,000	8,000
Dividends	(8,000)	(4,000)
	6,000	4,000

Home purchased 75% of Time S.A. many years ago. Ignore Goodwill.

Required

Prepare the consolidated income statement of the Home S.A. group.

Solution

Home S.A. Consolidated Income Statement	€
Revenues (49,000 + 31,200)	80,200
Cost of goods sold (28,000 + 20,000)	(48,000)
Operating Income	32,200
Dividend from Time Inc.	-
Income from continuing operations before taxes	32,200
Income taxes (10,000 +3,200)	(13,200)
Income from continuing operations	19,000
Non-controlling interests (25% × 8,000)	(2,000)
	17,000

Points to Note

- 100% of the results of the subsidiary are consolidated from Revenue to Profit after tax.
- Dividend income from Time S.A. is not reflected in the consolidated income statement. Dividend income has been replaced by earnings. To include dividend income would be to double count.
- The group tax figure is just an amalgamation of the individual company tax expenses. Group accounts are tax neutral, i.e. have no impact on tax. Tax is levied at the individual company level.
- Non-controlling interest is the share of earnings after tax of the subsidiary.

4 Technical Issues

4.1 Inter-Company Trading

The consolidated income statement must reflect transactions with entities outside the group. Adjustments must be made to eliminate the impact of any trading as illustrated below.

Eliminate on consolidation to achieve:

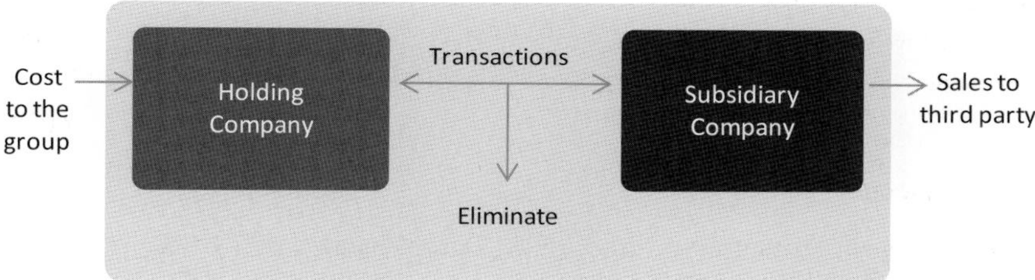

4.2 Example Adjustments for Inter-Company Trading

Assume Home S.A. had sold goods to Time S.A. for €15,000, mark up 20%. These goods remain in closing inventory at year end.

Required: Prepare the amended income statement of Home S.A. using the income statement data from paragraph 3.

Solution

Home S.A. Consolidated Income Statement	**€**
Revenues (49 + 31.2 − 15)	65,200
Cost of goods sold (28 + 20 − 15 + 2.5)	(35,500)
Operating Income	29,700
Dividend from Time Inc.	-
Income from continuing operations before taxes	29,700
Income taxes	(13,200)
Income from continuing operations	16,500
Non-controlling interests (25% × 8,000)	(2,000)
	14,500

Points to Note

Both revenue and cost of goods sold are reduced by the effect of the transaction. This adjustment is very similar to the cancellation of intercompany balances when preparing the consolidated balance sheet. The original transaction would have been recorded as follows:

	Home SA	Time SA
	€	€
Revenue	15,000	-
Purchases	(12,000)	15,000
Closing inventory	-	(15,000)
Profit	2,500	-

Home S.A. has recorded a profit of €2,500. This profit, however, has not yet been realised outside the group. It will only be realised when Time S.A. sells the inventory to a third party. Both purchases, and therefore, closing inventory are overstated from the group perspective. The cost to the group was €12,500. Two adjustments are therefore required:

1. Cancel intercompany sales and purchases of €15,000.
2. Reduce closing inventory on the consolidated income statement by €2,500 and on the consolidated balance sheet.

Income taxes are not affected by the unrealised profit as tax is levied at the individual company level.

Non-controlling interest is not affected by the unrealised profit as the profit was recorded by the parent company. If it was Time S.A. that had made the sale to Home S.A. then the same adjustments would need to be made but minority interest would be calculated as:

$$25\% \times (8{,}000 - 2{,}500) = €1{,}375$$

4.3 Preference Dividends and Non-Controlling Interest

The non-controlling interest calculation in the income statement is calculated as:

Net income × Non-controlling interest %

If the holding company owns both common stock and preferred stock then, unless it holds some percentage of both, this has an impact on our calculations in a similar way to the calculation of non-controlling interest on the consolidated balance sheet.

4.4 Preference Dividend and Non-Controlling Interest Example

The following is an extract of the income statement of Analytic S.A.

	€m
Revenues	150
Cost of goods sold	(50)
Income from continuing operations before taxes	100
Income taxes	(30)
Income from continuing operations after taxes	70

Analytic S.A. is 75% subsidiary of Ultra S.A. The stockholders' equity note of Analytic S.A. is as follows:

	€m
Common stock	300
Additional paid in capital	200
8% Preferred stock (Ultra S.A. owns 40%)	70
Retained earnings	360
	930

Required

Calculate the non-controlling interest to be included in the Ultra S.A. consolidated financial statements.

Solution

	€m
Share of preference dividend 60% × 8% × 70 =	3.36
Share of remaining net income (70 − 5.6) × 25% =	16.10
	19.46

Points to Note

- Ultra S.A. has control because of the majority holding of common stock of Analytic S.A.
- Actual ownership of the subsidiary can be analysed as follows:

	Analytic Common Stock	Preferred Stock
Ultra SA	75%	40%
∴ Non-controlling interest	25%	60%

- Non-controlling interest share of earnings is share of preferred dividend plus common stock share of any retained earnings i.e.

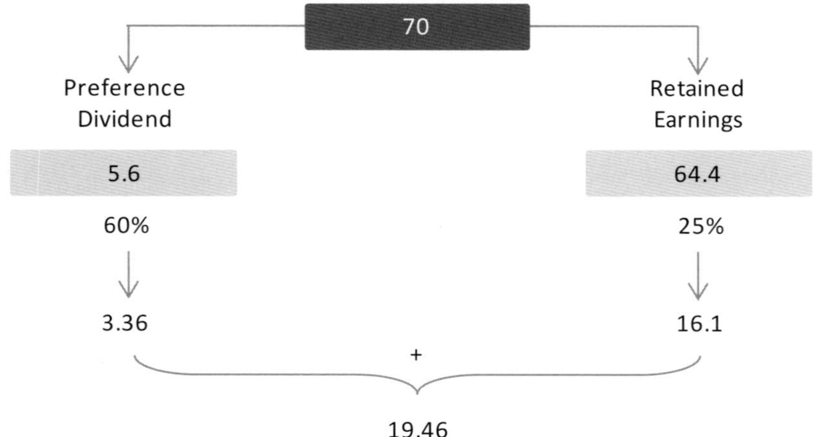

- Note, it is a coincidence that the €70m earnings figure is the same as the preferred stock in the balance sheet!

4.5 Mid-Year Acquisitions

If an acquisition takes place during an accounting year then all the subsidiary income statement captions must be time apportioned. This is to ensure that only post-acquisition earnings are consolidated. The calculation of minority interest is based on the time apportioned post-acquisition earnings of the subsidiary.

Illustration

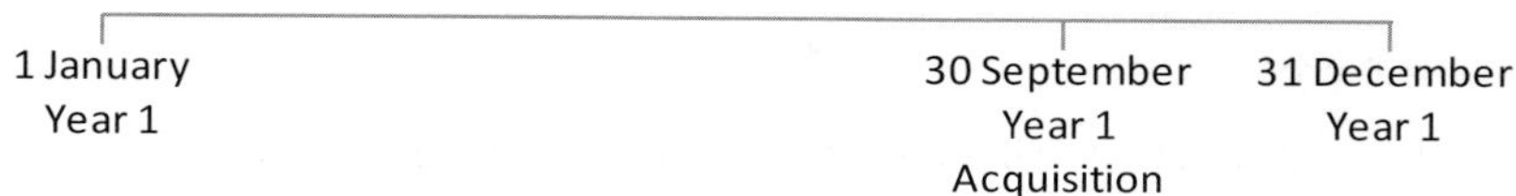

Any earnings prior to 30 September Year 1 are not consolidated as control was not obtained until that date. Pre-acquisition earnings are used in the calculation of goodwill. Only 3/12 of the earnings of Year 1 will appear in the consolidated income statement.

Chapter 11: Accounting for Associates

"Not everything that counts can be counted, and not everything that can be counted counts. " [12]

[12] Some people attribute this quote to Einstein but the fiendishly clever people at quoteinvestigator.com confirm that William Bruce Cameron, the sociologist, is indeed the source. Either way a good way of reminding ourselves that qualitative data is often richer and more interesting than numbers, but not always!

1 Introduction

This chapter covers the treatment of those investments that qualify as associates or joint ventures. The income statement and balance sheet treatment are covered. The chapter finishes with a comprehensive comparative example.

2 What is an Associate?

As we saw earlier in the text, the holding company can have different levels of influence over the affairs of its investment. These are typically illustrated by the level of the investment in ordinary shares.

- Control
- Significant influence (20% to 50%)
- None (less than 20%)

The need for the preparation of consolidated financial statements is driven by the need of users to understand the full amount of resources and earnings over which the parent company has control. There is a similar need for understanding the resources and earnings over which the parent company has significant influence. These investments are referred to as associates. Associates are a form of inter-corporate investment. Such investments possess the following characteristics:

- Long-term investment.
- Investing company exercises significant influence.
- Typically involves at least 20% ownership.

In determining whether or not significant influence exists, IAS 28 *Investments in Associates and Joint Ventures* states that the following may be indicative:

1. Representation on the board of directors.
2. Participation in policy-making process.
3. Material transactions between investor and investee.
4. Interchange of managerial personnel.
5. Provision of essential technical information.

By way of contrast, the following may be indicative of a lack of significant influence:

1. Opposition by other shareholders.
2. Majority ownership by a small group of investors.
3. Inability to achieve representation on the board or to obtain information on the operations of the investee.

Given that an associate is influenced but not controlled by the investing company the purchase method is not appropriate. Instead a technique called equity accounting is employed. Equity accounting is only required in the consolidated financial statements of the investor. Therefore, equity accounting is not required where the investor does not prepare consolidated accounts, for example because the investor has no subsidiaries.

3 Equity Accounting Mechanics

Whereas consolidation under the purchase method requires a line by line consolidation of the individual balance sheet and income statement of the subsidiary, the equity method is simpler. Under IFRS, the equity method requires accounting for the group **share** of resources and earnings and is reflected as a one-line entity in the consolidated income statement and balance sheet. The concept applied is that of substance over legal form in order to provide more meaningful information to the users.

Consolidated Balance Sheet
Include an 'investment in associates' in fixed assets
at cost adjusted for changes in the share of net assets after acquisition

Consolidated Income Statement
Include the group share of the associates net income

As with other fixed assets, the investment in associate is tested for impairment when indicators of impairment are identified.

4 Example – Income Statement

Stypen S.A. has a 40% holding in Standard S.A., which was acquired many years ago.

The group income statement of Stypen S.A., and its other subsidiaries, and the income statement of Standard S.A. for the year ended 31 January Year 1 are as follows:

	Stypen SA	Standard SA
	€	€
Revenues	2,200	1,200
Operating costs	(660)	(600)
	1,540	600
Finance charges	(200)	(40)
Income taxes	(340)	(100)
Net income	1,000	460

Required

Prepare the consolidated income statement for Stypen S.A. and its subsidiaries, for the year ended 31 January Year 1.

Solution

Stypen S.A. Consolidated Income Statement for 31 January Year 1

	€
Revenues	2,200
Operating costs	(660)
Income before interest and taxes	1,540
Finance charges	(200)
Income before taxes	1,340
Income taxes	(340)
Net income	1,000
Share of associate net income	184
	1,184

Points to Note

- The basic principle is to account for the share of associates' net income. The actual methodology of how this is achieved can vary from jurisdiction to jurisdiction and IFRS is not particularly clear on this matter
- No minority interest arises in this situation as the group has only accounted for its share of income

5 Example – Balance Sheet

The balance sheets of Home and Away many years after Home acquired Away are as follows:

	Home	**Away**
	€	**€**
Current assets	1,000	550
Plant, property and equipment	3,250	160
Investment in Away	500	-
Total assets	4,750	710
Current liabilities	750	200
Debt	1,000	120
Common stock	2,500	240
Retained earnings	500	150
	4,750	710

Home acquired 40% of Away for €500 when retained earnings were €200.

Required

Show the balance sheet if the investment is accounted for under the equity method.

Solution

Home Consolidated Balance Sheet

	€
Current assets	1,000
Plant, property and equipment	3,250
Investment in Associate (W1)	480
Total assets	4,730
Current liabilities	750
Debt	1,000
Common stock	2,500
Retained earnings (W2)	480
	4,730

Working

W1 Associates

	€
Cost of investment	500
Share of net assets at acquisition	
(240 + 200) × 40%	(176)
Share of net assets at asset at balance sheet date	
(240 + 150) × 40%	156
	480

W2 Retained Earnings

		€
Home		500
Away (post-acquisition)	(150 − 200) × 40%	(20)
		480

Points to Note

- The equity accounted investment in Away is incorporated in the group balance sheet and replace the cost of the investment.
- Net assets of Away at the date of the investment are calculated by reference to stockholder's equity at that date.
- Share of post-acquisition earnings are incorporated into group retained earnings.

Analysis Focus

Apples, Pears and Cash Flow

From the text, it is clear that the equity (rather than proportionate) method of consolidation creates a strange outcome in group consolidated amounts. Profit includes the share of profits from associates, but assets and liabilities are netted off in the group balance sheet, which just shows a share of net assets. The cash flow statement **excludes** the associate, except to the extent of dividends received from it. This means that analysts, when building cash flow models of companies with associates, must exclude the associate completely from the analysis and value the interest separately.

6 Proportionate Consolidation

There is still an argument that the equity method of accounting for an associate in the consolidated financial statements does not produce meaningful information. As there is no line by line consolidation, it is difficult to establish the asset and liabilities position of the investment. These are captured within the one-line entry. It is for this reason that in some jurisdictions (but not under IFRS) investments in associates are accounted for using the proportionate consolidation method. This involves consolidating the investing company's share of each caption in the balance sheet and income statement.

The advantage of this approach is that it disaggregates the equity investment and provides analysts with more information. This is illustrated by the example below.

7 Comprehensive Comparative Example

Balance Sheet as at 1 January Year 2

	Ajax SA	Axis SA
	€	€
Current assets	240	100
PP&E	120	420
Investment in Axis	100	-
	460	520
Current liabilities	90	60
Debt	140	240
Common stock	70	100
Retained earnings	160	120
	460	520

Ajax S.A. invested in 50% of the common stock of Axis S.A. on 1 January Year 1.

Income statement data for Year 1 is as follows:

	Ajax SA	Axis SA
	€	€
Revenues	440	800
Operating expenses	(366)	(732)
Operating income	74	68
Dividend income from Axis	10	-
Interest paid	(14)	(8)
Net Income	70	60
Dividends	-	(20)
Retained profit	70	40

Required

Prepare the income statement and balance sheet using

a) Cost method

b) Equity method

c) Proportionate method

Assume there has been no goodwill impairment.

Solution

Ajax S.A. Balance Sheet as at 1 January Year 2

	Cost Method	Equity Method	Proportionate Consideration
	€	€	€
Current assets	240	240	290
Investment in Axis S.A. (W3)	100	120	-
PP&E	120	120	330
Goodwill (W1)			10
	460	480	630
Current liabilities	90	90	120
Debt	140	140	260
Common stock	70	70	70
Retained earnings (W2)	160	180	180
	460	480	630

Ajax S.A. Income Statement for Year Ended 1 January Year 2

	Cost Method	Equity Method	Proportionate Consideration
	€	€	€
Revenue	440	440	840
Operating expenses	(366)	(366)	(732)
Operating income	74	74	108
Dividend income	10	-	-
Interest paid	(14)	(14)	(18)
Net income	70	60	90
Share of associate income	-	30	-
Net income	70	90	90

Points to Note

- There is no change under the cost method.
- Under the equity method the investment is reflected at €120 vs. cost of €100.
- Under the proportionate method, the key impact is on the debt balance. Neither the cost nor equity method reflect the heavy borrowing of the associate. This is one of the key problems with the equity method.
- The impact of the proportionate method is also highlighted in the income statement. The net income amount is the same as under the equity method but the operating income is higher to reflect the earnings over which significant influence has been exercised.
- Below is a summary of the impact of each method on certain key ratios:

	Cost Method	Equity Method	Proportionate Consolidation
Operating margin	74/440 = 16.8%	74/440 = 16.8%	108/840= 12.9%
Net income margin	70/440 = 15.9%	90/440 = 20.4%	90/840 = 10.7%
ROE	70/230 = 30.4%	90/250 = 36%	90/250 = 36%
Asset turnover	440/460 = 0.96	440/480 = 0.92	840/630= 1.33
Gearing	140/230= 61%	140/250= 56%	260/250= 104%

- In particular, note the higher gearing and lower operating and net income margins.

Workings

W1 Goodwill	**€**	**€**
Cost of investment		100
Net assets acquired		
Common stock	100	
Retained earnings (120 – 40)	80	
	180	
	× 50%	(90)
		10

W2 Group Retained Earnings	**€**	**€**
Ajax S.A.		160
Axis S.A. past acquisition		
New	120	
At acquisition	(80)	
	40	
	× 50%	20
		180

W3 Investment in Axis SA	**€**
Cost of investment	100
Share of net assets at acquisition (100 + 80) × 50%	(90)
Share of net assets at balance sheet date (100 + 120) × 50%	110
	120

Joint Ventures

IFRS 11 *Joint Arrangements* requires the use of equity accounting for joint ventures (i.e. using the same approach as for associates). This is a relatively recent change as, until 2013, joint ventures could be accounted for using either equity accounting or proportionate consolidation.

Full consolidation is not warranted on the basis that the investor has significant influence but not control. The nature of a joint venture is usually such that there are at least two ventures bound by a contractual arrangement and that the agreement establishes joint control of the entity.

Chapter 12: Advanced Issues in Consolidations

"Accounting isn't dead, just depreciating" [13]

[13] Foley, J. (2016), Reuters online, 26 November. This cheeky headline appeared in a book review. The thesis of the book was that accounting is dead or at the very least on life support. There are some good points made in the book, but accounting remains critical even with its flaws around how to deal with issues such as intangibles.

1 Introduction

Up to this point, we have concerned ourselves with the fundamentals of consolidation. For many analysts this will be more than sufficient. However, there is a lot of other technical material that may be required from time to time. This chapter provides a detailed overview of these advanced issues. In particular, this section addresses the following:

- Negative goodwill
- Fair values
- Piecemeal acquisitions
- Disposal of subsidiaries and associates
- Overseas subsidiaries (including hedging implications)
- Non-subsidiaries

2 Goodwill Amortisation

2.1 Positive and Negative Goodwill

As we have seen already goodwill is a key feature of the purchase method of consolidation. It is calculated as follows:

	€
Fair value of consideration	x
Fair value of separable net assets	(x)
Positive/negative goodwill	x/(x)

Fair values are discussed in more detail in the next section.

IFRS 3 introduces more detail into the disaggregation of a premium on acquisition between identifiable intangibles (such as brands, trademarks) and unidentifiable (i.e. goodwill). As a result, an acquirer will separately recognise more intangible assets (rather than just subsuming their value within "goodwill"), provided they meet the definition of an asset and their fair value is reliably measurable. The acquirer must also recognise the contingent liabilities assumed in the business combination, assuming their fair value is reliably measurable.

The normal treatment for positive goodwill is for it to be capitalised and reviewed for impairment. Under IFRS 3, treatment of negative goodwill has been significantly simplified. It is now recognised immediately in the income statement, after its calculation has been reviewed to ensure it really exists.

2.2 Impairment of Goodwill

The value of goodwill must be reviewed annually for any impairment. Such a reduction in value can be triggered by specific events or changes in circumstances specific to the subsidiary.

Undertaking an impairment for something as 'intangible' as goodwill is not straightforward. In particular, it is difficult to isolate and test an asset which is not separable. Therefore, a somewhat different approach to impairment testing is required. Goodwill must be valued as part of a larger group of assets, termed a cash generating unit (CGU). Impairments on a CGU are then allocated back to specific assets in the CGU such as goodwill.

The following diagram summarises the goodwill impairment review process:

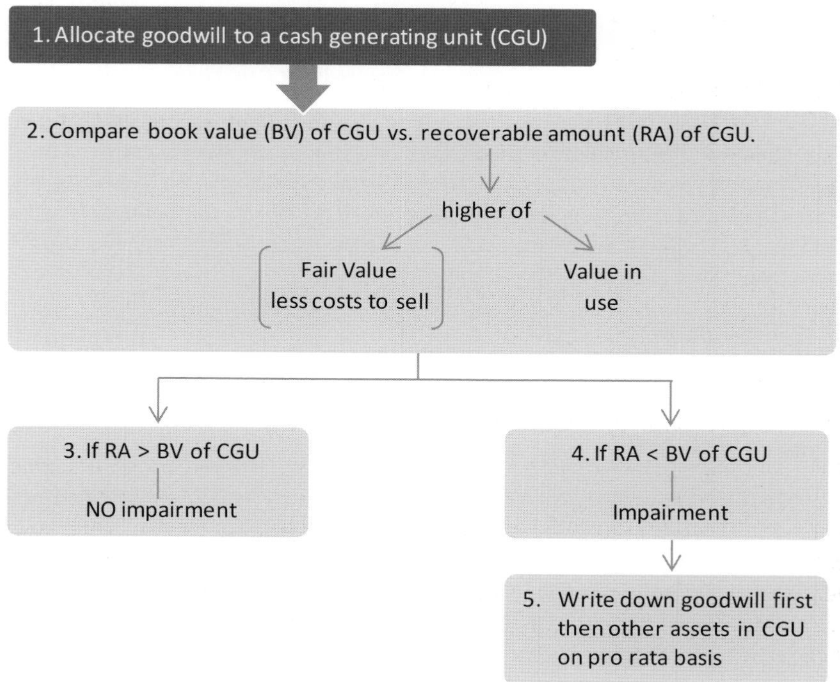

3 Fair Values and Deferred Tax Implications

3.1 Concept of Fair Values

The issue of fair values is important to the purchase method of consolidation. This method is based on the concept that the acquiring company has, in substance, purchased the underlying assets and liabilities of its investment rather than shares. The assets and liabilities of the investee company are consolidated at the value they are worth to the acquirer rather than their book value. The examples given so far have assumed that book value is the same as fair value. The determination of these values is vital for the very reason that they in turn determine the amount of goodwill that arises on acquisition.

	€'000
Fair value of consideration	x
Fair value of separable net assets acquired	(x)
Positive/negative goodwill	x/(x)

3.2 Fair Value of Consideration Including Contingent Consideration

If the shares in the subsidiary acquired were bought for cash, then fair value is not an issue. It is only when the consideration takes a form other than of cash that issues arise. For example, consideration may also take the form of shares, debt, deferred or contingent consideration. Where there is a market value available for any of these items then it should be used. This rule applies even when the acquiror swaps any of its own assets for shares in the acquiree.

There are additional issues for deferred and contingent consideration. In the case of deferred consideration, the time value of money must be taken into account. The cost of the acquisition is therefore the present value of future payments discounted at the normal cost of borrowing of the acquiring company.

Contingent consideration poses the problem that neither value nor future performance of the new subsidiary can be determined at the date control is obtained. Therefore, the solution is to estimate the fair value of the contingent consideration based on the likelihood of the subsidiary meeting its target future performance.

This means that the contingent consideration is included even where the likelihood of payment is less than 50% (though this would result in a lower fair value).

Once the fair value of the contingent consideration has been determined, any subsequent changes to the amount expected to be paid, or eventually paid, are recognised as either a gain or a loss in earnings.

Example

Zaragoza S.A. acquired 80% of Jerez S.A. on 1 January Year 1. The consideration paid on that date comprised 100,000 €2 common stock with a market value of €2.50 and €90,000 in cash. A further €18,000 will be payable in Year 3 if profit of Jerez S.A. exceeds €30,000 for the next three years. All forecasts indicate that Jerez S.A. will easily exceed these targets. Zaragoza S.A. can borrow money at 10%.

The discount factors are:

- Year 1 0.909
- Year 2 0.826
- Year 3 0.751

Requirement

Calculate the cost of the investment in Jerez S.A. as at 1 January.

Solution

	€'000
Common stock issued	250
Cash	90
Contingent consideration	
(€18,000 × 0.751)	13
	353

Points to Note

- The amount of €353,000 is shown as the cost of the investment in the financial statements of Zaragoza S.A. It is this amount which is in turn used to calculate goodwill arising on consolidation of Jerez S.A. The contingent consideration is included at fair value and the accounting treatment in relation to this in the records of Zaragoza S.A. is:

  ↑ Cost of the investment €13,000

  ↑ Liabilities €13,000

- The contingent consideration is discounted at the company's normal cost of borrowing in order to derive its fair value at the date control is achieved.

3.3 Fair Value of Separable Net Assets Acquired

In accordance with IFRS, the purchase method requires that a fair value be attributed to the identifiable assets and liabilities at the date control is achieved.

Fair value is defined as:

"the amount for which an asset could be exchanged is a liability settled between knowledgeable, willing parties in an arm's length transaction."

Table of Fair Values Attributed to Key Assets and Liabilities

Asset/Liability	Fair Value Measure
Land and buildings	Market value
Plant and equipment	Market value or depreciated cost
Identifiable intangible assets (example, patents)	Market value or best available information
Pensions	Actual present value of promised benefits net of fair value of assets
Taxation	Net of tax effect fair value adjustments
Liabilities	Present value of amounts to be paid

A contentious issue arises when the acquiring company creates provisions for future losses, post-acquisition reorganisation costs arising from the acquisition.

The creation of these provisions at the date of acquisition would increase the liabilities acquired and as a result increase goodwill. These provisions could then be released to the income statement post-acquisition.

Illustration

	€'000
Reorganisation costs	100
Provision for reorganisation	(120)
Costs	(20)

Overestimating provisions at acquisition may lead to an increase in post-acquisition profits. This may give a misleading impression of the group performance. Earnings are not generated by productivity but rather as a result of provisions which in turn do not result in cash flows. They are simply accounting entries. As a result, the accounting world has taken strict steps to address this issue.

Provisions for future losses or restructuring costs expected to be incurred as a result of the business combination cannot now be included as part of the goodwill calculation. They can only be included if they are a bona fide provision in the books of the acquiree at the date of acquisition and recognised in accordance with IAS 37. Restructuring provisions must be treated separately as post-combination expenses.

It should be noted that determining fair values involves making estimates and with the passage of time it may become evident that the original fair values assigned to assets and liabilities were inaccurate. In accordance with IFRS 3, if new information relating to fair values comes to light after the date of acquisition then adjustments should be made. The treatment of these adjustments depends on how soon they are identified after the date of acquisition as is illustrated below.

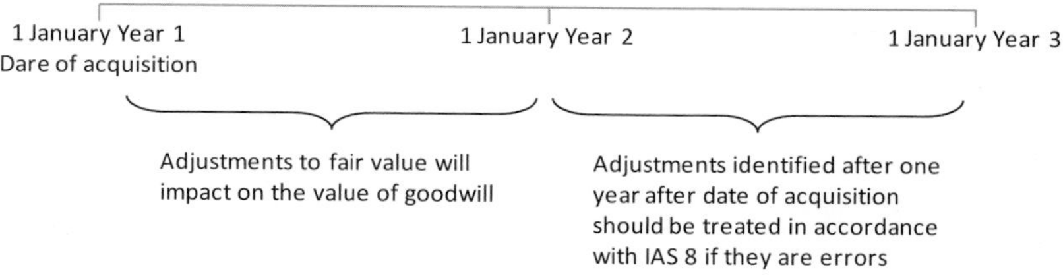

Example

In addition to the information in Example 1.3, the balance sheet of Jerez S.A. showed net assets of €249,000 at 1 January Year 1. The fair values of the net assets of Jerez S.A. were equivalent to the book values except for:

	Book Value €'000	Fair Value €'000
Plant and machinery	60	72
Inventory	46	51

Requirement

Calculate the fair value of net assets at acquisition and the goodwill arising on consolidation. Assume the company values the non-controlling interest based on the value of Jerez S.A.'s identifiable assets.

Solution

	€'000
Net assets	249.00
Plant and machinery adjustment (72 – 60)	12.00
Inventory adjustment (51 – 46)	5.00
Fair value of net assets	266.00
Fair value of consideration	353.00
Value of non-controlling interest (266 × 20%)	53.20
Fair value of subsidiary net assets	(266.00)
Goodwill	140.20
Non-controlling interest	53.20

Points to Note

- Under the 'full goodwill' method, goodwill is calculated as the purchase consideration plus the value of the non-controlling interest less 100% of the fair value of the subsidiary's net assets.
- Plant and machinery and inventory remain at book value in the accounts of Jerez S.A. The adjustments are only made for the purpose of preparing consolidated financial statements.

- Disclosure of fair value adjustments is made in consolidated financial statements.
- US GAAP requires the non-controlling interest to be valued at fair value. This generally results in a larger value for goodwill and non-controlling interest.

3.4 Deferred Tax Implications

Companies within a group are assessed on an individual basis for the purposes of taxation. These taxation amounts are then consolidated into the group financial statements. It must be noted, however, that fair value adjustments made at the date of control have deferred taxation implications for the group.

Assets and liabilities are revalued to fair values for the purposes of consolidation, and consolidated financial statements must reflect the temporary timing differences that arise. As a result, the consolidated financial statements must reflect any deferred tax asset or liability which arises from these additional revaluations.

4 Piecemeal Acquisitions

4.1 Determination of Control

Not every subsidiary is acquired by a single purchase of shares. Some equity interests are acquired over a period of time. These piecemeal acquisitions are sometimes known as "step acquisitions".

The investee company can only be consolidated under the purchase method once control (majority of votes) has been achieved. Under IFRS rules, at the point where control is achieved, any existing stake in the business is treated as if it has been disposed of and re-acquired at fair value. Any resulting gain or loss is recognised in earnings. This applies regardless of whether the previous stake was classified as an equity investment (and accounted for under IFRS9) or an associated investment.

4.2 Comprehensive Example

Azure S.A. acquires a 55% holding in Zapata S.A. as follows:

Year	Holding Acquired %	Consideration Paid €m	Net Assets Value of Zapata S.A. €m
1	10	5	10
2	15	8	14
3	30	20	16
	55%	33	

Requirement

Calculate the goodwill arising on acquisition of Zapata S.A. assuming that the consideration paid in Year 3 does not include a control premium and that the company values the non-controlling interest at fair value.

Solution

	Year 3 €m
Consideration	20.00
Fair value of existing stake (20 × 25% ÷ 30%)	16.67
Value of non-controlling interest (20 × 45% ÷ 30%)	30.00
Fair value of subsidiary net assets	(16.00)
Goodwill	50.67

Points to Note

- Azure S.A. has no subsidiaries in Years 1 and 2 and so Zapata S.A. would not have been accounted for using the equity method, as there would be no need to prepare consolidated financial statements. Zapata S.A. reaches subsidiary status in Year 3 and it needs to be consolidated. Consequently, the net assets acquired are those in Year 3.
- Goodwill is calculated as the consideration plus the value of any existing stake and the value of any non-controlling interest less the fair value of the total net assets of Zapata S.A.
- In Year 3, Azure S.A. will also recognise a gain or loss of earnings to represent the change in value of its existing 25% stake in Zapata S.A. since the stake was acquired.

4.3 Changes in Ownership Once Control is Achieved

In accordance with IFRS, the treatment is as follows:

a) Control is achieved once a majority holding has been obtained. The investee entity can only be consolidated into the group financial statements from this date.

b) If a further equity stake is acquired once control is achieved (i.e. by purchasing some or all of the non-controlling interest) this does not affect the value of goodwill, assets or liabilities in the consolidated balance sheet. This is because the consolidated balance sheet already reflects 100% of the goodwill, assets and liabilities of the investee. The transaction is accounted for in equity as follows:

   i) Reduce the value of the controlling interest to reflect the percentage change in ownership.

   ii) Any premium paid for the additional stake is **not** recognised as goodwill and is instead treated as a reduction to retained earnings.

5 Complex Groups Including Disposals

5.1 Determination of Control

The holding company is required to prepare consolidated financial statements in respect of each subsidiary it controls whether directly or indirectly. Holdings Inc. 60% Blowup Inc. 75%.

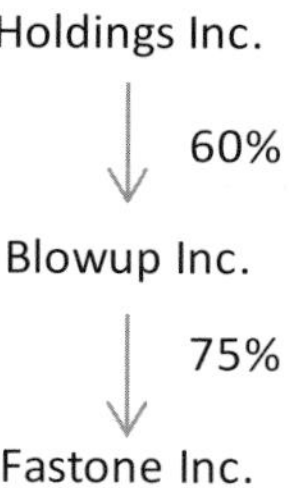

Whilst Holdings Inc. indirectly has a 45% equity interest in Fastone Inc. (60% × 75%), it controls Blowup Inc. and therefore controls Blowup Inc. investment in Fastone Inc. The parent company must consolidate the sub-subsidiary from the date it controls the subsidiary.

5.2 Example – Consolidated Balance Sheet

Balance sheet as at 31 December Year 4.

	Azure S.A.	Zapata S.A.	Rioja S.A.
Investments	**€m**	**€m**	**€m**
Zapata S.A.	100	-	-
Rioja S.A.	-	125	-
Other net assets	550	325	350
	650	450	350
Stockholders' Equity			
Common stock €1	200	100	100
Retained Earnings	450	350	250
	650	450	350

Azure S.A. acquired 60% of common stock of Zapata S.A. on 1 January Year 1. At that date retained earnings of Zapata S.A. were €25m.

Zapata S.A. acquired 60% of Rioja S.A. on 1 January Year 3. At that date retained earnings of Rioja S.A. were €80m.

As at 31 December Year 4, the goodwill that arose on the acquisition of Zapata S.A. has been impaired by €10m, and that on the acquisition of Rioja S.A. by €3.4m.

Requirement

Prepare the consolidated balance sheet of Azure S.A. group as at 31 December Year 4. Assume the non-controlling interests are valued based on the proportionate share of net identifiable assets.

Solution

Consolidated Balance Sheet as at 31 December Year 4:

	€m
Intangible Assets	
Goodwill (W2)	28.60
Other Net Assets	1,225.00
	1,253.60
Stockholders' Equity	
Common Stock	200.00
Retained Earnings (W4)	694.16
Non-controlling interest (W3)	359.44
	1,253.60

Workings

1. Group structure

∴ effective ownership of Rioja = 60% × 60% = 36%

∴ minority interest 64%

2. Goodwill

	€m	€m	€m	€m
Cost of investment				
Zapata S.A.		100		125
Rioja S.A. 40% × (100 + 25)		50	40% × (100 + 80)	72
Fair value of net assets at acquisition				
Common stock	100		100	
Retained earnings	25		80	
		(125)		(180)
		25		17

€10m to income statement

€15m Balance Sheet

€3.4m to income statement

€13.6 Balance Sheet

3. Non-controlling interest

	€m
Zapata S.A. 40% × (450 + 13.6 – 125)	135.44
Rioja S.A. 64% × 350	224.00
	359.44

4. Consolidated retained earnings

	€m	€m
Azure S.A.		450
Zapata S.A.		
Now	350	
At acquisition	(25)	
	325	
	× 60%	195

	€m	€m
Rioja S.A.		
Now	250	
At acquisition	(80)	
	170	
	× 36%	61.2
Goodwill impaired (10m + 60% × 3.4m)		(12.04)
		694.16

Points to Note

- Azure S.A. has control of Zapata S.A. from Year 1, but the latter company does not achieve control of Rioja S.A., which can only be consolidated by Azure S.A. from Year 3 onwards. If the situation had been the reverse:

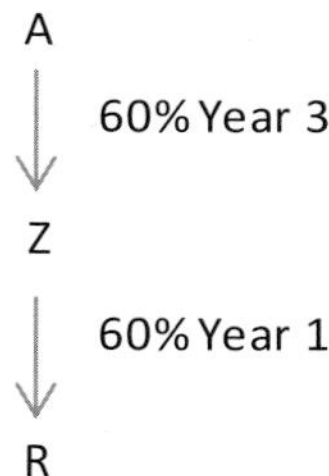

  Then both Zapata S.A. and Rioja S.A. became subsidiaries of Azure S.A. in Year 3 only.

- Even though effective ownership of Rioja S.A. by Azure S.A. is 30%, the latter controls the former through its control of Zapata S.A.
- Goodwill arising on each acquisition is calculated separately. Under the full goodwill method, 100% of the goodwill acquired with Rioja S.A. is considered by Azure even though Azure has effected ownership of 36%.
- Non-controlling interest is calculated by percentage of ownership. The €125m is deducted from net assets of Zapata. To exclude the cost of investment of Rioja S.A. Instead it has been replaced by the underlying net assets & goodwill of Rioja S.A. as the minority interest are given their appropriate share.
- Earnings are calculated separately for each acquisition and percentage is based on ownership not control.

5.3 Example – Consolidated Income Statement

Using the information in example 5.2, the income statements of each of the three companies for the year ended 31 December Year 4 are:

	Azure S.A.	**Zapata S.A.**	**Rioja S.A.**
	€m	**€m**	**€m**
Sales	750	755	459
Cost of sales	250	551	289
Gross margin	500	204	170
Depreciation and interest expense	75	60	15
Other operating expenses	250	19	75
Net income	175	125	80

Requirement

Prepare the consolidated income statements for the year ended 31 December Year 4, if in that year, goodwill was impaired by €3.52m.

Solution

	€m
Sales	1,964.00
Cost of sales	1,090.00
Gross margin	874.00
Depreciation and interest expense (150 + 3.52)	153.52
Other operating expenses	344.00
Minority interest (40% × 125) + (64% × 80)	101.00
Net income	275.48

Points to Note

- The impairment charge to goodwill is expensed in the income statement
- The minority interest is calculated based on actual ownership of earnings of each subsidiary

5.4 Disposal of a Subsidiary

There are two key issues to deal with:

a) Treatment of profit or loss on disposal of equity interests

b) The dilution of control

The sale of equity interests could result in any of the following treatments:

Investment Status Pre-Sale	Investment Status Post-Sale	Treatment	
		Balance Sheet	**Income Statement**
Subsidiary (e.g. 70%)	Subsidiary (e.g. 60%)	• Full consolidation • Remaining non-controlling interest of 40%	• Full consolidation Profit/loss on sale
Subsidiary (e.g. 70%)	Associate (e.g. 40%)	• Equity method	• Pro rata • Consolidate for period as subsidiary • Equity for period as associate • Profit/loss on sale
Subsidiary (e.g. 70%)	Investment (e.g. 15%)	• Financial asset* (see earlier)	• Pro rata • Consolidate for period as subsidiary • Investment gains only after sale • Profit/loss on sale
Subsidiary (e.g. 70%)	None	• Derecognise in full	• Pro rata • Consolidate for period as subsidiary • Profit/loss on sale

* As these are likely to be long-term investments, they are likely to be classified as "FVOCI".

6 Foreign Subsidiaries

6.1 Exchange Rates for the Purpose of Consolidation

Firms that have subsidiaries overseas are required to consolidate these entities. However, the financial statements of such overseas entities may be in another currency. Therefore, a set of rules is required in order to translate financials into currency of the parent. These rules are set out in IAS 21, the effects of changes in foreign exchange rates.

The table below summarises the key terminology that is used when consolidating foreign subsidiaries.

Term	Definition
Functional Currency	Primary currency of the commercial and economic environment in which the firm operates.
Reporting Currency	Currency of the financial statements of the holding company.
Local Currency	A particular subsidiary's reporting currency.
Foreign Currency	Any currency other than the functional currency.
Current Rate/ Closing Rate	Exchange rate as at the balance sheet date.
Average Rate	Average rate over a particular period.
Historical Rate	The rate that existed when a particular transaction was made.
Translation Exposure	Changes in exchange rates impact on financial results.
Transaction Exposure	Change in exchange rates impact on unsettled transactions such as accounts receivable and payable.
Operating Exposure	Potential exposure due to future possible exchange rate changes.

Below is an overview of the method used to translate the financials of subsidiary with a different functional currency to its parent.

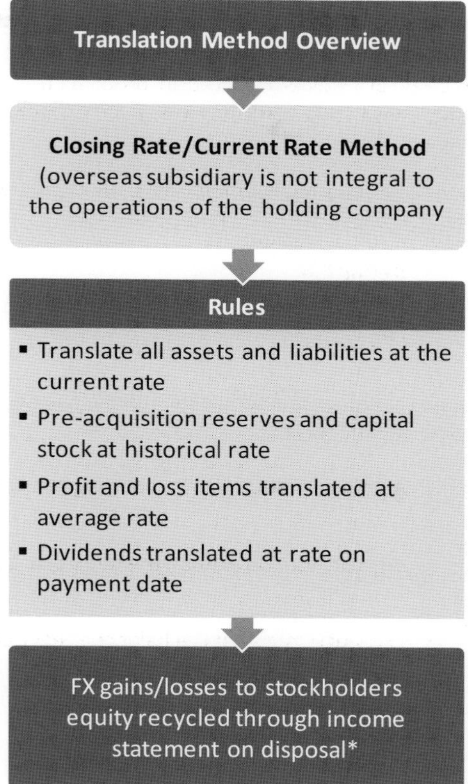

* Under the closing rate method, the FX gains/losses are held in a separate component of equity and the cumulative gain/loss is recycled through the income statement on disposal of the foreign operation.

6.2 Comprehensive Example

Olbas Inc. has a wholly owned Irish subsidiary, Failte Ltd. The relevant exchange rates (1€=$) and functional statement extracts are as follows:

Current Rate	=	**.9389**
Historical rates		
Ending inventory	=	.9026
Dividend pay date	=	.9426
Common stock	=	.9527
Fixed assets	=	.8725
Opening rate/opening inventory	=	.9550
Average for the year	=	.9650

Approach to Translation

You should bear in mind that the actual process of foreign currency translation is very mechanical and involves the use of 'balancing figures'.

Closing Rate Method

1. Translate the income statement using the average rate.
2. Translate the balance sheet using the closing rate/historical rate as appropriate.
3. Solve for closing retained earnings:

	US$
Opening retained earnings (US$)	X
+ Net Income (US$ – translated)	X
-Dividends (US$)	(X)
Retained earnings before adjustment	X
+/- Translation adjustment	PLUG
Closing retained earnings	X

Failte Ltd Balance Sheet as at 31 December 2007

		Current Rate	
	€	Rate	US$
Assets			
Cash	7,000		
Inventory	8,000		
Land	5,000		
Building – net	13,000		
Equipment – net	7,000		
Total assets	40,000		

Liabilities and Stockholders' Equity

		Current Rate	
	€	Rate	US$
Current liabilities	10,000		
Long-term liabilities	10,000		
Stockholders' equity			
Capital stock	9,000		
Retained earnings	11,000		
* FX gain/loss			
Total liabilities and stockholders' equity	40,000		

Required

Translate the balance sheet of Failte Ltd using the Closing Rate Method.

Solution

Failte Ltd Balance Sheet as at 31 December 2007

		Current Rate	
	€	Rate	US$
Assets			
Cash	7,000	0.9389	6,572
Inventory	8,000	0.9389	7,511
Land	5,000	0.9389	4,695
Building – net	13,000	0.9389	12,206
Equipment – net	7,000	0.9389	6,572
Total assets	40,000		37,556

Liabilities and Stockholders' Equity

		Current Rate	
	€	Rate	US$
Current liabilities	10,000	0.9389	9,389
Long-term liabilities	10,000	0.9389	9,389
Stockholders' equity			
Capital stock	9,000	0.9527	8,574
Retained earnings	11,000	P&L	10,075
* FX gain/loss		Plug	129
Total liabilities and stockholders' equity	40,000		37,556

Points to Note

- Under the closing rate method the exchange difference is taken to equity. This is because it is more like a "revaluation" due to changes in exchange rates rather than as a result of operating activity

Failte Ltd Statement of Income for Year Ended 31 December 2007

		Current Rate	
	€	Rate	US$
Sale	35,000		
Cost of sales	(17,000)		
Depreciation	(5,000)		
Other expenses	(3,200)		
Translation (loss) gain			
Income before taxes	9,800		
Income tax	(5,800)		
Net income	4,000		
Retained earnings			
Opening balance*	9,000	given	8,100
	13,000		
Dividends	(2,000)		
Retained earnings			
Closing balance (per B/S)	11,000		

* In practice, this would be in the prior year translated financials.

Requirement

Translate the income statement of Failte Ltd using the Closing Rate Method.

Solution

Failte Ltd Statement of Income for Year Ended 31 December 2007

		Current Rate	
	€	Rate	US$
Sale	35,000	0.9650	33,775
Cost of sales	(17,000)	0.9650	(16,405)
Depreciation	(5,000)	0.9650	(4,825)
Other expenses	(3,200)	0.9650	(3,088)
Translation (loss) gain		-	-
Income before taxes	9,800		9,457
Income tax	(5,800)	0.9650	(5,597)
Net income	4,000		3,860
Retained earnings			
Opening balance	9,000	(given)	8,100
	13,000		11,960
Dividends	(2,000)	0.9426	(1,885)
Retained earnings			
Closing balance	11,000		10,075

Points to Note

- In the case of the current rate, the income statement exchange difference would be calculated first then transferred to the balance sheet in order to derive the foreign exchange difference.

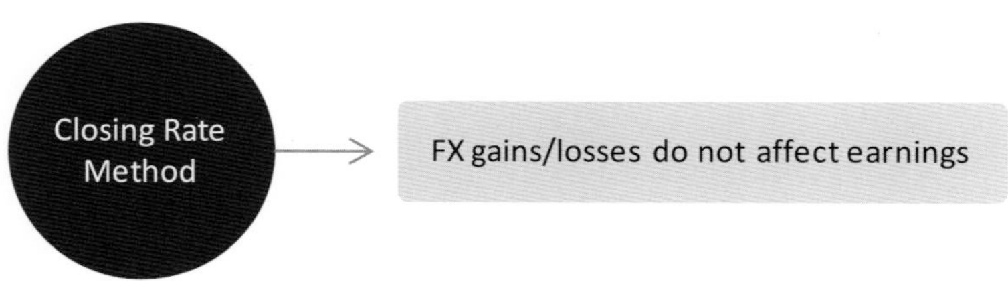

6.3 Hedging Treatment of Foreign Equity Investments

This accounting treatment relates to a very specific transaction. The foreign equity investment has either been financed or hedged by a foreign currency loan (not necessarily in the same currency). The basic principle is that gains or losses on the equity investment should be protected by gains or losses on the foreign borrowing. Below is a summary of the principles of this hedge issue, which are broadly based on the principle of matching income with expenditure in the accounting period. Note that this area is covered by IFRS 9, rather than IAS 21. A hedge of a net investment in a foreign operation is now accounted for similarly to a cash flow hedge.

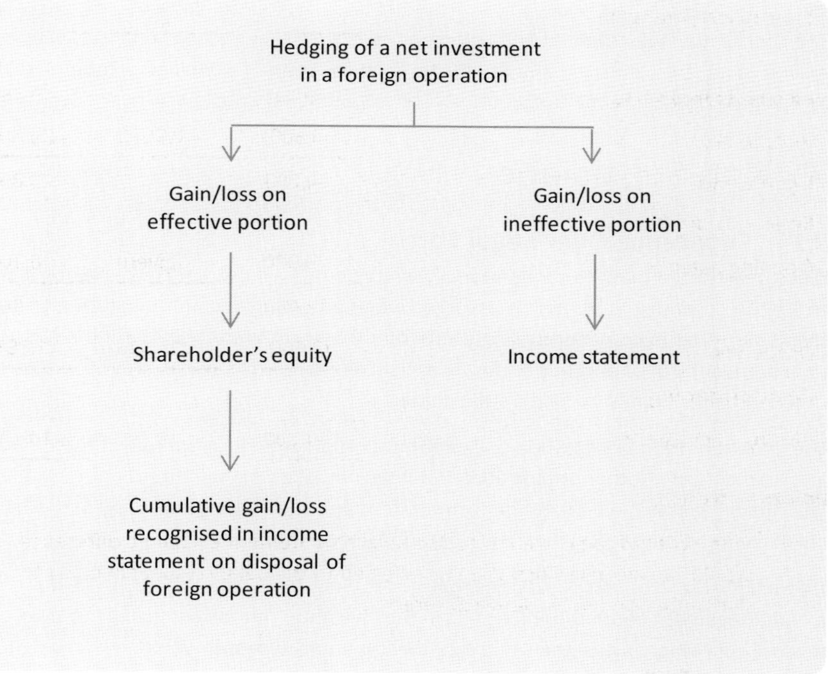

Example

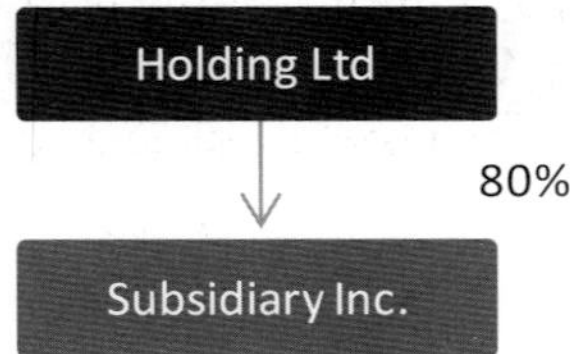

The cost of the investment in Subsidiary Inc. was $2million and was financed with a $2 million loan. It is clear that any fluctuations on the loan of $2million will be offset by any gains or losses on the translation of the net assets of Subsidiary Inc.

7 Non-Subsidiaries

7.1 Substance Over Legal Form

It has been noted that the conventional way to identify a subsidiary undertaking is that of control. In principle, control is assumed when a holding in common stock is greater than 50%. It has become increasingly apparent that legal ownership is not the only way to acquire control of another entity. These subsidiary undertakings are often referred to as 'non-subsidiaries' or 'quasi subsidiaries'.

The situation often arises when one organisation plays an integral role in the creation and financing of another organisation but does not take up a significant equity interest. The financing may have taken the form of debt and the holding company may also be involved in the management of the operations of the 'subsidiary'.

Under IFRS, these quasi subsidiaries may be required to be consolidated if the financing and management of operations results in the investing company enjoying the 'risks and rewards' of ownership, in the same way that an equity investor would.

Chapter 13: Financial Instruments

"You have to understand accounting and you have to understand the nuances of accounting. It's the language of business and it's an imperfect language, but unless you are willing to put in the effort to learn accounting - how to read and interpret financial statements - you really shouldn't select stocks yourself" [14]

[14] We needed at least one Warren Buffett quote so voila! It could be a useful marketing quote for this book! Many thanks for this from the sage of Omaha.

1 Introduction

In 1995, IASC reached agreement with IOSCO on the content of a work programme to complete a core set of IFRSs that could be endorsed by IOSCO for cross-border capital-raising and listing purposes in global markets. These included standards on recognition and measurement of financial instruments, off balance sheet items, hedging and investments. Eventually, the IASC issued IAS 39 as an interim solution, to serve until a comprehensive standard was completed. Work on a more comprehensive standard was already underway when the global financial crisis occurred in 2008; arguably this crisis exposed some of the flaws in the accounting rules as banks appeared to have a great deal of flexibility in how they valued their financial instruments, whilst providing only minimal disclosure around how these valuations were derived.

These events put significant pressure on standard setters to accelerate their work on a new, more robust standard to replace IAS 39. This new standard – IFRS 9 – was recently finalised and became mandatory in 2018. In addition to this, a number of enhancements have been made to the disclosure standard on financial instruments, IFRS 7. Although IFRS 9 retains the mixed measurement model of IAS 39 (with some assets and liabilities measured at cost and some at fair value), it provides greater clarity over when and how the different measurement models should be applied.

Although the new standard undoubtedly improves the consistency and transparency of financial instruments accounting, the fact remains that the instruments themselves can be extremely complex and exposed to a variety of financial risks. Therefore, the material in this chapter has been pitched at an intermediate level. This should be more than enough to enable most analysts to attain a good working knowledge of the issues involved.

2 Summary of IFRS9

In overview, IFRS 9 promulgates:

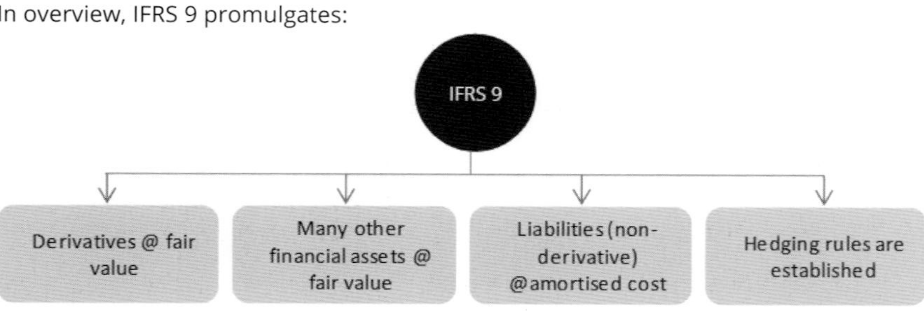

- **All** financial assets and financial liabilities should be recognised on the balance sheet, including all derivatives. They should **initially be measured** at cost (which is the fair value of the consideration given or received to acquire the financial asset or liability).
- Subsequent to initial recognition, **all financial assets should be re-measured to fair value**, except for debt instruments where the following criteria are satisfied:
  - the contractual cash flows give rise solely to payments of principal and interest on specified dates; and
  - the objective of the business model is to collect contractual cash follows (i.e. hold until maturity rather than for trading purposes).
- After acquisition, most financial liabilities should be measured at original recorded amount less principal repayments and amortisation. Only derivatives and liabilities held for trading should be re-measured to fair value.

3 Definitions

IFRS 9 (and the related standard, IAS 32) contain a number of key definitions, which we summarize below.

3.1 Financial Instrument

A financial instrument is any contract that gives rise to both a financial asset of one enterprise and a financial liability, or equity instrument, of another enterprise.

3.2 Equity Instrument

An equity instrument is any contract that evidences a residual interest in the assets of an enterprise after deducting all of its liabilities. This is a reasonably standard definition of equity.

3.3 Derivative

A derivative is a financial instrument:

- Whose value changes in response to the change in a specified interest rate, security price, commodity price, foreign exchange rate, index of prices or rates, a credit rating or credit index, or similar variable (the 'underlying').
- That requires no initial net investment or little initial net investment relative to other types of contracts that have a similar response to changes in market conditions.

- That is settled at a future date.

The first part of this definition is the cornerstone of most text book definitions of derivatives. The price of a derivative (such as an equity option) is a function of the price of something else (i.e. the underlying, in this case an equity share).

3.4 Financial Assets

A financial asset is any asset that is:

- Cash
- A contractual right to receive cash, or another financial asset, from another enterprise.
- A contractual right to exchange financial instruments with another enterprise under conditions that are potentially favourable, or;
- An equity instrument of another enterprise.

4 Accounting Treatment of Financial Assets

4.1 Overview

IFRS 9 has various categories for financial assets, with the accounting being determined by the categories. The different treatment for these categories, in overview, is as follows:

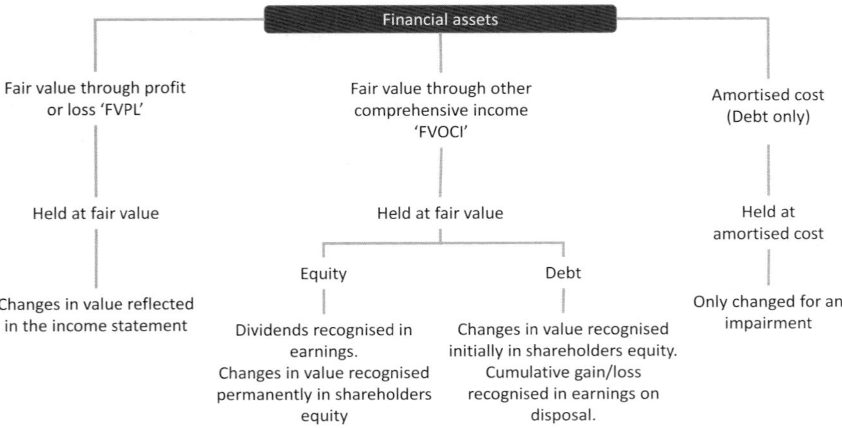

The accounting for equity investments described here should be familiar territory from Chapter 7.

4.2 Categories of Financial Assets

As demonstrated above, there are three categories for financial assets: FVPL, FVOCI and amortised cost, though the amortised cost category is only available for debt instruments.

The default classification for equity instruments is FVPL. Debt instruments are classified as FVPL, FVOCI or amortised cost depending on the instrument characteristics and the business model.

A more formal taxonomy of financial assets follows.

Fair Value Through Profit and Loss (FVPL)

This is the default classification for all derivatives and equity instruments. Debt instruments are also classified here if they have any additional payment features (so they don't just pay interest and principal to the holder on specified dates) or if they are held exclusively for trading purposes. However, companies may also elect to use this category for other debt instruments if it helps to reduce earnings volatility/ mismatches between the measurement of financial assets and financial liabilities.

Fair Value Through Other Comprehensive Income (FVOCI)

This is the main category for debt instruments. It is applied only for 'traditional' debt instruments (that only pay interest and principal to the holder on specified dates) and where the company's objective when holding this type of asset is to hold them until maturity **and also** for trading purposes.

For debt instruments in this category, all value changes are recognised in equity until the instrument matures, is sold or if there is an impairment in its value.

In addition, companies can make a permanent election to use this category for certain equity instruments (those not held for trading purposes). However, this will result in only dividend income being recognised in earnings; value changes are recognised in equity.

Amortised Cost

As highlighted in section 2, this category is only available for loans and receivables and 'traditional' debt instruments, and is applied whenever the company's business model is to hold these them until maturity. Changes in the asset value are not reflected in the balance sheet; an adjustment is only made (and a loss recognised) if there is an impairment in its value. The impairment of assets in this category is discussed in more detail in Chapter 16.

4.3 Issues in Accounting for Financial Assets

In order to understand the fundamental accounting treatment of financial assets we need to establish rules for the following:

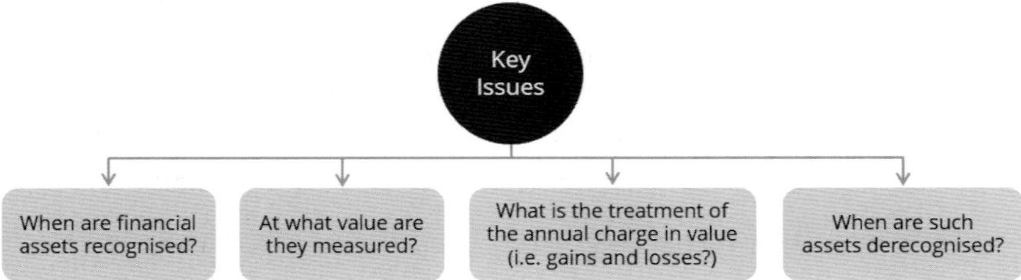

Recognition

An enterprise should recognise a financial asset when it becomes a party to the contractual provisions of the instrument. For example, financial options are recognised as assets (or liabilities) when the holder (or writer) becomes a party to the contract.

Initial Measurement

A financial asset is recognised initially at cost (fair value of consideration given plus transaction costs).

Subsequent Measurement

As highlighted above, the subsequent measurement depends on the classification:

Category 1: Financial assets at fair value through profit and loss (FVPL)

A gain or loss on remeasurement to fair value is included in net income for the period in which it arises ('mark-to-market' accounting).

If an enterprise recognises purchases of financial assets using settlement date accounting, any change in fair value between trade date and settlement date is recognised in net income.

Category 2: Financial assets at fair value through other comprehensive income (FVOCI)

For debt instruments in this category, a gain or loss on remeasurement to fair value is recognised directly in equity until the financial asset is sold or it matures. At this point the cumulative gain or loss is recognised in earnings (known as 'recycling' to earnings).

For equity instruments in this category, a gain or loss on remeasurement to fair value is recognised directly (and permanently) in equity. However, any dividend income received each year is included in net income. When the equity instrument is sold, the previously recognised fair value gains or losses remain in equity (no recycling).

If an enterprise recognises purchases of financial assets using settlement date accounting, any change in fair value between trade date and settlement date is recognised in net income or equity.

Category 3: Financial assets at amortised cost

Fair value gains and losses are not recognised for this category. However, if the asset is impaired (or a previously impairment needs to be reversed) the impairment loss (or the gain from an impairment reversal) is recognised in net income.

Derecognition

An enterprise should derecognise a financial asset or a portion of a financial asset when, and only when, the enterprise loses control of the contractual rights that comprise the financial asset (or portion thereof). An enterprise loses such control if it realises the rights to benefits specified in the contract, the rights expire, or the enterprise surrenders those rights.

On derecognition, the difference between:

- The carrying amount of the asset (or portion thereof) transferred to another party.
- The sum of the proceeds received or receivable.

Should be included in net profit or loss for the period.

For debt instruments (but not equity instruments) classified at FVOCI, any cumulative gains and losses recognised previously in equity are also transferred (recycled) to net income on disposal.

5 Financial Liabilities

5.1 Definition and Overview

A financial liability is any liability that is a contractual obligation:

- To deliver cash or another financial asset to another enterprise or
- To exchange financial instruments with another enterprise under conditions that are potentially unfavourable.

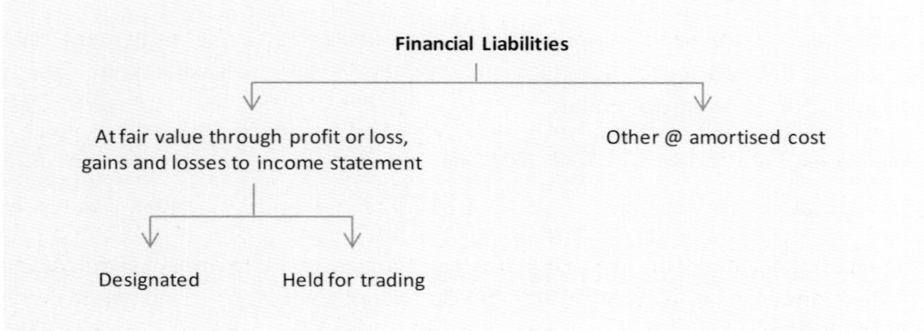

5.2 Categories of Financial Liabilities

Financial Liabilities at Fair Value Through Profit and Loss

A financial liability held for trading is one that was acquired or incurred principally for the purpose of generating a profit from short-term fluctuations in price or dealer's margin. Derivative financial liabilities are deemed to be held for trading unless they are designated and effective hedging instruments. Remember this category also includes instruments 'designated' to be within this classification.

Other

Other financial liabilities are those that are not held for trading or designated at fair value through profit and loss.

5.3 Accounting Treatment of Financial Liabilities

Recognition

In exactly the same way as financial assets, an enterprise should recognise a financial liability when it becomes a party to the contractual provisions of the instrument.

5.4 Measurement

Initial Measurement

A financial liability is recognised initially at cost (fair value of consideration received less transaction costs).

Subsequent Measurement

- Financial liabilities are measured at amortised cost, except:
  - Liabilities held for trading.
  - Derivatives that are liabilities.
  - Designated hedges.
- Derivative liabilities and liabilities held for trading purposes are measured at fair value.

Amortised Cost

The initial carrying amount (i.e. net proceeds) is increased by finance charges (at the effective interest rate) in respect of the period and reduced by payments made in the period. We have seen this in the section on accounting for bonds in Chapter 4. The following example further illustrates the accounting treatment.

Illustration

Bonds with a nominal value of €1.25m, paying interest at 4.7% per annum, are issued for €1m (transaction costs are negligible). The bonds are redeemable at par in five years' time. The effective interest rate is 10%.

Year	Balance	Interest @ 10%	Cash Paid	Balance
1	1,000,000	100,000	(58,750)	1,041,250
2	1,041,250	104,125	(58,750)	1,086,625
3	1,086,625	108,662	(58,750)	1,136,537
4	1,136,537	113,654	(58,750)	1,191,441
5	1,191,441	117,309*	(1,308,750)	0
		543,750	(1,543,750)	

*Due to rounding error.

Gains and Losses

Financial Liabilities at Fair Value Through Profit and Loss

A gain or loss on remeasurement to fair value is included in net profit for the period in which it arises ('mark-to-market' accounting).

However, IFRS 9 requires that any changes in fair value that arise from changes in own credit risk (referred to as 'own credit adjustment') are recognised in other comprehensive income, rather than profit and loss, to prevent companies recognising a gain if their credit risk increases. Other changes in fair value (e.g. resulting from movements in interest rates) are recognised in net profit.

Other Financial Liabilities

Finance costs are allocated to periods over the term of the debt at a constant rate on the carrying amount (the effective interest rate, level yield to maturity or internal rate of return).

Derecognition

An enterprise should remove a financial liability (or a part of a financial liability) from its balance sheet when, and only when, it is extinguished – i.e. when the obligation specified in the contract is discharged, cancelled or expires.

6 Hedge Accounting

Hedge accounting is a crucial part of financial instrument accounting. Essentially, hedge accounting facilitates the establishment of a linkage between two transactions for the purposes of accounting. For example, this might be one transaction with a customer in a foreign currency and an associated foreign currency forward contract or option.

Analysis Focus

Valuation of industrial companies (but not financials) is generally done for the operations, with financial liabilities netted off to derive a value for the equity. This implies that the cash flows to be discounted will precede financial items, such as interest and gains/losses on financial swaps. In this case, all the analyst needs is to be sure that the liabilities they deduct include fair value of financial swaps. But what if the company sells electricity and is taking gains and losses on its forward electricity contracts through its profit and loss account as operating profit?

The hedging provisions of IFRS 9 utilise the nature of the hedging relationship as the driver for the accounting treatment. There are three types of hedge.

Fair Value Hedge

A hedge of an exposure to changes in the fair value of a recognised asset or liability (or an identified portion of such an asset or liability) that is attributable to a particular risk and that will affect reported net income.

Cash Flow Hedge

A hedge of the exposure to variability in cash flows that is attributable to a particular risk associated with a recognised asset or liability (e.g. all or some future interest payments on variable rate debt) or a forecast transaction (e.g. an anticipated purchase or sale); and will affect reported net profit or loss.

A hedge of an unrecognised firm commitment to buy or sell an asset at a fixed price in the enterprise's reporting currency is accounted for as a cash flow hedge, even though it has a fair value exposure.

Hedge of a Net Investment in a Foreign Entity

A foreign currency liability used to finance or hedge against a net investment in a foreign entity. Some aspects of this are covered in Chapter 12. Hedge accounting recognises symmetrically the offsetting effects on net profit or loss of changes in the fair values of the hedging instrument and the related item being hedged.

7 Conditions for Hedge Accounting

A hedging relationship qualifies for hedge accounting if, and only if (i) formal hedge documentation is in place and (ii) the company can demonstrate that the hedge will be effective. These criteria are discussed below (and note that they are much less onerous than the previous rules under IAS 39):

7.1 Formal Documentation/Designation

At the inception of the hedge, there is formal documentation of the hedging relationship and the enterprise's risk management objective and strategy for undertaking the hedge.

That documentation should include:

- Identification of the hedging instrument.
- The related hedged item or transaction.
- The nature of the risk being hedged.
- How the enterprise will assess the hedging instrument's effectiveness in offsetting the exposure to changes in the hedged item's fair value or the hedged transaction's cash flows that is attributable to the hedged risk.

7.2 Hedge Effectiveness

Companies must be able to demonstrate that the hedge will be effective as follows:

- An economic relationship must exist between the hedging instrument and hedged item. Even where such a relationship exists, the effects of credit risk changes for these items must not dominate the value changes associated with the hedged risk (as this would limit the effectiveness of the hedge).

There is no prescriptive approach for assessing hedge effectiveness; qualitative assessment would suffice for simple hedges, but quantitative analysis would be required for more complex ones. For quantitative assessment, the hedge ratio (the relationship between the quantity of the hedging instrument and the quantity of the hedged item) is determined by the company but must be aligned with the company's risk management objectives. The company must make an ongoing assessment at each balance sheet date of whether the hedge continues to meet the hedge effectiveness criteria.

7.3 Impact if Conditions are not Met

The hedged item is accounted for as a stand-alone financial asset or liability (i.e. at amortised cost or at fair value with gains or losses recognised directly in equity).

Fair value adjustments of a hedging instrument that is a derivative are reported in net profit or loss.

7.4 Hedge Accounting Impact if Conditions are Met

Fair Value Hedges

The gain or loss from remeasuring the hedging instrument at fair value is recognised immediately in net profit or loss.

The gain or loss on the hedged item attributable to the hedged risk adjusts the carrying amount of the hedged item and is recognised immediately in net profit or loss (for a perfectly effective hedge, there will be no net effect on earnings).

Cash Flow Hedges

The portion of the gain or loss on the hedging instrument that is determined to be an effective hedge is recognised directly in equity.

The ineffective portion is reported immediately in net profit or loss, if the hedging instrument is a derivative; or as for gains or losses arising from changes in the fair value of financial assets and liabilities, in the limited circumstances in which the hedging instrument is not a derivative.

Example 1 – Fair Value Hedges

Six months before year end, a company issues a three-year €10m fixed interest note at 7.5%, with semi-annual interest payments. It also enters into an interest rate swap to pay LIBOR and to receive 7.5% semi-annually; swap terms include a €10m notional principal, three-year term and semi-annual variable rate reset.

LIBOR for the first six-month period is 6%. By year-end, interest rates have fallen and the fair value of the swap (after settlement) is €125,000 (asset).

Requirements

- Indicate the accounting entries that would be made in the financials for the swap and the underlying borrowing, both at initiation and at year end. Assume the transaction is accounted for using the traditional transaction based (historic cost) approach.
- What would be the impact of no hedge accounting but use of fair values for the derivative?
- What would be the impact of hedge accounting but use of fair values for the loan and derivative?

Solution

1. Traditional Transaction Approach

Borrowings

1. Loan is recognised at net proceeds:

↑ Cash	€10,000,000
↑ Creditors	€10,000,000

2. Interest on loan for period:

↓ P&L account – net interest payable	€375,000
↓ Cash	€375,000

Derivatives

1. Swap is recognised, measured at cost:

↑ Financial asset – held for trading	€0
↓ Cash	€0

2. Settlement under swap in period:

↑ Cash (€375,000-€300,000)	€75,000
↑ P&L account – gain on hedge	€75,000

Balance Sheet

	€000
Cash	↑9,700
Swaps	0
Borrowings	(10,000)
Equity	↓300

P&L Account

	€000
Interest payable	(375)
Gain on hedge	75

Balance sheet fails to reflect fair value of swap

Cash Flow Statement

	€000
Interest paid	(375)
Swap receipt	75
Financing	10,000

P&L account is effectively charged with LIBOR

2. Accounting with Derivative at Fair Value

Borrowings

1. Loan is recognised at net proceeds:

↑ Cash	€10,000,000
↑ Creditors	€10,000,000

2. Interest on loan for period:

↓ P&L account	
– net interest payable	€375,000
↓ Cash	€375,000

Derivatives

1. Swap is recognised, measured initially at cost:

↑ Financial asset	
– held for trading	€0
↓ Cash	€0

2. Settlement under swap in period:

↓ Cash (€375,000-€300,000)	€75,000
↑ P&L account	
– gain on hedge	€75,000

3. Swap is subsequently remeasured to fair value:

↑ Financial asset	
– held for trading	€125,000
↑ P&L account	
– gain on hedge	€125,000

Balance Sheet	
	€000
Cash	↑9,700
Swaps	125
Borrowings	(10,000)
Equity	↓175

P&L Account	
	€000
Interest payable	(375)
Gain on hedge	200

Balance sheet reflects fair value of swap

Cash Flow Statement	
	€000
Interest paid	(375)
Swap receipt	75
Financing	10,000

P&L account fails to reflect true interest suffered (LIBOR)

Documentation and Effectiveness Testing

Changes in the fair value of the swap are designated as a hedge of changes in the fair value of the debt due to changes in LIBOR. The principal/notional amounts, currencies, maturity and interest payment dates of the note and the swap are the same. The basis of the variable leg of the swap (LIBOR) is the underlying exposure on the note. Therefore, changes in the fair value of the debt and the swap, due to the hedged risk, will exactly offset each other. The swap is assumed to be fully effective.

7.5 Hedge Accounting with the Derivative and Underlying at Fair Value

Borrowings

1. Loan is recognised at net proceeds:

↑ Cash	€10,000,000
↑ Creditors	€10,000,000

2. Interest on loan for period:

↓ P&L account	
– net interest payable	€375,000
↓ Cash	€375,000

Derivatives

1. Swap is recognised, measured initially at cost

↑ Financial asset	
– held for trading	€0
↓ Cash	€0

2. Settlement under swap in period

↑ Cash	€75,000
↑ P&L account	
– gain on hedge	€75,000

3. Swap and loan are subsequently remeasured to fair value

↑ Financial asset	
– held for trading	€125,000
↑ Financial liability (loan)	€125,000

Balance Sheet

	€000
Cash	↑9,700
Swaps	125
Borrowings	(10,125)
Equity	↓300

P&L Account

	€000
Interest payable	(375)
Gain on hedge	75

Balance sheet reflect fair value of swap and borrowings

Cash Flow Statement

	€000
Interest paid	(375)
Swap receipt	75
Financing	10,000

P&L account is effectively charged with LIBOR

Example 2 – Cash Flow Hedges

Delta Limited has tendered for a contract. The price quoted is $10m. However, Delta's functional currency is the Euro. Therefore, as prices would be fixed, Delta wishes to hedge this exposure. It enters into an FX future with a nominal value of $10m.

The treatments under various scenarios are summarised below:

1. Traditional Transaction Approach

The hedge will be ignored until the contract flows occur at which point the gain/loss on the derivative would be recognised. If the contract tender is not successful, the derivative would be settled and reported in income.

2. Hedge Accounting Conditions NOT Met

The FX derivative is marked to market at period end through the income statement as it is classified as speculation per IFRS 9.

3. Hedge Accounting Conditions ARE Met

Phase I: Derivative is marked to market on the balance sheet with gains/loss going to equity.

Phase II: Once cash flows occur, the gain/loss on derivative is matched with the relevant portion of the hedged inflows.

Chapter 14: An Introduction to Off Balance Sheet Finance

"The basic needs of humans are simple: to get enough food, to find shelter and to keep debt off the balance sheet." [15]

[15] Forbes, 1980. Incredibly this quote is almost 40 years old, and yet it captures the essence of just how strong the desire to get assets and debt off the balance sheet is.

1 Introduction

This chapter explains the meaning and impact of off balance sheet finance (OBSF). It addresses the motivations behind off balance sheet financing and how it provides significant advantages in terms of balance sheet representation. The remaining sections of the chapter address the various techniques that can be employed to gain off balance sheet treatment. Throughout, consideration is given to the impact of IFRS rules on the viability of these techniques.

2 Definition and Nature of OBSF

2.1 Impact of Funding Transactions with Debt

Typically, the acquisition of an asset (resource) will be funded by debt or equity. OBSF is fundamentally about the treatment of debt and similar commitments. If an entity borrows funds to finance a €100m transaction, then the entries (excluding the cash inflow and subsequent outflow) would be:

- ↑ Assets €100m
- ↑ Debt €100m

Note that there is no impact on net assets. The increase in assets is offset by the increase in liabilities (i.e. debt).

Off balance sheet 'financing' means structuring transactions in such a way that neither the loan nor the asset appear explicitly on the balance sheet. In practical terms, this would mean that, in our €100m transaction, there would be no asset and no debt finance recognised. Typical methods to achieve this include the use of JV arrangements, securitisation transactions, leasing contracts and working capital finance.

It is worth noting that the upcoming lease accounting change under IFRS and US GAAP will prevent leases being used as a form of off balance sheet finance (since the new rules will force all leases to be recorded on balance sheet). Nonetheless, we have retained this example below as it illustrates the mechanics of how OBSF changes the balance sheet.

Example

A company is considering leasing an asset. The lease term and the useful life of the asset are six years. Its cash equivalent price is €300,000, €60,000 is repayable within 12 months.

	Effect of Lease Capitalisation	
	€'000	**€'000**
Fixed assets	400	
Current assets	260	
Creditors: < 1 year	(180)	
Creditors: > 1 year	(160)	
	320	
Shareholders' funds	320	
Effect on ratios		
Capital employed		
Debt/equity		

Requirement

Redraft the company's balance sheet bringing in the asset and leasing obligation and calculate the impact on the above accounting ratios.

Solution

	Effect of Capitalisation
	€'000
Fixed assets (400 + 300)	700
Current assets	260
Creditors: < 1 year (180 + 60)	(240)
Creditors: > 1 year (160 + 240)	(400)
	320
Shareholders' funds	320
Capital employed (TALCL)	= 720 (v 480)

Gearing D/E

$$= \frac{400}{320} = 125\% \left(\text{v} \frac{160}{320} = 50\%\right)$$

2.2 Why Should Companies Seek to use Financing Off Balance Sheet?

Key Benefits

- **Reduction in gearing.** Although net assets and hence equity are unchanged irrespective of whether a transaction is on or off-balance sheet, debt is always higher if on balance sheet. Therefore, achieving OBSF treatment should lower gearing.
- **Improved efficiency ratios.** Total assets will be lower with OBSF. Therefore, ratios such as asset turnover will be enhanced. This will give the impression of a more efficient, leaner company.
- **Improved risk metrics.** OBSF will result in the company reporting lower interest expense as there is no loan as such in the accounts. This will result in an improved interest cover ratio.
- **Avoidance of covenant breach.** Debt covenants are restrictive conditions imposed on a company by its lenders. The company must avoid breaking these covenants to avoid default, which can result in expensive coupon increases and possibly receivership. OBSF techniques help with a number of these covenants (e.g. maximum debt/equity, minimum interest cover, etc.).

2.3 Accounting Rules

There is no one IFRS standard that addresses OBSF. Instead, a variety of standards are of relevance. This makes understanding the accounting issues more complex. However, this is the case in most jurisdictions (e.g. US).

The key detailed IFRS requirements are contained in the following standards:

- IFRS 7 – Financial instruments: disclosure
- IFRS 9 – Financial instruments
- IFRS 11 – Joint arrangements
- IFRS 12 – Disclosure of interests in other entities

3 The Accounting Principles of OBSF

Although an analyst is typically concerned with what schemes will work to achieve off balance sheet treatment and how these might be identified. It is still useful to examine the approach adopted in the accounting rules. This is especially appropriate for OBSF as the accounting framework is rather odd.

The key starting point is whether an asset should be recognised or not. It is the asset that tends to be the driver for the on/off balance sheet decision rather than the liability. The reason for this is that the asset tends to be more complex than the liability (except perhaps in the case of derivative instruments).

An asset should not be recognised if the entity does not have control over the risks and benefits of the asset. Therefore, an asset can only be derecognised if there is a passing of its risks and rewards to a third party. If an asset is derecognised then a net profit or loss should be recognised in the income statement as the difference between the carrying amount transferred asset and the proceeds received or receivable. This is a standard profit on disposal calculation.

What if an asset is transferred to another party but the de-recognition criteria are not met? In this case, the asset remains on balance sheet and the transferor will account for the monies received as borrowing secured on that asset.

These principles may well appear simple, straightforward and appropriate. In reality, our interest mainly surrounds the application of these principles to transactions. The next section follows such an approach.

3.1 Transaction I – Outright Sale

A sale of an asset which involves the transfer of benefits with no right to repurchase would qualify for derecognition. In many ways, this is simply a disposal with a profit and loss to be recognised and an asset to be taken off the balance sheet (i.e. derecognised). The potential off balance sheet finance is obvious – sell an asset to a bank for cash to raise finance. No asset and no loan would be recognised. However, we are left with a practical problem. Typically, the bank will not want the asset and the corporate will need the asset. Therefore, an outright sale with no repurchase dimension is often a non-starter from a practical standpoint.

3.2 Transaction II – Sale and Repurchase

IFRS 9 states that derecognition is not appropriate if there is a right of repurchase. For example, a sale together with an option to repurchase. There are exceptions to this. First, if the asset is readily obtainable in the market. Second, if the reacquisition is at the fair value at date of re-acquisition. In practical terms an asset (say a bundle of mortgage loans) is sold with a right to repurchase at a fixed price. As this fixed price may not be market price, derecognition will not take place. However, if the right was to repurchase at fair value (i.e. market price) then this is similar to a right of first refusal and may well qualify for derecognition.

3.3 Transaction III – Sale with Right and Obligation to Repurchase

IFRS 9 is concerned that a transaction could be structured in such a way as to provide a purchaser of an asset with merely a lender's return. This concept of lender's return is a level of return not significantly different from the return a bank (or lender) might obtain on a collateralised loan to the seller. In such cases and where a right and obligation to repurchase exists (e.g. by using put and call options), no derecognition takes place.

3.4 Transaction IV – Transfer Subject to Performance Guarantees

This might occur if a company guaranteed the creditworthiness of customer receivables in a factoring contract. These types of arrangements are considered further in section 5 on working capital finance.

4 Recognition of Another Financial Asset/Liability after Derecognition

As discussed in transactions two and four above, where derecognition occurs another financial asset or liability may be recognised. In order to do this the following entry would be made:

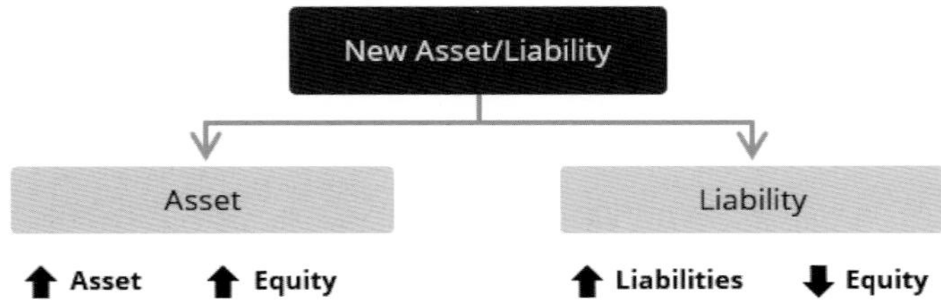

Example

Duplex Inc. transfers an amount of receivables to Culture Inc. for a cash payment. Duplex guarantees the payments from the customers if receipts are below a certain level.

Entries:

- Duplex Inc. will derecognise the receivables.
- Culture Inc. will recognise the receivables.
- Guarantee is recognised as a financial liability in Duplex Inc. (contingent liability).
- Guarantee is a financial asset for Culture Inc.

Analysis Focus

If the market is misled, as it seems to have been in some cases, then it clearly cannot value off balance sheet finance properly. Where it is not misled, and the evidence of financial guarantees is in the notes to the accounts, experience suggests that the market will treat the liability as if it were consolidated, as happens with operating leases.

5 Working Capital Finance

Working capital finance covers a broad range of different arrangements all related to accelerating the receipt of cash to aid funding working capital needs. It includes factoring, receivables financing and reverse factoring. The accounting disclosures on these arrangements are often opaque and so they are difficult to unpick. There is evidence to suggest that the use of these techniques is increasing, which heightens the concern that significant amounts of leverage remain unrecognised on corporate balance sheets.

5.1 Factoring

A factoring arrangement would involve the following common features:

- A company has $100m outstanding customer balances (accounts receivable) with a maturity of (say) 90 days.
- A company could raise finance by 'selling' these receivable balances to a factor (e.g. financial institution).
- The company would receive $100m net of a fee from the factor.
- The customer would then settle the invoice directly to the factor.

The fee charged by the factor could include:

- Administrative costs
- Financing costs
- Bad debt protection costs
- Arrangement fees (may be a one off)

There are two fundamental forms of factoring as illustrated below:

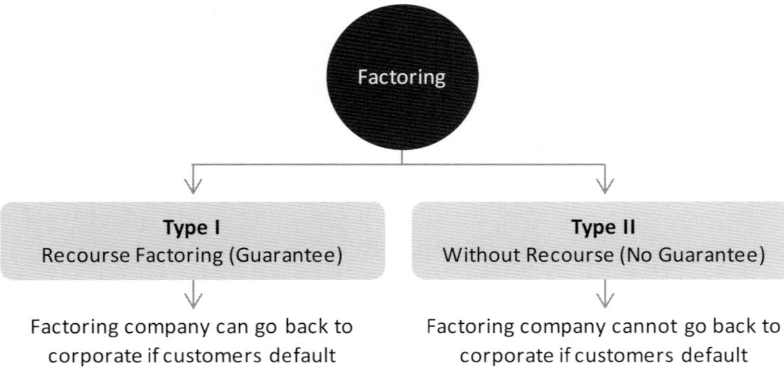

In type I, full recourse factoring, the risk remains with the company, whereas in the second type there appears to be a genuine transfer of risk to the factor. IFRS guidance indicates that, in general terms, Type I factoring does not require derecognition whereas typically Type II would require derecognition.

However, the situation can be clouded somewhat if receivables are transferred but there is some residual guarantee made by the seller (e.g. compensation for late payment, factor only responsible for a limited amount of bad debts). We refer to this as 'partial recourse'. In this case, the guidance is unclear. It appears to suggest that the accounts receivable balances should be derecognised in most of these cases. However, if it can be shown that the company and the factor share the risks then 'continuing involvement' accounting would be appropriate. In this case receivables would no longer be recorded on the company's balance sheet but a 'continuing involvement' asset and liability would be recognised to capture the bad debts that the company remains liable for under the arrangement.

5.2 Reverse Factoring

Reverse factoring differs from the above arrangements in that:

- Normally initiated by the customer rather than company (supplier).
- Financing costs are not necessarily borne by the company (supplier) (even given they are the principal beneficiaries of the arrangement). They can be shared or borne by either party to the arrangement.

These arrangements are often led by large corporates with a multitude of small suppliers. These small companies could not necessarily afford the costs of factoring and so it helps these companies manage their working capital.

5.3 Impact on Key Financial Metrics[16]

Arrangement	Receivable Days	Payable days	EBIT/Interest cost	Net debt/EBITDA
Full recourse	=	=	LOWER	HIGHER
Non-recourse	LOWER	=	LOWER	=
Reverse factoring	=	Depends on arrangements	Depends on arrangements	=

[16] Both full recourse and non-recourse are from the supplying company's perspective whereas reverse factoring is from the customer's.

6 Special Purpose Entities (SPEs)

SPEs have achieved significant notoriety in the media especially given the actions of, for example, Enron and Elan Corporation.

6.1 Why Use SPEs?

Advantages can accrue by using a separate company to undertake the activity (e.g. borrowing). Often SPEs can conveniently hide gearing.

Example

Airport Engine Manufacturer 1 (AEM_1) and AEM_2 decide to set up a joint venture (SPE) to undertake research and development work on a new audio resistant jet engine casing. Both companies invest €100m in the venture.

The structure can be shown as follows:

The SPE then borrows €1,000m from a bank. The structure now looks like:

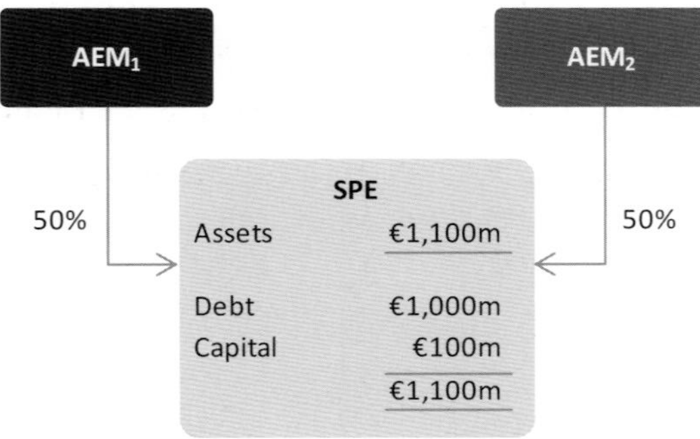

In order to borrow these funds, AEM_1 and AEM_2 were required to provide guarantees:

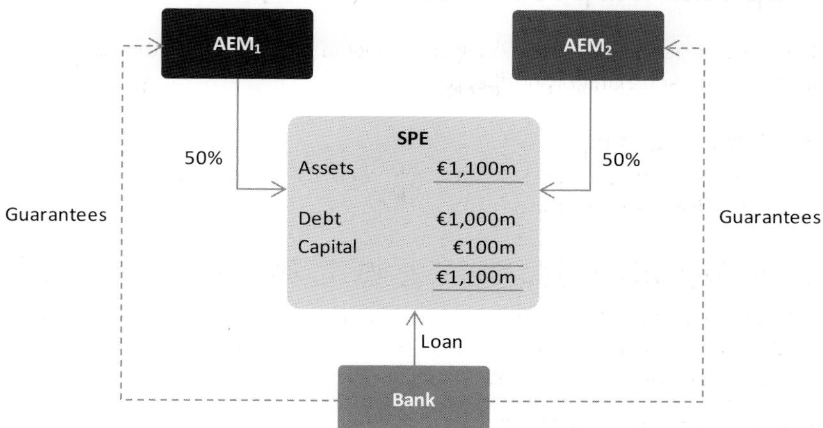

How is this reflected in AEM_1 and AEM_2 accounts? Assuming the equity method is used then the investment in AEM_1 and AEM_2 is shown in fixed assets as:

		€
	Cost of investment	0
+	Change in net assets (50% × 0)	
		0

Even if it had net assets there would be no explicit recognition of the debt element.

The crucial issue is what is an SPE, that does not meet the definition of a subsidiary but is under the direct or indirect control (or quasi-control) of an enterprise. SIC-12 addresses the treatment of SPEs. The following two points are relevant:

- A SPE can be a corporate entity, trust, partnership or unincorporated entity.
- An entity may transact with a SPE. If so, then that entity may, in substance, control the SPE.

Under IFRS, establishing if an enterprise controls a particular entity (in this case SPE) is a matter of judgement depending on the facts in each case. However, SIC-12 lists certain circumstances that may indicate an entity does indeed control a SPE.

- The activities of the SPE are being conducted on behalf of the sponsoring entity.
- The sponsoring entity has, by whatever means, the decision-making power to obtain the majority of the benefits of the SPE.
- The sponsoring entity retains the majority of the residual or ownership risks of SPE.

The following article provides a little bit of historical context. Off balance sheet vehicles appear to have been central to what happened at Enron. Many of these problems arose specifically from the non-consolidation of these SPEs.

Enron – How the Fraud Worked

The full details of what happened at Enron have yet to emerge. But bits and pieces of the picture have come out over the past few months, and while some of this is anecdote and hearsay, it all seems to fit together. There is enough available now at least to paint a rough picture of how Enron managed to rig its accounts.

A good place to start is Enron's published annual report, for the year 31 December 2000. Sadly, a fraudulent set of accounts does not carry a big red warning label stuck on the cover, but with the benefit of hindsight one or two points in these accounts stand out.

First, Enron's turnover was growing at a fantastic rate. This was largely because it had significantly changed the nature of its business during the year. While its turnover in 1999 was $40bn, not only did its turnover in 2000rise to $101bn, but in the last quarter alone it reported turnover of $41bn – more than in the whole of the previous year. What happened was that during the year Enron had gone heavily into market-making in energy – buying and selling wholesale contracts, including derivatives. Activities of this sort, what Enron refers to as 'Wholesale Services', can easily generate astronomical turnover figures without anything ever actually being delivered. Looking at the turnover numbers alone, therefore can give a completely misleading view of the company's size. What is in substance a small company can, if it adds together all the deals that it's done as 'turnover', appear very large.

Enron was not a small company, but the changing nature of its business meant it had a turnover figure that mislead as to both its size and its rate of growth. This had its uses. The apparently rapid growth rate fuelled its image as a dynamic company. And the huge turnover figure earned it number seven place in the Fortune 500. Hence all the reports that described Enron as the 'seventh biggest company in America'. It was nothing of the sort if you look at any other criteria – profitability or capital employment, for example – but the label was useful to a business that relied increasingly on its image. What could be more solid or dependable than a Fortune top 10 company?

It's also worth noting at this stage (a) that Enron's total profit for the year was $979m and (b) it's statement that 'Contracts associated with [Wholesale Services] are accounted for using the mark-to-market method of accounting' – more on that in a moment.

'Other operating activities'

In the cash flow statement, in the section that reconciles 'net income' (ie, profit) with 'net cash provided by operating activities', there are several features of interest. In spite of its extraordinary growth in turnover, the company managed to reduce its working capital by $1.769bn – the opposite of what one would expect and a tribute to the company's management skills, no doubt. Then there is an item, contributing $1.113bn to cash flow, simply described as 'other operating activities'. What on earth is this? And what is it doing in reconciliation between profits and cash flows? Then there is an item labelled 'net assets from price risk management activities', which contributes a negative $763m in the reconciliation.

At least this item makes sense. The price risk management activities are the Wholesale Services that we saw earlier, and which we have been told are valued on a mark-to-market basis. The $763m represents the additional net assets created in Enron's accounts by making these contracts up to market value, and appears in reconciliation because, while it's included in the company's profit, it's not cash, it's simply a revaluation amount. So we now know that $763m profit comes from writing up the value of its contracts.

In view of the importance that marking-to-market has for Enron's profits, it's worth taking a look at the accounting polices note on the subject. These say: 'The market prices used to value these transactions reflect management's best estimate considering various factors including closing exchange and over-the-counter quotations, time value and volatility factors underlying the commitments'. This is very odd. In an active market trading a commodity (energy) or derivatives of a commodity, there isn't a lot of doubt about what the market price is. Different trader may briefly quote marginally different prices, but not by very much – if they're still going to be in business the next day. So how does 'management's best estimate' come into it? One can only imagine the intense grilling on this point that the stock market analysts must have given Enron's director.

The real fraud

Having got that much from the published accounts, we need to abandon them and get down to the real fraud. As everybody knows, unconsolidated 'special purpose entitles' or SPEs lie at the heart of the story. There were a vast number of them – reports vary from 3,500 to 4,300 – and they had a variety of uses. One of their lesser purposes was simply to transfer money into the hands of Enron executives in the shape of 'fees'. Andrew Fastow, the company's chief financial officer, received at least $30m in this way. Another executive, Michael Kopper (and a friend who he brought into the feast), received at least $10m. The other received $1m each and two more received payments amounting to hundreds of thousands of dollars.

But for Enron the SPEs served far more important purposes. According to an Enron report filed with the US Securities and Exchange Commission after the company's collapse, the SPEs allowed Enron 'to conceal from the market very large losses' by giving the appearance that key exposures were hedged with third parties. In fact, the third parties were Enron's SPEs, and in substance they were merely extension of Enron. The SEC filing puts these losses at about $1bn.

By trading with SPEs, Enron could also generate profits and cash that appeared directly in its own accounts. Trading with the SPEs had indirect benefits too. The prices set in the deals could be taken as 'market prices' that Enron then used to revalue other contracts in its own accounts, helping to generate the $763m we saw earlier. Enron also apparently entered into long-term energy supply contracts that it would then mark to market, effectively taking credit now for the value of contracts that would be fulfilled over a number of years in the future. It has been alleged that Enron started doing this early in the 1990s.

How much Enron lost in the SPEs is unclear, but one estimate is that it managed to hide $40bn liabilities in these 'independent' entities. Enron managed to persuade major banks to put large sums into the SPEs, which could then flow into Enron itself and into accounts. Persuading the banks does not seem to have been terribly difficult, as they market SPEs to companies as a matter of course. They naturally wanted security for the money they put into the SPEs, but Enron supplied the necessary guarantees backed by its own highly-rated shares.

The banks which received hundreds of millions dollar of fees from Enron, also employed the analysts who encouraged others to invest in the company and keep its stock price up. Dissenting analysts were moved on to other work or left the bank. So possibly the directors weren't grilled that hard about the oddities in the accounts.

The high share price also provided a useful source of remuneration for Enron's directors. Between May 2000 and August 2011, Chairman Kenneth Lay sold stock worth $38m, CEO Jeffery Skilling realised $15m and Lou Pai a divisional CEO, made $63m from share sales.

The great thing about the SPEs, the whole point of them in fact, was that if you set them up right, they stayed off balance sheet under US GAAP. Unaccountably, Enron made some technical errors on some of the SPEs, which meant that they should have been on balance sheet. When this was discovered, Enron had to disclose a $1.2bn write-off against shareholders' funds. Its share price was already in trouble following Skilling's resignation last August 'for personal reasons' and a botched presentation to analysts of poor third quarter results. The SPEs disclosures destroyed what remained of the market's confidence. And as confidence in the company and its share price was what kept the house of cards standing, it collapsed.

Where were the auditors while all this was going on? The answer appears to be that they genuinely believed, or perhaps more accurately, succeeded in convincing themselves that Enron's accounts met the requirements of US GAAP. When last autumn Enron itself admitted that some of its SPEs should have been consolidated. Andersen's reaction was to admit that in at least one case its judgement was wrong. But Andersen also claimed that Enron had not supplied it with all the information it needed to make the right judgments. Enron has denied this.

Evidence emerging from various US investigations of Enron shows that there was internal debate at Andersen about certain SPEs and that doubts were expressed about their accounting treatment. In an apparent repetition of the pattern at Enron's banks, doubters at Andersen were taken off the case. This does not mean that Andersen colluded in a gigantic accounting fraud. More likely, either it did not see the big picture or perhaps thought the big picture was irrelevant as long as Enron complied with the detailed requirements of US GAAP.

Brian Singleton-Green

Reproduced with kind permission of Accountancy Magazine

Chapter 15: Accounting for Employee Benefits and Pension Obligations

"Money is better than poverty, if only for financial reasons." [17]

[17] A Woody Allen quote! It does not really mean a great deal and yet it conveys much. For a variety of reasons, society has decided that measurement is everything, a subtext to the Allen quip.

1 Introduction

IAS 19 *Employee Benefits* addresses a wide range of accounting issues associated with compensating employees. Most compensation schemes are very straight forward and do not in reality require an accounting standard as such. Bonuses, profit sharing and similar arrangements merely require the application of the matching (or accruals) concepts. This involves allocating the compensation to the appropriate accounting period. This will generally be the period in which the services were rendered by the employee. The one area of potential complexity relates to compensation schemes that involve equity compensation benefits (e.g. stock options) and those that include certain types of pension benefit.

2 Equity Compensation Benefits – Stock Options

IFRS 2 *Share-based Payment* addresses this issue.

The key issues relating to stock options from an accounting perspective are:

- What is the compensation charge to be recognised in the income statement?
- What is the impact on diluted EPS?

This section addresses both issues.

Compensation Charge

IFRS 2 requires that stock option compensation is fair valued and charged to the income statement over the vesting period. This is broadly consistent with the treatment under US GAAP.

In the rare cases that fair value cannot be reliably determined, both IFRS and US GAAP allow the use of intrinsic value. However, the value must be remeasured regularly until settlement date.

Intrinsic Value Approach

The intrinsic value of a stock option is calculated as:

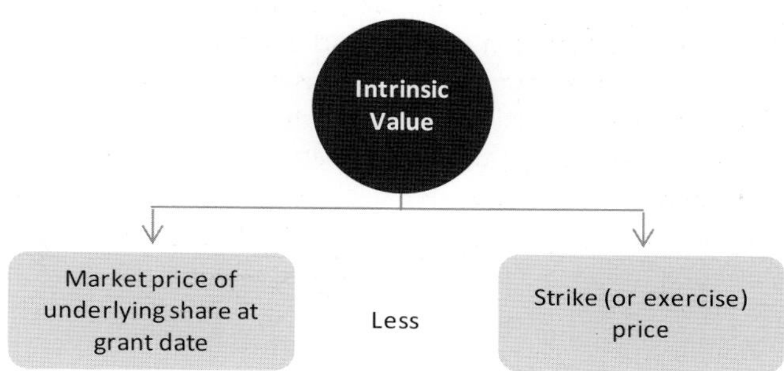

So, if a share is trading in the market at €5 and an option offers the holder the right to buy it for €4, then this option has an intrinsic value of €1. Options with intrinsic value are termed **in the money**. If the right to buy (strike or exercise price) is the same as the current market price, then the option is said to be **at the money**. If the market price is lower than the strike, it is called an **out of the money** option. Intrinsic value can never be negative, it is just zero.

Historically, this option was favoured by companies. This is because it is easy to ensure that intrinsic value equals zero, and therefore no expense is recognised upfront. However, in practice this option is now rarely used since it is presumed that a fair value can be estimated using one of a number of options pricing methodologies.

Fair Value Approach

The intrinsic value approach fails to recognise that options have more than intrinsic value. Even if an option is out of the money, its price could rise and bring it into the money. This other element of value is termed **time value**. The normal method of calculating the fair value of an option is to use Black Scholes model.

$$C_t=N(d_1) \times S_t\text{-}N(d_2) \times Xe^{-r(T-t)}$$

where:

N = Cumulative normal distribution function

(T – t) = Time to maturity of time option

S = Spot price of underlying asset

X = Strike price of the option

r = Risk free rate

σ = Volatility of returns on underlying asset

$$d_1 = \frac{\ln\left(\frac{S_t}{X}\right) + (r + 0.5\sigma^2)(T\text{-}t)}{\sigma\sqrt{T\text{-}t}}$$

$$d_2 = d_1 - \sigma\sqrt{T\text{-}t}$$

This is a fairly daunting formula! For our purposes, we merely need to appreciate that Black Scholes provides a means of ascertaining the fair value of an option and has six key inputs:

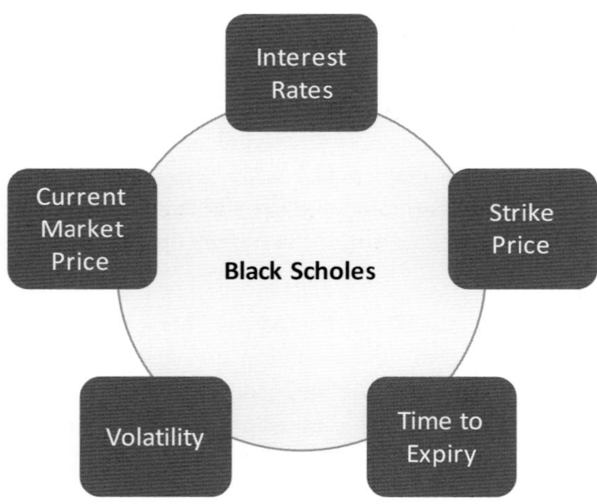

IFRS 2 does not require the use of any specific valuation approach for stock options. However, it does outline the advantages of the binomial lattice approach.

US companies have been keen to adopt more conservative accounting policies in order to reassure investors. A number of significant US corporations have chosen to adopt the fair value approach. These include Boeing, Coca-Cola and The Washington Post.

A few simple examples will illustrate the fair value approach enunciated in IFRS 2.

Example 1

- Johnson Plc gives 2000 options to a member of staff.
- The options have a strike price of €5. The current market price is €5.
- The options are given to the staff member in return for his services.
- The vesting period is three years.
- A Black Scholes model of the option would produce a fair value per option of €3.

Total Options	**2,000**
Value (at fair value)	€6,000
Vesting period	3 years
Annual charge to EBIT	€2,000

Note that in the example above, the vesting period is the period between option grant date and vesting date.

The Vesting Period

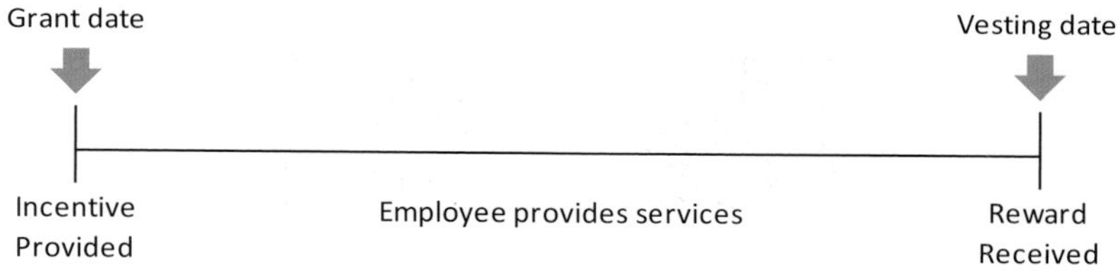

Example 2

A corporate grants 100 share options to each of its 500 employees (50,000 options). The vesting period is three years and binomial lattice model of the option gives a fair value of €15. The expectation is that 20% of employees will leave over the period and therefore the forfeiture rate is 20%.

Year	Calculation	Expense	Cumulative Expense
1	[50,000 × 80% × €15] × 1/3	€200,000	€200,000
2	[[50,000 × 80% × €15] × 2/3] – 200,000	€200,000	€400,000
3	[50,000 × 80% × €15] – 400,000	€200,000	€600,000

Example 3

If the forfeiture estimate changes as time progresses, then the company will make adjustments in each year to ensure the overall result is up to date on a cumulative basis.

The example is as above, except:

- In Year 1, 20 people leave and the company reassesses its estimated forfeiture rate at 15%.
- In Year 2, a further 22 employees leave and the company reassesses the forfeiture rate at 12%.
- In Year 3, a further 15 employees leave meaning that over the three years, 57 employees left.

So eventually 44,300 (443 employees at 100 options each) options vest at the end of Year 3.

Year	Calculation	Expense	Cumulative Expense
1	[50,000 × 85% × €15] × 1/3	€212,500	€212,500
2	[[50,000 × 88% × €15] × 2/3] – 212,500	€227,500	€440,000
3	[50,000 × 88.6% × €15] – 440,000	€224,500	€664,500

How are Options Reflected in Diluted EPS?

IAS 33 *Earnings per Share* states that the treasury stock method should be used. Numerical examples are included in Chapter 6. The key point to note is that options are only reflected under this method if they are in the money. Out of the money or at the money options are not included at all. Therefore, there is potential for 'latent dilution'.

Should Stock Options be Expensed?

Irrespective of what SFAS 123 or IFRS 2 states there is no unanimity about whether options should be expensed. The following table illustrates some of the closely balanced arguments.

Argument in favour of expensing stock options	Argument against expensing stock options
▪ Do not get something for nothing! ▪ Comparable EBIT (to cash bonus paying companies) ▪ Dilution of ordinary shareholders so it is a cost from their perspective	▪ Already in DEPS ▪ Not a cash flow ▪ Merely a redistribution of wealth

Types of Pension Fund and Associated Terminology

3 Introduction

Providing retirement benefits for employees is a significant cost for many firms. In addition to this high cost there may also be a high level of uncertainty associated with the ultimate liability and, hence, how it should be funded. Whether this latter point is an issue depends upon the type of pension scheme.

In relation to financial reporting, there are two key issues:

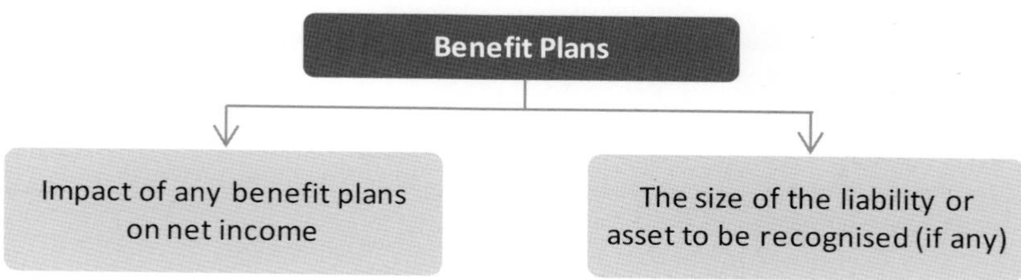

4 Pension Terminology

There are various forms of pension schemes but, in essence, there are two major categories:

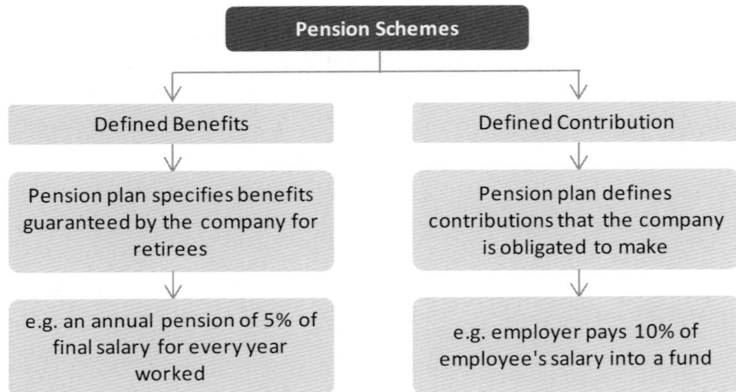

The key impact of the two schemes rests in the residual liability facing the employee. The nature of defined contribution schemes is such that, once the fixed percentage of salary is paid into the fund, the company has no further liability. This is not the case with defined benefit schemes where the residual risk rests with the employer.

Defined Contribution Plans

5 Accounting Issues

5.1 Effect on Income Statement and Balance Sheet

There are few, if any, accounting complications with defined contribution schemes. IAS 19 simply requires the following:

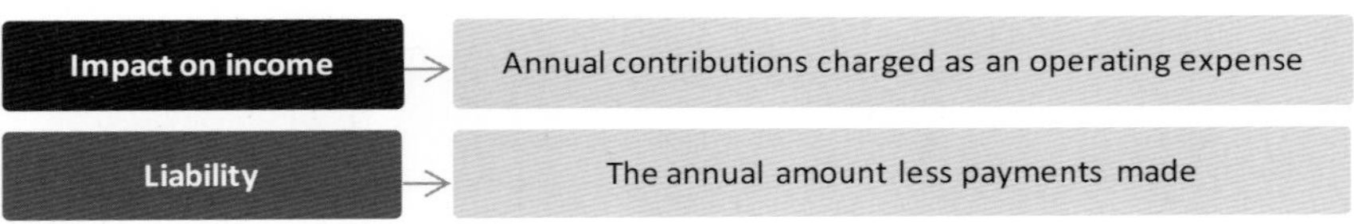

In a similar manner to wages and salaries, as contributions are normally paid monthly there will often be no residual liability.

Defined Benefit Plans

6 Background and Context

These are much more problematic. The first issue of confusion emanates from the fact that such schemes may be funded or unfunded. In the US and the UK, it is mandatory for defined benefit plans to be funded. This means that any contributions that the actuary determines are necessary must be made to a separate funding vehicle. Therefore, a scheme will have both a fund (i.e. the equities, bonds and cash invested to satisfy future obligations) and an obligation (i.e. amounts to be paid to employees on retirement). The difference between the actuaries' current estimation of the fund and obligation can either be a deficit or surplus. In other jurisdictions, there is no funding requirement (e.g. Germany and Japan). Therefore, there is only an obligation with such schemes, and the assets are part of the corporate's assets.

7 Deficits and Surpluses

7.1 The Variables

The level of funding required for a defined benefits pension plan is determined by the actuary. The actuary will base his estimate on forecasts of various factors such as:

- Salary levels.
- Retirement age.
- Life expectancy.
- Employee turnover.
- Investment performance of the fund's assets.
- Level of benefits guaranteed.

Due to the difficulty of forecasting such variables, deficits (under funding) and surpluses (over funding), commonly arise on defined benefit plans.

For example, for a funded scheme the relevant deficit or surplus could be ascertained by comparing the current market value of the plan assets ('fair value') with the present value of the obligations. This can be illustrated as follows:

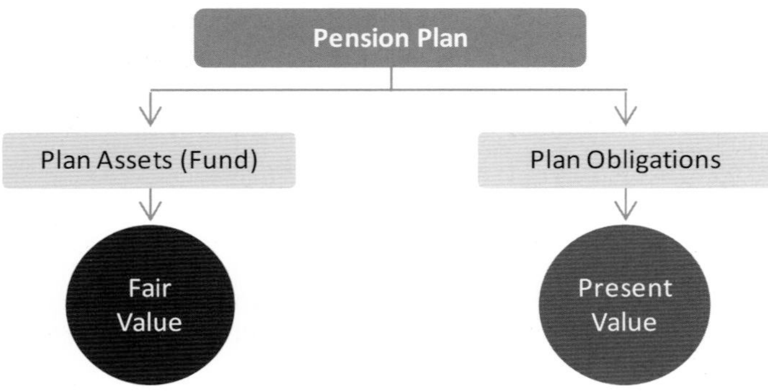

Over/Under Funding

The funded status of any pension plan can be identified by comparing the balance of plan assets with the obligation (e.g. PBO).

Plan assets > PBO = *over* funding	→	Net asset position
Plan assets < PBO = *under* funding	→	Net liability position

8 The Two Elements: Benefit Obligations and Pension Plan Assets

A defined benefit scheme consists of two elements – the obligation and the plan assets. The following sections examine the approaches to establishing and measuring both.

9 Pension Obligations

9.1 Types of Obligation

The level of salary at retirement has a significant impact on the ultimate defined benefit plan obligation. There are two alternative approaches to estimating this.

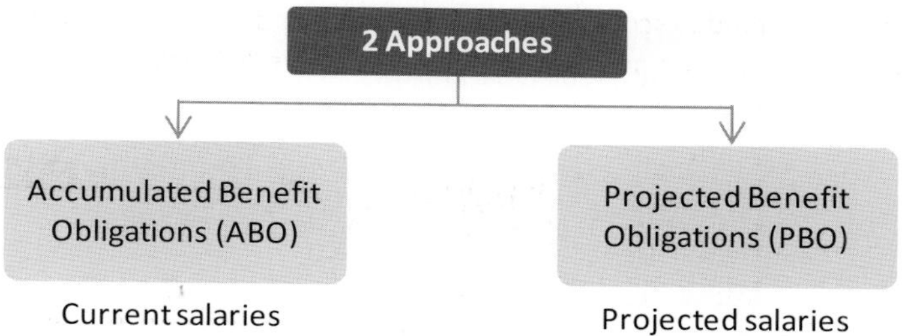

Current salaries

Projected salaries

Note

- IAS 19 uses the term DBO (defined benefit obligation) but this is the same as the more widely used PBO.
- ABO and PBO are identical in schemes not related to pay (flat benefit plans).
- Both of these measures are based on present values and hence each measure is very sensitive to the discount rate used. The required discount rate is that for a high-quality corporate bond of equivalent maturity and currency. IAS 19 suggests a corporate bond with an AA (so called double 'A' rating).
- IAS 19 requires the application of the PBO approach. However, under US GAAP, despite the fact that PBO is required, the ABO is important for establishing what is known as the minimum liability. This is examined in a later section of the chapter.

9.2 The Calculation of the PBO

The benefit obligation can be calculated as follows. Remember IAS 19 requires the use of the PBO.

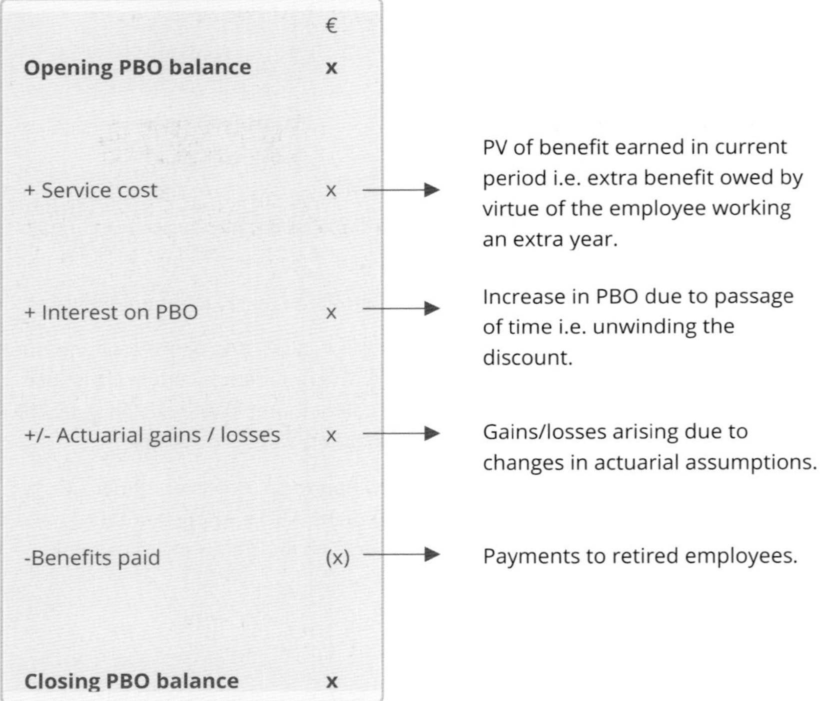

9.3 Pension Plan Assets

This can be calculated as the assets at the start of the year plus returns and contributions less the payments to pensions.

	€
Opening balance of plan assets	X
+ Return on plan assets	X
+ Contributions	X
– Benefits paid out	(X)
Closing balance of plan assets	X

10 Accounting for Defined Benefit Plans

10.1 Overview

A defined benefit pension scheme will be reflected in the financials as follows:

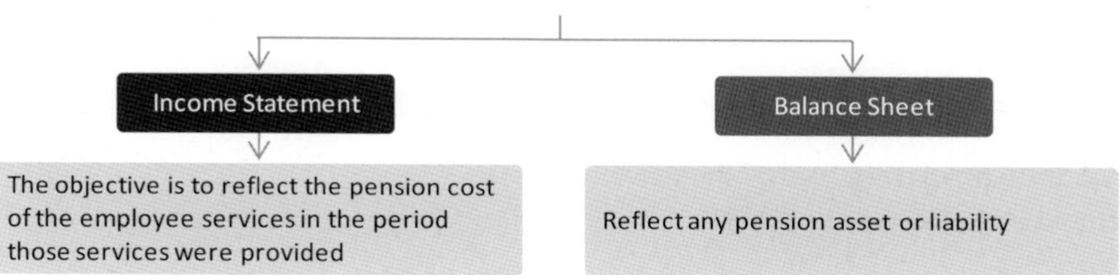

10.2 Income Statement Charge

The actual cost of providing a defined benefit scheme in any year will be the increase in the obligation minus the increase in the fund assets. This concept is reflected in the income statement calculation below.

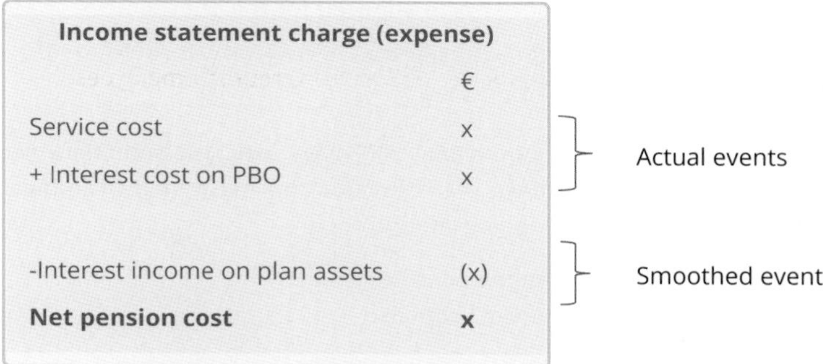

Income statement charge (expense)	€	
Service cost	x	Actual events
+ Interest cost on PBO	x	
-Interest income on plan assets	(x)	Smoothed event
Net pension cost	**x**	

The interest cost on the PBO less the interest income on plan assets is referred to as the net interest cost. The net interest cost is generally included within finance costs whilst the service cost is included in operating costs (in EBIT).

Notes:

- The interest income on plan assets is a 'smoothed' number rather than representing the actual return on fund assets (as this will be volatile from one year to another). It is calculated by applying the discount rate used to determine the PBO to the value of the pension assets.

- Under US GAAP (and until relatively recently under IFRS), the income statement charge includes the expected return on plan assets, rather than the interest income on plan assets. This is calculated using management's expectation of the rate of return that the plan assets will generate each year. The IFRS switched to the interest income number because of a concern that management could 'game' the assumption to boost earnings.

11 Balance Sheet Asset/Liability

11.1 Computation of Asset/Liability

The balance sheet asset or liability is calculated thus:

	€
PV of future obligation (i.e. the PBO)	X
– Fair value of plan assets	(X)
+ Effect of asset ceiling	X
Pension liability/ (asset)	X

Essentially, this is the funding status of the plan adjusted for the effects of the asset ceiling (discussed below).

11.2 The Asset Ceiling

If the fair value of the plan assets exceeds the PBO, IFRS may restrict the potential asset that can be recognised in the balance sheet. This restriction applies where the company cannot access the benefits of surplus funding either through:

(i) A refund of contributions from the pension fund.
(ii) A reduction in future pension contributions.

Therefore, where a company has a surplus in its pension fund, this might not be reflected in full in balance sheet assets.

Special Case for Asset Ceiling Increasing the Pension Liability

The asset ceiling can also apply even where the fair value of the plan assets does not exceed the PBO today. This special case occurs if a contractually agreed funding plan is in place that, when added to the fair value of the plan assets, would exceed the current value of the PBO.

If this arises and the company cannot access the benefits of any future surplus (as described above), then the value of the pension liability on the balance sheet is increased, to reflect the present value of the contractually agreed funding plan.

12 Impact of Key Variables

The following table illustrates the impact of changes to key assumptions on the balance sheet liability.

Impact of changes on key accounting variables:

Assumptions Underlying Pension Accounting						
Variable	**Disclosed in Financial Statements**	**Pension Accounting Elements**				
		Pension Cost	**ABO**	**PBO***	**FV of Plan Assets**	**Plan Status**
Discount rate increase	Yes	Decrease	Decrease	Decrease	-	Improved
Rate of compensation increase	Yes	Increase	-	Increase	-	Dis-improved

* Called DBO in IAS 19

13 Comprehensive Example

Lamy Plc has the following disclosures in its notes regarding its pension fund on 1 January 2017:

	€
Pension fund assets (@ fair value)	10,000,000
Pension fund liabilities (@ present value)	(10,600,000)
	(400,000)

The following information relates to the year ended 31 December 2017:

Current service cost	€900,000
Contributions to the fund	€1,020,000
Pensions paid	€500,000
Actual return on assets	€400,000

The present value of liabilities at 31 December 2017 is estimated to be €11,000,000. The relevant discount rate is 5%.

Required

What would be the treatment under IAS 19?

Solution

Income Statement	**€**
Service cost	900,000
+ Net interest cost (W2)	30,000
	830,000

Balance Sheet Liability	**€**
PV of future obligation	(11,000,000)
– FV of plan assets (W1)	10,920,000
	(80,000)

W1 Fund Assets	**€**
Opening balance	10,000,000
+ Actual return	400,000
+ Contributions paid	1,020,000
– Pensions paid	(500,000)
	10,920,000

W2 Net Interest Cost	**€**
Interest cost on PBO	530,000
Interest income on plan assets	(500,000)
Net interest cost	(30,000)

14 Analysis

14.1 The Considerations in Analysis

In an environment where there is a shortage of highly skilled and experienced staff, pension benefits can be used as a means of attracting employees. However, offering generous pension terms can be very expensive. Therefore, analysts will want to closely examine the underlying assumptions and status of the plan. Such analysis may well involve going beyond the financial statements data and adjusting the financials.

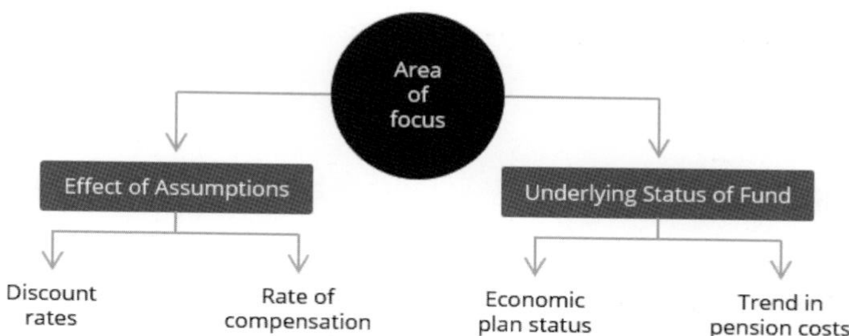

One of the key problems for analysts is the significant amount of 'netting off' that occurs under IAS 19. Given the smoothing nature of some of these numbers, there is an argument that, if the numbers are significant, some level of disaggregation should be undertaken by the analyst. Typical adjustments that might be made would include:

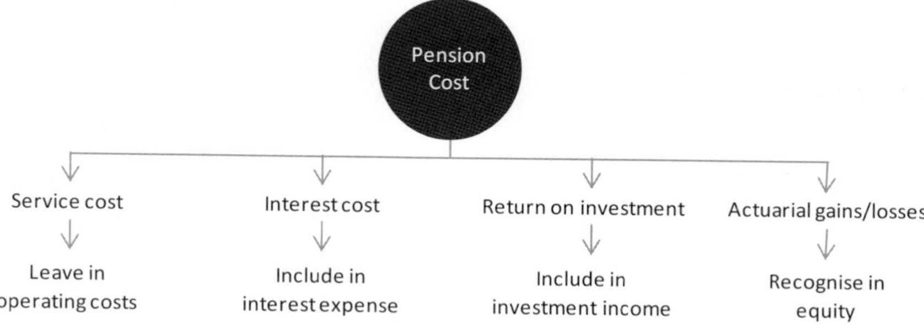

Analysis Focus

Valuing Pension Obligations

There are two elements to the correct treatment of pensions – the balance sheet and future free cash flows. Unfunded or under-funded pensions (measured using PBO) should be deducted from the value of the assets alongside debt. They represent a loan from employees to the company. But, if the pension is unfunded, then future profits will also incorporate a provision for future liabilities. This cannot be ignored in valuations. Free cash flow should exclude the pension service charge, even though this will be shown in the accounts as a non-cash item.

15 Overview

15.1 Summary of Issues

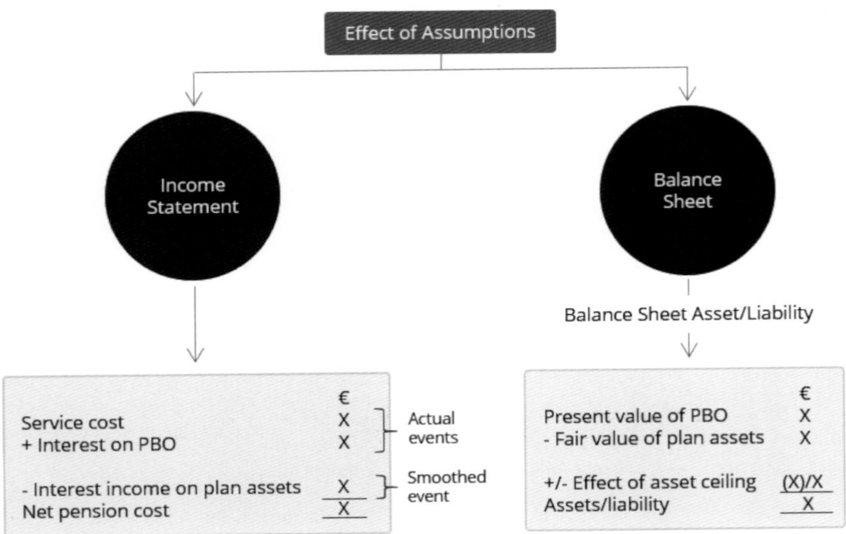

Accounts Commentary

Note 32 on page 140 details the make-up of pension provisions. The pension schemes are far and away the largest provision here and this note provides lots of detail on these schemes.

There is a suite of tables that provide the information, and these are provided in turn in the note. Perhaps the most salient table is the reconciliation of funded status on the left-hand side of page 143. This includes:

- PV of funded obligations, i.e. the PV of the PBO
- Plan assets – recorded at fair value
- PV of unfunded obligations, i.e. the PV of the PBO for those schemes where there is no fund set up to pay the employees

Another next key note is the calculation of the pension expense on page 144. This mainly consists of the four key components outlined in the chapter.

The actuarial assumptions on page 145 are useful for comparing companies and getting a feel for the adequacy of the numbers.

Chapter 16: Accounting for Banks

"A bank is a place that will lend you money if you prove you don't need it" [18]

[18] Bob Hope gets the credit (no pun intended) for this one. The financial crisis, which happened well after Bob's passing, turned this on its head as loans were written to people that did not need them, often did not really want them and, as it sadly transpired, had almost no hope of paying them back.

1 Introduction

Why are banks different from industrial companies? And why do they deserve a specific chapter in this book?

Banks are involved in a very specific form of business:

- In the most traditional form, banks collect deposits from individuals and other providers and lend these funds to corporations to finance their growth, i.e. they intermediate the flow of funds from providers to users and make money on the interest spread between deposits and loans. On the other hand, industrial companies invest in property, plant and equipment, inventories and people to be able to provide goods and services to their customers.
- Property, plant and equipment and working capital hardly play any role in the case of banks, being dwarfed by, for example, loans as the major assets. Similarly, whereas it makes sense in the case of industrial companies to separate operations (providing goods and services) from financing activities (debt and equity), the same does not apply in the case of banks. Banks make money both from the asset and the liability side of their balance sheet and, in particular, depositors are not only providers of finance but also customers of banks. Therefore, operating and financing activities cannot easily be split in the case of banks.
- For these reasons, financial statements of banks look very different from those of industrial companies and need to be interpreted differently.

Banks are subject to specific regulation, which is more stringent than that applicable to industrial companies:

- Banks are the key source of credit for both corporations and individuals and without a properly functioning financial sector, overall economic growth would grind to a halt.
- Governments, aware of the importance of the sector, subject banks to very strict supervision and regulation aimed at minimising the risk of bank failures.

As financial markets have become increasingly global, banks have been at the centre of continuous reform and harmonisation of both their accounting and regulatory treatment:

- The introduction of IFRS 9 on 1 January 2018 has had a significant impact on the accounts of banks, by changing the classification and measurement of their financial assets and financial liabilities.
- The ongoing introduction of new banking regulations, Basel III, in response to the financial crisis of 2007-09. Like their predecessor regulations, Basel I and Basel II, these regulations are internationally agreed minimum standards and were developed by the Basel Committee on Banking Supervision. The implementation started in 2013 and will be completed by 1 January 2019.

This Chapter examines a typical detailed balance sheet and income statement of a large European Bank. Each key area of the balance sheet and income statement is examined and contrasted with that of an industrial company.

2 Consolidated Financial Statements

The key components of banks' financial statements are:

- The balance sheet
- The income statement
- The statement of changes in equity
- Notes to the consolidated accounts
- The cash flow statement

3 Overall Structure of the Balance Sheet

In its most basic form, a bank balance sheet can be summarised as follows:

Assets	**Liabilities and Equity**
Cash	Deposits
	Other financial liabilities
Loans	Miscellaneous liabilities
	Subordinated debt
Other financial assets	Non-controlling ('minority') interests
Miscellaneous assets	Equity

A bank raises funds through deposits, other financial liabilities and equity capital (i.e. shareholders' equity and non-controlling interests) and uses them to lend, invest in financial assets and cash. Similarly, to the balance sheet of industrial companies, banks' assets and liabilities should be ranked by decreasing liquidity.

4 Balance Sheet Description

BNP Paribas - At 30 June 2018[19]	**(€ m)**
Cash and balances at central banks	211,441
Financial assets at fair value through profit and loss	709,239
Hedging derivatives	11,750
Financial assets at fair value through equity	52,784
Financial assets at amortised cost	841,664
Financial investments of insurance activities	233,617
Accrued income and other assets	102,346
Equity method investments	5,787
Property, plant and equipment and investment property	25,773
Intangible assets and goodwill	11,801
Other assets	28,283
Total assets	**2,234,485**
Deposits from central banks	5,948
Financial liabilities at fair value through profit and loss	717,012
Hedging derivatives	13,535
Financial liabilities at amortised cost	1,060,465
Accrued expenses and other liabilities	88,037
Technical reserves and other insurance liabilities	214,317
Provisions for contingencies and charges	10,236
Other liabilities	20,690
Shareholder' equity	98,711
Minority interest	5,534
Total liabilities and equity	**2,234,485**

[19] Note that we have condensed some line items from the published accounts to simplify the presentation

4.1 Cash and Balances at Central Banks

This category represents the most liquid assets of a bank; they generally have a maturity of less than 90 days from the date of acquisition and can be converted into cash at short notice and with limited cost. They represent a bank's first source of liquidity to satisfy cash demands from deposit withdrawals or applications for fresh loans. They would generally include deposits held with central banks and other banks, short term treasury bills and short-term money market deposits.

Valuation and Link with the P&L

Liquid assets should be accounted for at market value. They generate little or no interest income and are expensive to maintain because they need to be funded by deposits or share capital. In addition, cash has significant storing, transporting and custody costs. Therefore, banks would ordinarily try to maintain liquid assets at a minimum level.

However, Basel III contains new liquidity regulations (the liquidity coverage ratio is discussed later in this chapter) which has increased the proportion of liquid assets on a bank's balance sheet in recent years. In the case of BNP Paribas, this balance represents almost 10% of total assets.

4.2 Loans and Advances

Loans and advances sit within the 'Financial assets at amortised cost' category, representing 92% of this balance sheet caption. They incorporate two types of balance:

- Loans and advances to credit institutions.
- Loans and advances to customers.

Loans and advances to credit institutions can be further split into short-term deposits with other banks, loans to central banks, including the mandatory reserve requirement, and other loans to banks, including time deposits and repurchase agreements.

Banks maintain short-term deposits with banks located in foreign countries as part of their "correspondent banking" relationships. A bank needs a network of correspondent banks to offer its clients international payment services in countries where it is not directly present.

Banks are also required to maintain mandatory reserve deposits with the central banks of the countries in which they operate. In addition, central banks have the authority to demand higher reserve deposits to regulate money supply in the overall economy. Such mandatory reserves with central banks cannot be used by the bank in its day-to-day activity and therefore cannot be considered liquid resources.

Customer loans often represent the single largest asset of a banks' balance sheet. In the case of BNP Paribas, customer loans represent 33% of total assets.

Loans can be split according to different criteria, namely purpose or type of customers (mortgages v commercial loans), maturity (short vs. long term), or pricing terms (fixed vs. floating interest). One of the most important classifications is the quality of the counterparty, which determines credit risk exposure. Accordingly, there are:

- Performing loans, where there are no significant concerns about the credit quality of the counterparty.
- Under-performing loans are where the bank has observed a significant increase in the credit risk of the loan. This could be because a scheduled repayment is past due by more than 30 days or because of increased credit risk associated with the counterparty, instrument type or the geographical location of the borrower.
- Non-performing loans, where any scheduled repayment (interest or principal) is past due for more than 90 days. Non-performing loans also include restructured loans, i.e. when interest and principal repayments have been restructured to accommodate the borrower's deteriorated circumstances.

As explained below, the classification of the loans in each of these categories is a key driver in determining the calculation of credit loss provisions under IFRS 9 (also referred to as 'impairment provisions').

Valuation and Link with the P&L

1) Interest Income

Loans are recognised only after the credit is advanced to the borrower either with cash or with accreditation of the borrower's account. Once they are recorded, the income they generate is accounted for using the **amortised cost method**. For example, if a borrower pays some of the interest upfront, such interest is considered unearned because the borrower has not yet benefited from the use of the principal. Similarly, if interest accrues but is not yet paid, it is earned and can be recognised in the P&L. Over time, temporary discrepancies between accrued and paid interest disappear and eventually all accrued interest should be earned and paid (received).

Gross loan balances are recorded at **amortised cost**, i.e.

+	**Original Principal Amount** **(or price in the case of loans purchased in the secondary market)**
+	Accrued interest
-	Repaid interest and Principal
–	Write Offs (+ Writebacks)
=	**Gross loan balance**

- Any earned but unpaid interest (also called overdue interest) increases the carrying amount on the balance sheet
- If the loan becomes uncollectible, it needs to be written off the books

2) Credit Losses

A key risk for banks is when customers are unable to repay the full amount of principal or interest on a loan (referred to as 'credit losses').

The accounting rules provide banks with a framework for how (and when) they should recognise credit losses. IFRS 9 introduced significant changes to this framework in 2018 when it replaced IAS 39, as it forced banks to recognise credit losses as soon as they are expected, rather than waiting until the bank has evidence of the loss (e.g. late payment of interest of principal). This 'expected loss model' under IFRS 9 requires banks to recognise credit losses earlier in the credit cycle than under the previous standard.

IFRS 9 applies a staged approach to credit loss provisioning, as follows:

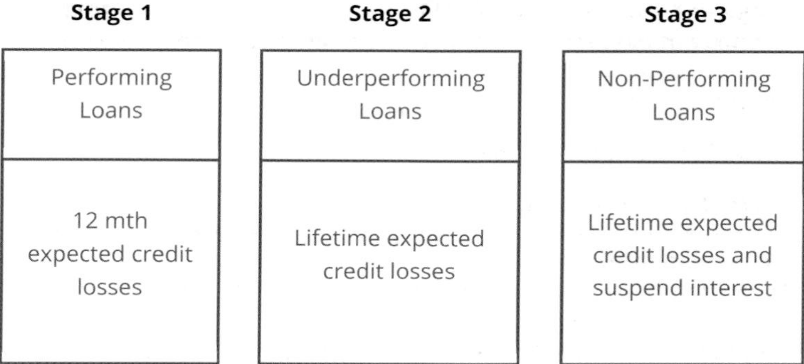

- Stage 1 is at origination of the loan. The bank recognises a provision for the credit losses that are expected if a loss event occurs in the next 12 months;
- Stage 2 occurs when there is a significant increase in the credit risk of the loan. The bank recognises a provision for all expected credit losses on the loan but interest income continues to be calculated on the gross loan balance; and
- Stage 3 occurs where there is evidence of impairment of the loan. The bank continues to recognise a provision for all expected credit losses on the loan, but interest income is now calculated on the net loan balance (this is sometimes referred to as 'suspending interest').

Loans are recorded at the **net realisable value**, defined as:

+	**Gross loan balance**
–	Provision for credit losses
=	**Net loan balance**

This reflects the conservatism concept.

When a bank incurs a credit loss, it has to reduce its P&L profit by a non-cash loan loss charge, which increases the provisions for loan losses, a contra-asset account reducing the net loan value on the balance sheet. A contra-asset account is merely a liability account that, instead of being recognised in liabilities, is set off against assets. Subsequently, if the loss materialises, the P&L is not further impacted.

Instead, gross loans are written off by the loss, the impairment provision for loan losses declines by the same amount and, therefore, the net loan carried on the balance sheet remains the same. If the loss does not materialise or is less than expected, then the net loan outstanding increases either with a writeback of the gross loan or with a reduction of the impairment provision for loan losses.

Loan loss impairments can be individual (specific) or portfolio level (generic). In the first case they cover the risk of individual loans defaulting because of deteriorated credit profile of the borrower, or because of deteriorated economic conditions in the country where the borrower operates. Portfolio allowances are created with lump-sum adjustments to performing loans. Again, there is a similarity with provisions against accounts receivable for industrial companies.

Whenever the risk of loss is removed, individual loan impairments must be reversed and loans must be written back, otherwise the bank is building hidden reserves, which could be used to manipulate profits in the future.

However, rating agencies and regulators monitor the ratio of loan loss provisions over gross loans outstanding and over non-performing loans (non-performing loan ratio) and expect banks to maintain a minimum level of provisions, as a safety margin.

Example

A bank has granted €10bn of loans. It already has a €50m credit loss provision. During the next year, the bank identifies further expected credit losses of €1m.

		(€m)
+	Gross loan balance	10,000
-	Credit loss provision	(51)
=	**Net loan balance**	**9,949**

+	**Opening credit loss provision**	**50**
+	Loan loss charge	1
=	**Closing credit loss provision**	**51**

Subsequently, the bank discovers that out of €1m losses, €500,000 are worthless loans which must be written off. The write-off simultaneously reduces the gross outstanding amount and the allowance for loan losses. However, the net loans outstanding are not impacted as they have already been adjusted for expected losses.

		(€m)
+	Gross loan	10,000
–	Write-offs	(0.5)
=	Adjusted gross loans	9,999.5
–	Credit loss provision	(50.5)
=	Net loan balance	9,949.0

+	**Opening credit loss provision**	**50.0**
+	Provisions for expected credit losses	1.0
–	Write-offs	(0.5)
=	Closing credit loss provision	50.5

Note that the net realisable value of loans does not represent their **market value**. The recoverable amount reported in the books is the present value of expected cash flows discounted at historical, not current, interest. However, if the credit worthiness of a borrower deteriorates, the borrower would not be able to get a similar loan at the same interest, but rather at a higher rate reflecting the higher risk. For example, if the original one-year €1m loan is priced at a 10% rate and, subsequently, the borrower moves to a higher risk customer group which is offered only 15% interest, the market value of the loan declines to €956,500. Therefore, in case of a deterioration of borrowers' quality, the book value of the loan portfolio, in spite of all adjustments for loan losses, still overestimates its market value.

3) Other Considerations

In addition to interest income and credit losses, loans can generate some commissions, e.g. for committing un-drawn funds or providing other services.

Securitisations are designed to allow banks to transfer the credit risk of homogeneous categories of loans (such as mortgage loans) to capital markets investors and, therefore, remove securitised loans from the balance sheet. Therefore, securitisations provide funding, risk transfer and improved capital structure.

4.3 Other Financial Assets

In addition to providing loans, banks gather significant amounts of financial assets. They need liquid investments to meet loan requests or deposit withdrawals. They take proprietary short-term positions in traded securities or derivatives to realise short-term profits and they use derivatives to hedge risks. They also need suitable long-term investments for their permanent equity capital. They underwrite security issues or contribute to price stabilisation in the secondary market. They might be brokers or market makers for specific securities, though they would typically perform this function through separately incorporated subsidiaries.

Pre-IFRS, financial assets used to be separated on the face of the balance sheet by nature (i.e. bonds, equities, other) and derivatives positions were kept off balance sheet.

IFRS completely changed this presentation, with the recent implementation of IFRS 9 introducing further changes. Financial assets are broadly accounted for as follows:

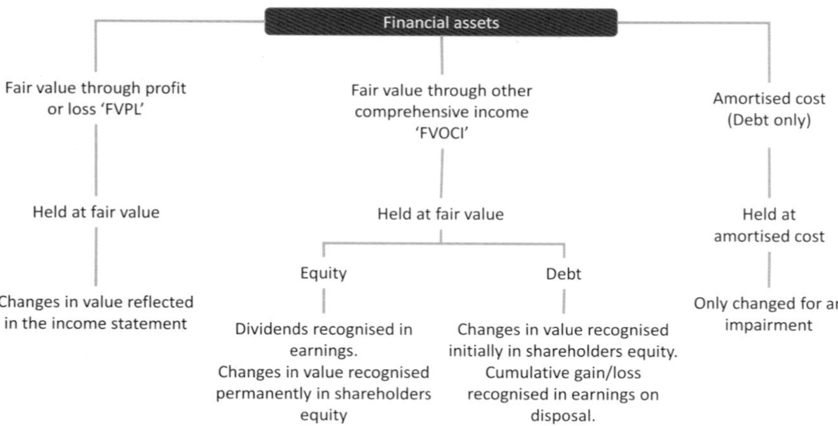

As we saw in Chapter 13, the default classification for equity instruments is FVPL. Debt instruments are classified as FVPL, FVOCI or amortised cost, depending on the instrument characteristics and the business model.

Classification of debt (or 'fixed income') instruments at amortised cost is permitted only where the following criteria are satisfied:

- Payment test – the contractual cash flows give rise solely to payments of principal and interest on specified dates.
- Business model test – the objective of the business model is to collect contractual cash flows, rather than held for trading purposes.

Where debt securities meet the payment test, but don't meet the business model test, they are either classified as FVOCI (if the business model is to hold these assets both for contractual cash flows AND for trading purposes) or as FVPTL, where they are held only for trading purposes.

As a result of the changes introduced by IFRS 9, more financial assets (and particularly fixed income instruments) are now held at fair value in the balance sheet than under IAS 39.

Amortised Cost Assets

Valuation and Link with the P&L

Debt securities which meet the 'payment test' and 'business model test' highlighted above are accounted for under the **amortised cost** method. This requires the calculation of the **effective interest rate** inherent in the financial asset, which is defined by IFRS 9 as the "rate that exactly discounts estimated future cash payments or receipts through the expected life of the financial asset...to the gross carrying amount of a financial asset".

Therefore, the effective interest rate represents the internal rate of return[20] on the financial asset.

For loans and receivables, this is relatively straight forward as the loans are initially reported at the gross loan balance at inception (net of fees and costs), interest is accrued (and recognised in earnings) based on the effective interest rate; any actual interest paid is deducted. The effective interest rate is calculated based on the expected life of the financial asset and the expected principal and interest payments (excluding the effects of any credit losses anticipated at inception).

---

[20] In general terms the internal rate of return is the discount rate which when applied to a series of cashflows returns a net present value of zero.

For fixed income investments, the situation is slightly more complicated. The investments mean that they are initially reported at purchase price (including commissions and other purchase-related expenses), and amortised towards the redemption value (or face value). If securities have a maturity date and are issued at a discount to face value, the discount is added to the historical price over the life of the security and included in the effective interest rate.

After inception, the gross book value is the net present value of expected future cash flows discounted at the effective interest rate.

The table below shows an example of a zero-coupon bond amortised according to the effective yield method. The book value increases to reflect the approaching principal repayment.

Example

Assumptions						
Par value	100					
Maturity (years)	5					
Coupon annual	0					
Effective Interest Rate	*6.0%*	*6.0%*	*5.4%*	*4.9%*	*4.4%*	*4.0%*
Year	**0**	**1**	**2**	**3**	**4**	**5**
Cash flow	(74.73)	0.00	0.00	0.00	0.00	100.00
Bond at book value	74.73	79.21	83.96	89.00	94.34	0.00
Interest income		4.48	4.75	5.04	5.34	5.66
P&L impact		4.48	4.75	5.04	5.34	5.66
B/S impact						
Bond		79.21	83.96	89.00	94.34	0.00
Equity		4.48	9.24	14.27	19.61	25.27
Debt		74.73	74.73	74.73	74.73	(25.27)
Total liabilities & equity		79.21	83.96	89.00	94.34	0.00

Although the security does not pay any coupon, it generates a positive interest income which is the effective yield applied to the opening book value of the bond.

The security book value does not reflect its changing market value. In particular, a decline in market interest rates of similar securities would results in an increase in the market value of the security[21], which the bank cannot reflect in its balance sheet.

However, the bank should still adjust the book value of financial assets for impairments.

The amortised cost method has the advantage that the banks' results are not affected by market volatility and are therefore more stable and predictable. On the other hand, the amortised cost method generates an incentive for banks to hold on to a security with a declining market value in order to postpone the capital loss, and to sell a security with an increasing market value to manipulate earnings and equity. Therefore, this method would not be appropriate to measure income generated by actively managed assets.

In the case of BNP Paribas, debt securities at amortised cost represent only 3% of total assets.

Financial Assets at Fair Value Through Profit or Loss (FVPL)

Financial assets at fair value through the profit or loss is a broad category which includes four groups of assets:

- Actively managed assets, i.e. all those previously classified as 'held for trading' securities. Any assets held by banks' treasury departments or trading floors is recorded here.
- Derivatives, excluding derivatives used for hedging purposes. In other words, the presumption is that banks invest in derivatives for trading or speculative reasons, unless they prove that they are used for risk management purposes and that they are effective hedges for specific risks.
- Equity investments, excluding those designated at FVOCI. Also, any fixed income investments which don't satisfy the 'payments test' (and are therefore not really considered debt instruments).
- Other financial assets which banks decide to nominate at fair value through the profit and loss under the fair value option. Banks have the option to classify and therefore measure at fair value through the profit and loss whatever asset they want, without substantial restrictions. They have the same options for financial liabilities, but more stringent conditions apply (see Chapter 13 for more details).

[21] This is because a lower discount rate gives a higher present value

In the case of more sophisticated banks, this category has become very significant, reflecting banks' increasing exposure to capital markets. BNP Paribas' financial assets at FVPL are the second largest asset of the balance sheet, representing 32% of total assets, which is just slightly lower than the value of customer loans.

Valuation and Link with the P&L

As the label says, financial assets at fair value through the profit and loss have to be marked to market on the balance sheet, with any changes immediately impacting the profit and loss. Therefore, the profit and loss reflect both realised and unrealised capital gains and losses on any trading securities and on all derivatives positions (unless hedging rules apply).

If the same zero-coupon bond as above is accounted for as a trading security, and yields decline, then the balance sheet will reflect the increased market value of the bond and a trading gain will be reported in the P&L even though the bond has not been sold.

In the example below, the bond is accounted for "as if" it was sold and re-purchased every year that it is held in the portfolio, thus reinforcing the concept that holding on to a trading security is an active decision.

Example

Par Value	**100**					
Maturity (years)	5					
Coupon annual	0					
Effective Yield	*6.0%*	*6.0%*	*5.4%*	*4.9%*	*4.4%*	*4.0%*
Year	**0**	**1**	**2**	**3**	**4**	**5**
Cash inflow		79.21	85.35	90.88	95.76	100.00
Cash outflow	(74.73)	(79.21)	(85.35)	(90.88)	(95.76)	0.00
Bond at market value	74.73	79.21	85.35	90.88	95.76	0.00
Bond at book value	74.73	79.21	83.96	89.98	95.33	0.00
Cumulative trading gain			1.39	0.90	0.43	0.00
Yearly trading gain			1.39	(0.49)	(0.47)	(0.43)

P&L impact					
Interest income	4.48	4.75	6.02	5.35	4.67
Trading gain		1.39	(0.49)	(0.47)	(0.43)
Total income	4.48	6.14	5.53	4.88	4.24
B/S impact					
Bond	79.21	85.35	90.88	95.76	0.00
Equity	4.48	10.63	16.15	21.04	25.27
Debt	74.73	74.73	74.73	74.73	(25.27)
Total liabilities & equity	79.21	85.35	90.88	95.76	0.00

Every year, the bond generates a total income equal to the increase in the bond market value. Therefore, the reported trading gains or losses from financial assets at fair value through the profit and loss include both an interest element and a pure trading gains/losses element. Since the bond in the example is maintained to maturity, it generates the same income over its life regardless of its accounting treatment at fair value through profit and loss or held to maturity. However, accounting for it as a trading security allows the bank to recognise some unrealised trading gains in Year 2, which are reversed into trading losses in the following years.

The benefit of marking to market financial assets is that it reflects the current value of the bank's exposures and that it prevents profit manipulation by correctly rewarding management for actively managing its portfolio of liquid assets. On the downside, market-marking can contradict the principle of prudence as it allows a bank to report gains in the P&L before they are effectively realised. This might result in a reported profit number that significantly deviates from actual cash generated.

Fair Value Through Other Comprehensive Income (FVOCI)

This category applies to financial assets held for an indefinite period of time with the possibility of being sold in case of need for liquidity. In the case of BNP Paribas, FVOCI financial assets represent 2% of total assets.

The measurement of this category reflects their status as in between amortised costs assets and the FVPL category. The balance sheet reflects their fair value (based on approved methodologies), but the profit and loss is shielded from volatility because any change in fair value is recorded in a fair value reserve directly in shareholders' equity. This distorts the return on equity ratio, because of the different measurement in the numerator (P&L return) and denominator (BS equity).

4.4 Equity-Method Investments and Miscellaneous Assets

Investment in group companies and most miscellaneous assets such as goodwill, intangibles, tangible fixed assets, own shares (or treasury stock) are not specific of banks. Therefore, they are accounted for exactly in the same way as for industrial companies (refer to the other relevant chapters of the book).

4.5 Deposits

Deposits include the following categories:

- Deposits from central banks.
- Deposits from credit institutions.
- Deposits from customers.

The last two of these sit within the 'Financial liabilities at amortised cost' category in the balance sheet.

Deposits represent a major source of funding for banks, and the most important source of funding for traditional institutions. As a general trend in the banking sector, customers are becoming more sophisticated and reluctant to leave a lot of money on deposits which give them very little interest. As a result, customer deposit funding is growing at a slower pace than customer loans, and banks are forced to look for other more expensive sources of funding, such as bank deposits or securities issued on the capital markets. Analysts monitor the customer loans to customer deposits ratio and the speed at which it increases over time.

In the case of BNP Paribas, bank deposits and customer deposits covered 4% and 35% of total liabilities and equity respectively.

Given banks' dependence on deposits to finance their activities, and the fact that deposits can usually be withdrawn at creditors' request, banks are exposed to significant liquidity risk. For this reason, banks have to manage their deposits very carefully and are bound by a "duty of care towards depositors" which limits the use of such deposits on the asset side of the balance sheet. Closely matching assets and deposit liabilities by maturity ("asset liability management") is a strategy designed to minimise both liquidity risk and interest. Diversifying the depositor basis, with a large number of retail customers, corporate customers and banks, also reduces risk of failure.

Valuation and Link with the P&L

Current account deposits tend to pay very limited interest, whilst interest on time deposits might be slightly higher. In any event, deposit proceeds are the nominal amount on which interest due is calculated and there is no difference between coupon and yield (as opposed to debt securities which can be issued at discount or premium, thus generating a difference between coupon and yield).

For this reason, the accounting of deposits is straightforward. Deposits are usually accounted for at nominal value (net of any transaction costs), which simultaneously represents the net proceeds, principal outstanding as well as the amortised cost. See example below.

Example

Par Value	**100**					
Maturity (years)	5					
Coupon annual	2					
Yield	2.0%					
Year	**0**	**1**	**2**	**3**	**4**	**5**
Cash flow deposits	100.00	(2.00)	(2.00)	(2.00)	(2.00)	(102.00)
Deposits (book value)	100.00	100.00	100.00	100.00	100.00	0.00
Interest expense		(2.00)	(2.00)	(2.00)	(2.00)	(2.00)
P&L impact		(2.00)	(2.00)	(2.00)	(2.00)	(2.00)
B/S impact						
Cash	100.00	98.00	96.00	94.00	92.00	(10.00)
Equity		(2.00)	(4.00)	(6.00)	(8.00)	(10.00)
Deposits		100.00	100.00	100.00	100.00	0.00
Total liabilities & equity		98.00	98.00	94.00	92.00	(10.00)

4.6 Other Financial Liabilities

Securities issued represent the third source of financing after customer deposits and interbank deposits. They are included within both the 'Financial instruments at fair value through profit or loss' and 'Financial instruments at amortised cost' categories.

Securities issued have increased in importance over time and represent an increasing proportion of banks' liabilities. Compared to customer deposits, they have the advantage of being an easily and quickly accessible form of financing. On the other hand, they are more expensive than customers' accounts and pay a higher and more volatile market interest. In case of deterioration of a bank's solvency, its debt capital markets investors will deny financing much faster than account depositors.

The most important type of fixed income securities issued are Eurobonds, which give banks access to foreign currency investors. Securities issued include also certificates of deposit, which are short-term tradable fixed income securities. Another important source of financing is represented by "repos", which are essentially short-term borrowings collateralised by securities (the bank lends securities it owns in exchange for cash). As for deposits, notes to accounts need to provide a breakdown of securities issued by maturity.

As highlighted above, financial liabilities are split between two categories:

- Financial liabilities at fair value through profit and loss. Securities in this category include:
    - Short security trading positions (including repurchase agreements).
    - Issued debt securities that the bank has designated at fair value through the profit and loss under the fair value option.
    - Derivatives with a negative fair value, excluding hedging derivatives.
- Financial liabilities at amortised cost. Securities and issued debt in this category include:
    - Issued debt securities.
    - Subordinated debt.

Liabilities at fair value through the profit and loss are marked to market on the balance sheet with changes through the profit and loss. However, IFRS 9 has introduced a new restriction on recognising the effects of changes in a company's own credit risk in earnings (since a deteriorating credit rating can result in a company recognising gains as their issued securities are worth less than before). Therefore, fair value changes relating to own credit risk are recognised in equity, whilst the balance sheet still reflects the full fair value of the liabilities.

Financial liabilities at amortised cost are accounted for using the effective interest rate method.

Subordinated debt is so called because it is subordinated to the payment of claims by depositors, financial creditors and other parties, covered by the provisions for risks and charges described in the paragraph above. In addition, it can absorb banks' losses without triggering insolvency. It is normally listed separately on the balance sheet because, unlike all other liabilities, it can qualify for capital ratios calculations under specific circumstances (refer to the section on Regulatory Requirements for further details). Subordinated debt generates a higher interest expense than other debt to compensate creditors for the higher risk associated with it.

In the case of BNP Paribas, financial liabilities at fair value through the profit and represent 32% of total liabilities and equity, whilst debt issued and accounted at amortised cost represents just 8% of total liabilities and equity. Financial liabilities at FVPL are therefore almost as significant a form of financing as deposits from banks and customers.

4.7 Other Liabilities

Other liabilities include items such as accrued expenses and deferred income and negative goodwill, which are not specific to banks and therefore follow general accounting standards.

In addition, they include public funds under administration, received from the Government and other public authorities, and write-downs of off balance sheet transactions.

4.8 Provisions for Contingencies and Charges

Provisions for contingencies and charges include some provisions which are common to industrial companies and some bank specific provisions.

The first type encompasses items such as deferred tax liabilities and pension provisions. The second type includes provisions to cover losses related to off balance sheet guarantees and commitments, provisions for risks in regulated savings products and for litigation relating to banking transactions.

Some provisions for contingencies and charges cover risks which are expected to materialise (with the exception of deferred tax liabilities), although there is some uncertainty with regards to their exact amount and timing, and therefore should be considered as quasi-debt items. For this reason, such provisions do not contribute to the calculation of capital for capital ratios purposes. As deferred tax liabilities might not materialise under certain circumstances (see Chapter 4), they might be considered quasi-equity items, although they do not contribute to the calculation of capital ratios.

4.9 Minority Interests and Equity

Minority interests are a liability generated whenever banks fully consolidate subsidiaries in which they own less than 100%. They follow the same accounting principles established for industrial companies.

Similarly, equity is the same for financial and non-financial companies. Equity has a particular relevance for banks because it is the basis used to calculate banks' capital and capital ratios (refer to the section on Regulatory Requirements for more details).

The only difference between the way equity is presented in banks' accounts and industrial companies' accounts is that it is quite common for banks providing more detail on the components of shareholders' equity i.e.

- Share capital.
- Share premium reserve.
- Retained earnings.
- Fair value reserve (relating to the cumulative effective of gains and losses on items classified as FVOCI).
- Hedging reserve (relating to the cumulative gains and losses on hedging instruments designated as cash flow hedges).
- Liability credit reserve (relating to the cumulative effect of own credit adjustments recognised in OCI).
- FX translation reserve.
- Net income for the period.

4.10 Off Balance Sheet Items

Off balance sheet items include "Guarantees and Commitments" quantified either at the bottom of the balance sheet or as a separate note in the accounts.

As soon as banks realise guarantees and commitments might generate future losses, they provide for them through a non-cash charge in the P&L included in "Adjustments to loans and provisions for guarantees and commitments", which builds up a corresponding liability in the balance sheet included in "Provisions for Risks and Charges".

Chapter 14 addresses off-balance sheet transactions.

5 Income Statement Description

IFRS accounting standards are rather prescriptive in terms of the measurement of assets and liabilities and the quantitative impact on the income statement, but they are less prescriptive with regards to the layout of the income statement.

The old IAS 30 gave some indications on the layout of banks' profit and loss requiring, for instance, the separate presentation of interest income from interest expense, commission income from commission expense.

There are no compulsory rules with regards to relevant sub-totals, but there is a widely accepted definition of banks' top-line (or revenues, or what is indicated below as net banking income) and operating profit. Analysts are used to slightly different implementations of these key lines of the profit and loss.

BNP Paribas – 6 months Ended June 2018	**(€ m)**
Interest income	17,948
Interest expense	(7,495)
Net interest income	**10,453**
Commission income	6,502
Commission expense	(1,842)
Net commission income	**4,660**
Net gain on fin. instruments at fair value through profit and loss	3,545
Net gains on fin. Instruments at fair value through equity	170
Net gains on derecognised financial assets at amortised cost	14
Other income	8,745
Other expense	(5,583)
Revenues	**22,004**
Total operating expenses	(15,628)
Cost of risk (credit losses)	(1,182)
Operating profit	**5,194**
Share of earnings of equity-method entities	294
Net gain on non-current assets	206
Goodwill	15

Profit before tax	**5,709**
Tax	(1,476)
Net income	**4,233**
Minority interests	(273)
Net income attributable to shareholders	**3,960**

5.1 Net Interest Income

Net interest income is the difference between interest income on loans and interest expense on deposits, and this spread represents the main source of banking revenues. Since the financial crisis, this income stream has become more significant as a revenue driver as other banking activities (especially securitisation and investment banking) have been scaled back across the banking industry. In the case of BNP Paribas, it generates 48% of revenues.

Interest Income

Interest income is generated by interest earning assets which include:

- Cash and balances at central banks.
- Loans and advances.
- Debt securities classified at amortised cost.
- Some off-balance sheet transactions.

Interest income is calculated on an accruals basis, using the effective interest rate method (see earlier in this chapter for more details) i.e. interest earned but not yet received in cash has to be reported in the P&L.

As previously mentioned, when loans become non-performing, the accrual of interest is suspended, and interest income cannot be reported until it is actually received.

Interest Expense

Interest expense is generated by interest bearing liabilities, namely:

- Deposits from banks.
- Deposits from customers.
- Securities issued.
- Subordinated debt.
- Off balance sheet transactions.

Interest expense is also accounted for on an accruals basis, using the effective interest rate method.

5.2 Net Fee and Commission Income

Net fee and commission income is the balance of fee and commission income and expenses, which have to be detailed separately in the consolidated P&L.

Fee and commission income is generated by a wide range of activities including:

- Fund management.
- Settling current account transactions.
- Credit card distribution and ATMs.
- Custody services.
- Dealing in and placing securities.
- Payment services.
- Loan securitisation.
- Distribution of third-party investment products.
- Providing guarantees and structuring credit derivatives.

Similarly, banks incur fee and commission expenses, related to:

- Management and distribution of investment products.
- Purchase of payment services.
- Use of credit cards and international circuits.

Recognition

The recognition of fee and commission income has changed under IFRS 15. Recognition has to be matched with the provision of the underlying services and, where fees cover a range of different services, these fees must now be 'unbundled'. IFRS 15 also provides new guidance on contingent fees (which are common in investment banking advisory contracts) and allows these payments to be anticipated when the service is delivered and where there is a low probability of revenue reversal.

5.3 Net Gains on Financial Instruments

Net gains on financial instruments at fair value through the profit and loss represent the sum of all positive and negative changes in the fair value of financial assets and financial liabilities at fair value through the profit and loss, including derivatives. For instance, if a derivative changes from a net positive value of 100 to a net negative value of −50 (liability of 50), the bank has overall incurred a loss of 150. They include both realised and unrealised capital gains/losses.

Notice that gains on debt securities at fair value through the profit and loss include an element of interest income and an element of 'pure' trading gain/loss. This is because the value of the security reflects in part the simple time value of money (interest income) and changes in market rates (trading gain). However, the split is usually not available because banks report the overall change in the security's fair value in trading gains.

Net gains on debt securities at fair value through equity represent only realised capital gains/losses when the instruments are sold. Unrealised gains on these investments affect the balance sheet and equity but not reported profits.

Net gains on equity investments at fair value through equity represent only dividends received from these investments, as fair value gains on these investments are recognised permanently in equity.

Refer back to Chapter 13 for further details on the treatment of fair value gains on financial instruments.

5.4 Net Other Income

This item collects other sources of income, which are part of banks' ordinary operations but are not included in either net interest, net fee or net capital.

For banks controlling insurance subsidiaries, this will include the income generated by the insurance operations.

5.5 Costs

Banks incur costs which can be specific to their banking activities or common to industrial companies. Bank specific costs include:

- Interest expenses.
- Fee expenses.
- Credit losses.

Non-bank specific costs include:

- Administrative costs, including staff costs and depreciation of fixed assets.
- Provisions for risks and charges, including pension provisions.
- Impairments of fixed assets, intangibles and goodwill.
- Taxes.

As mentioned in the previous paragraphs, interest expense and fee expense should be analysed as a deduction from net banking income, i.e. banks' true top-line, rather than as separate costs (as is the case for industrial companies).

Please refer to previous chapters for non-bank specific costs.

5.6 Credit Losses

As mentioned in previous paragraphs, credit losses are bank-specific non-cash costs which have significant impact on banks' profitability. Banks apply various labels to these losses, including impairment losses, loan losses, credit provisions or - in BNP's case - cost of risk.

IFRS 9 provides a framework for staged recognition of credit losses on loans and receivables, as the credit risk on the loan book increases. The balance sheet adjustment is a reduction of net loan balances for the expected loss and the corresponding losses in the income statement are included as a separate line, below interest income, non-interest income and operating expenses.

Similarly, for securities classified at amortised cost (remember that this will apply only to debt securities), IFRS 9 requires credit losses to be recognised using the same framework as for loans and receivables. An impairment provision is recognised against the value of the securities in the balance sheet and a credit loss recognised in the income statement.

When the expected loss does materialise (i.e. the counterparty defaults), then the loss does not appear in earnings because it is charged directly against the credit loss provisions, which have been created. If the expected loss does not materialise and the risk is no longer present, the provisions are reversed and a positive writeback entry is reported in earnings.

6 Regulatory Requirements

Banks are subject to strict requirements with regards to their capital position.

There are several reasons why banks require adequate capital ratios:

- To get regulatory approval and a banking license when they are set up.
- To absorb financial and operating losses resulting from the risks inherent in banking activities, namely:
  - Credit risk i.e. risk of loss on loans or similar activities due to counterparty default. Credit risk increases in periods of economic downturns, making banking a highly cyclical business.
  - Market risk i.e. risk of loss on investments and trading activities due to adverse changes in financial asset prices. It can be further split into interest rate risk and foreign exchange risk.
  - Operational risk i.e. risk of loss due to quality control failures and simple human error or fraud.
  - Liquidity risk i.e. the risk of losses because a lack of market participants (or an inefficient market) results in them trading or selling investments at distressed prices in order to meet their obligations as they fall due.
- To maintain depositors' and creditors' confidence in the bank, by protecting their savings and interests from risks above.
- To support growth of banking activities. Regulators require bank capital to increase in line with risky assets.
- To achieve desired credit rating from rating agencies and thus keep their cost of funding on capital markets under control.

Regulatory Framework for European Banks

Bank regulation has traditionally been the remit of national governing authorities. However, growing internationalisation of financial markets has increased the risk that the impact of a major bank failure spreads beyond the national banking system. In addition, regulators have become increasingly keen to prevent banks moving to less prudent jurisdictions to reduce their cost of maintaining minimum capital ratios.

These factors contributed to a trend towards increasing standardisation of capital regulations.

In 1975, the **Basel Committee on Banking Regulations and Supervisory Practices ("The Basel Committee")** was established to create a unified approach to capital regulation. In July 1988, the Basel Committee published the "International Convergence of Capital Measurement and Capital Standards" **("The Basel Capital Accord"** or **"Basel I")**, which provided a definition of capital (Tier I and Tier II) and minimum capital requirements in particular in relation to credit risk (measured rather crudely by risk weighted assets, see below). In January 2001, the Basel Committee proposed the development of regulations **("Basel II")** recognising the effectiveness of sophisticated internal risk models developed by large banks to assess capital adequacy, and also exploring further capital requirements related to operational risk. Basel II was implemented in Europe in 2007. However, shortly after this, the financial crisis of 2008/09 occurred, revealing significant shortfalls in the regulatory system with respect to the liquidity risk of banks. In response to this, further changes were proposed in 2009 **("Basel III")** which included the introduction of liquidity requirements and leverage ratios. Basel III implementation commenced in 2013, with full implementation by 2019 (as the implementation process is phased). However, this is not the end of regulatory changes for the sector, with further refinements currently being proposed by the Basel Committee (although these refinements don't officially represent a new regulatory regime, they are widely referred to as **"Basel IV"**).

Basel III uses a three-pillar approach to regulation:

- Pillar 1 requires banks to hold a minimum amount of regulatory capital that reflects the riskiness of banks' assets;
- Pillar 2 provides supervisors with the authority to evaluate risk management practices and impose more stringent capital requirements if they deem the current level of capitalisation to be inadequate; and
- Pillar 3 focuses on market discipline, requiring transparent reporting.

Regulatory Authorities

The Basel Committee comprises representatives from each of the G-10 countries but has no binding regulatory authority. However, the regulators of all the G-10 countries have enforced its provisions in their respective banking systems.

In particular, the **European Commission** has formulated capital regulations implementing and sometimes going beyond those published by the Basel Committee, in a series of Directives. The latest of these is the Credit Requirements Directive 2013 (2013/36/EU) which, together with the Capital Requirements Regulation 575/2013, are referred to as 'CRD IV', as they represent the fourth iteration of Capital Requirements Directives in the EU. CRD IV aims to implement the Basel III requirements across the EU, but also includes additional rules on corporate governance and remuneration.

Since 2014, the European Central Bank (ECB) has been responsible for supervision of the banking industry in Europe, with national regulators providing a supporting role.

7 Definition of Available Capital

Capital essentially represents a margin of net assets which is available to absorb losses. Although capital calculations are based on accounting numbers, certain adjustments are made ('prudential filters') to ensure that the available capital is adequately prudent.

A bank's available capital can be broadly described as net tangible asset value, i.e. the value of realisable assets (less goodwill and intangibles) in excess of expected commitments or liabilities.

The key components are therefore:

Equity + Non-controlling interests − Goodwill

However, there is a continuum of hybrid capital instruments between debt and equity, with varying degrees of ability to absorb losses and preserve creditors' and depositors' interests. For this reason, regulators have decided to define capital according to a tier structure, recognising that there might be different layers of capital ranging from higher quality (Common Equity Tier 1, essentially pure shareholders' equity) to poorer quality (Tier 2, hybrid instruments and long-term subordinated debt). Certain forms of capital are also eligible as 'Additional Tier 1 Capital'.

The EU is also in the process of introducing an additional requirement for loss absorbing capital ('Minimum Requirement for own funds and Eligible Liabilities' or 'MREL') to provide an extra layer of stability in the financial system.

Tier 1

Tier 1 capital consists of Common Equity Tier 1 capital (CET 1) and Additional Tier 1 capital. They are calculated as:

+	Permanent shareholders capital, including: Fully paid common stock Retained earnings Accumulated other comprehensive income and other disclosed reserves
+	Minority interests (i.e. non-controlling interest)
–	Goodwill and other intangible assets
-	Deferred tax assets and defined benefit pension assets
–	Shortfall on provision stock against expected losses
-	Cumulative reserves relating to cash flow hedges
-/+	Gains or losses on liabilities at fair value resulting from changes in own credit
=	Common Equity Tier 1
+	Perpetual instruments (e.g. non-cumulative preferred stock)
+	Contingent convertible securities
=	Additional Tier 1

Some comments on the calculation of CET 1:

- Disclosed reserves from cumulated retained earnings are part of CET 1, whereas cash flow hedge reserves are explicitly excluded, though they are part of shareholders' funds.
- Including minority interests in CET 1 recognises that minority interests represent equity invested by third parties in subsidiaries belonging to the group which can absorb part of the losses.
- Deducting goodwill (and other intangibles) reflects the fact that goodwill does not represent a separable asset which could be easily liquidated in case of losses and therefore does not help to protect depositors and creditors.

- Retained earnings will include credit losses calculated using accounting standards. Prudence requires a further adjustment for any shortfall in the accounting credit loss provisions (the 'provision stock') against the expected losses calculated using the regulatory methodology (i.e. using either the standardised approach or the internal ratings-based approach).

Additional tier 1 consists of hybrid instruments with more 'equity-like' characteristics (e.g. non-cumulative preferred stock).

Tier 2

Tier 2 is calculated as follows:

+	Undisclosed reserves
+	Perpetual, cumulative preferred stock
+	Perpetual subordinated debt
+	Term subordinated debt (maturity > 5 years)
+	Surplus on provision stock against expected losses
=	Tier 2

Some comments on the calculation of Tier 2 capital:

- Tier 2 capital tends to include hybrid instruments with more 'debt-like' characteristics (e.g. cumulative preferred shares and perpetual debt). Also, long term subordinated debt can qualify provided it has a long enough maturity.
- Tier 2 also allows as an 'add-back' adjustment where there is a surplus in the accounting credit loss provisions (the 'provision stock') against the expected losses calculated using the regulatory methodology (i.e. using either the standardised approach or the internal ratings-based approach). However, this adjustment is subject to certain limits.

Banks are obliged to publish their Tier 1, Tier 2 and Total Capital but they do not have to disclose a reconciliation of their calculation with the information contained in the balance sheet. However, many banks show a breakdown of the calculation of capital in the directors' report.

8 Definition and Purpose of Capital Ratios

Capital is required to cover the following types of risks:

- Credit risk.
- Market risk.
- Operational risk.
- Liquidity risk.

Credit risk is the risk of unexpected losses from customers' defaults in a worst-case scenario, and in excess of those expected and already covered by loan loss impairments.

Market risk is the risk of unexpected losses from adverse changes in interest rates, equity prices, FX rates in the trading book (although FX risk is covered both for the trading and the investment book).

Operational risk is the risk of expected and unexpected losses arising for systems or people's failure.

Liquidity risk is the risk of unexpected losses because a lack of market participants (or an inefficient market) results in them trading or selling investments at distressed prices in order to meet their obligations as they fall due.

The first three of these (credit risk, market risk and operational risk) are addressed using a risk-weighting approach to calculate 'risk-weighted assets'. One of the key regulatory ratios for banks is the ratio of Tier 1 capital to risk weighted assets, which is referred to as the 'Capital ratio'.

Liquidity risk is addressed through both the Liquidity Coverage Ratio and the Net Stable Funding Ratio.

In addition, the banks are required to comply with a leverage ratio, which is designed to prevent excessive build-up of on-and off-balance sheet leverage in the banking system.

The fact that the current framework covers credit risk, market risk, operational risk and liquidity risk represents a significant change from the original framework, which focused primarily on credit risk (which was estimated with a simple conversion of balance sheet and certain off balance sheet assets into risk-weighted assets).

On the following page we outline the calculation of the key capital ratios.

Capital Ratio

The capital ratio is considered the key regulatory ratio for banks. Although minimum levels are set for both CET 1 and Total Capital (see next section for details), Basel III has increased the focus on CET1 capital ratios.

The capital ratio is calculated as:

Capital ratio = Regulatory Capital / Risk Weighted Assets

With regulatory capital calculated as described in the previous section, for CET 1 or Total Capital.

The calculation of Risk Weighted Assets (RWAs) is complex. However, in general terms (and ignoring scaling factors), total RWAs are calculated as:

Risk Weighted Assets (RWA) = Credit Risk RWA + Market Risk RWA + Operational Risk RWA

The default approach (and the approach taken by most banks) for calculating RWAs is to use the 'Standardised Approach'. For credit risk and market risk, this involves applying a risk-weighting (as detailed in the Basel III documentation) to certain categories of asset, depending on how 'risky' each of those assets are considered to be; the credit risk categories are broadly aligned with the credit ratings provided by the rating agencies whilst the market risk groups assets by 'risk class' (e.g. interest rate risk, FX risk, commodity risk, credit spread risk etc). For operational risk, the standardised measurement approach involves applying risk weightings based on the size of certain items of income and expenditure, alongside information on historic operational losses.

However, as an alternative to this, for credit risk and market risk, banks can use internal credit ratings ('Internal Ratings Based Approach') and valuation models ('Internal Models Approach'). Since these alternative approaches rely on the bank applying its own judgements and estimation techniques, their use is allowed only where approval of the national regulator has been obtained. In order to approve these internal ratings and models, the regulator will review the robustness of the banks' models and the judgements and criteria that they rely upon.

Liquidity Coverage Ratio (LCR)

The LCR is designed to ensure that banks hold sufficient liquid assets to survive a 30 days stress period. It is calculated as:

LCR= High Quality Liquid Assets / Net Cash Outflow Over 30 days

Various limits are in place for the composition of high quality liquid assets, and they are sub-classified by quality: Level 1 assets include cash, central bank holdings and bond with a zero-risk weight whilst Level 2 assets include claims on sovereigns, central banks and public-sector entities.

The total net cash outflow is calculated as the cash outflow less the cash inflow, but the inflow is restricted to 75% of the outflow (thus acting as a floor).

Net Stable Funding Ratio (NSFR)

The NSFR's purpose is to ensure that banks maintain a stable level of funding in relation to the composition of their assets and off-balance sheet activities. It is calculated as:

NSFR = Total Available Stable Funding/ Total Required Stable Funding

The numerator and the denominator are calculated by applying pre-defined available stable funding factors and required stable funding factors to the bank's liabilities and assets respectively, as follows:

Available stable funding (ASF)	ASF Factor	Required stable funding (RSF)	RSF Factor
Regulatory capital and liabilities maturing > 1 yr.	100%	Cash and central bank reserves	0%
Stable retail deposits <1 yr.	95%	Highly quality liquid assets	5-50%
Less stable retail deposits <1 yr.	90%	Residential mortgages and loans > 1yr and RW<35%	65%
Funding from NFC and sovereigns < 1 yr.	50%	Other performing loans > 1yr and RW>35%	85%
All other liabilities	0%	Net derivative receivables, deferred tax assets and pension assets	100%

Leverage Ratio

The aim of the leverage ratio is to prevent the build-up of excessive leverage in the banking system and uses a relatively simple (non-risk based) formula:

Leverage Ratio = Capital Measure /Exposure Measure

The capital measure is the Tier 1 capital whilst the exposure measure incorporates exposures from: 1) on-balance sheet liabilities 2) derivative liabilities 3) securities financing transactions and 4) off-balance sheet items. Various prescriptive formulae (detailed in the Basel III rules) are used to calculate these exposures.

9 Minimum Capital Ratios

We summarise below the key minimum capital requirements under Basel III:

$$1.\quad \text{CET 1 capital ratio} = \frac{\text{CET 1 capital}}{\text{RWAs}} \geq 4.5\%$$

Additional buffers are applied in addition to this: (1) a 2.5% capital conservation buffer is applied outside periods of stress (so that additional reserves are built up when the economy is growing well) and (2) up to 2.5% countercyclical buffer is applied where deemed appropriate by national authorities. If both buffers are applied, this results in a minimum CET 1 capital ratio of 9.5%.

If capital levels fall below the core capital ratio but within the buffer amounts, the bank would be restricted from making further distributions (dividends, share buybacks, bonus payments).

$$2.\quad \text{Total capital ratio} = \frac{\text{Total capital}}{\text{RWAs}} \geq 8\%$$

Additional capital conservation and countercyclical buffers are applied in the same way as above, resulting in a minimum total capital ratio of up to 13%.

$$3.\quad \text{Liquidity coverage ratio} = \frac{\text{High Quality Liquid Assets}}{\text{Net Cash Outflow over 30 Days}} \geq 100\%$$

$$4.\quad \text{Net stable funding ratio} = \frac{\text{Available Stable Funding}}{\text{Required Stable Funding}} \geq 100\%$$

5. $\text{Leverage ratio} = \frac{\text{Tier 1 capital}}{\text{Exposure Measure}} \geq 3\%$

As demonstrated by the ratios above, regulatory requirements address both the minimum level of capital in proportion to the size of the banking book and the composition of capital. In practice, banks target higher capital ratios to give sufficient comfort to industry analysts and rating agencies.

Chapter 17: Accounting for Insurance Companies

"Any standard that takes away the perverse incentive of writing long-term business to achieve a day-one profit must be a good thing." [22]

[22] Getting a good quote on insurance accounting is not easy! This quote from Rob James of Old Mutual Global Investors in May 2017 (Financial Times) gets right to the point of how broken the existing model is.

1 Introduction

Insurance companies are a specialised group of financial institutions that sell life and non-life insurance policies. When an insurance policy is sold, the customer undertakes a contractual obligation to pay either a lump-sum or regular premiums for a pre-determined period of time, in exchange for the promise by the insurer for payment under pre-determined circumstances. In the case of life insurance policies, the payment is related either to the death of the policyholder, or simply to the contract reaching maturity. In the case of non-life insurance policies (also called general insurance policies), the payment is related to an accidental event, such as a car accident, a theft, or the policyholder's disease, in the case of car, property and health insurance, respectively.

This 'promise' by the insurer is one key aspect of why the insurance business is so unique; the exact cost of goods sold is not known when they 'sell' the policy. Therefore, insurance business (and in turn the accounting) is heavily reliant on the use of estimates. Insurance companies have access to detailed statistical tables which allow them to calculate the risk associated with each policy and charge a premium sufficient to cover the risk of claims, insurance expenses, and a profit margin for shareholders. Insurers make money thanks to asymmetry of information which allows them to price the risk undertaken.

The insurance business has traditionally been a highly profitable business, which has over time attracted an increasing number of players. More recently, increasing competition, maturing markets, increasing distribution costs, increasing claims costs and falling investment returns have eroded insurance margins and subjected insurance companies to increasing risk of failures.

Similar to banks, insurance companies receive policyholders' funds into their custody and have to manage them to protect their customers' right to be compensated and/or rewarded according to the contracted terms of the policy. For this reason, insurance companies are also subject to strict regulation, aimed at preventing insurers from managing customers' funds unwisely, failing to deliver on their promises and becoming insolvent. This regulation has undergone change in recent years in an effort to achieve a greater level of international standardisation, and to bring the solvency regime up to date with current views on assessing risk. The most significant of these changes was the introduction of the Solvency II regime across Europe in 2017.

All these factors contribute to explain why insurance companies' accounts are unique, as they need to reflect the nature of the insurance business and disclose relevant information on the risks that insurers, policyholders and insurers' creditors are exposed to.

An additional factor makes the life insurance accounting, in particular, very different from other forms of business. When a life insurance policy is sold, insurers pay substantial acquisition costs upfront to access a flow of revenues and profits over multiple years. Published accounts reflect only the flow of revenues and profits generated over a single year, and therefore do not give the full picture of the economic benefits arising from the sale of a life insurance contract. In other words, published accounts of insurance companies are specifically difficult to interpret, because they show only a snapshot of a multi-year business.

The issues listed above, combined with the variety of different types of insurance contracts written globally, has proven a significant challenge for accounting standard setters. The IASB spent almost two decades attempting to write a comprehensive insurance standard which is acceptable to both users and preparers of accounts. This standard was finally completed in 2017, with the publication of IFRS 17 Insurance Contracts. The new standard is due to take effect in 2021 and a summary of the new standard is provided in Section 10 below.

In the meantime, insurance companies rely on an interim IFRS standard (IFRS 4) which effectively ratifies local GAAP accounting for insurance contracts and liabilities. Some companies also choose to provide disclosures using 'embedded value' accounting (which provides an estimate of the net present value of future cash flows generated by life insurance business). However, embedded value accounting is not accepted in some European countries since there is no official standard prescribing the methodology.

2 Consolidated Financial Statements

Insurers have to publish the following components in their financial statements, namely:

- The balance sheet.
- The income statement.
- The statement of changes in equity.
- Notes to the consolidated accounts.
- The cash flow statement.

3 Overall Structure of the Balance Sheet

The macro-structure of an insurer's balance sheet can be represented as follows:

Assets	Liabilities and Equity
Liquid assets	Insurance provisions (also known as 'technical reserves')
Investments	Other liabilities
Miscellaneous assets	Equity

The single most important liability of an insurance company is represented by the claims of policyholders, covered by technical reserves. Technical reserves are managed by insurance companies and, together with shareholders' equity, they are invested in an appropriate mix of long and short term, equity, real estate and fixed income securities, in order to generate maximum investment return whilst fulfilling the liquidity requirements of insurance claims.

4 Balance Sheet Description

Generali

Assets	2017 (€m)
Intangible assets	8,784
Investments	471,232
Amounts ceded to reinsurers from insurance provisions	4,294
Tangible assets	4,075
Receivables	11,676
Other assets	30,170
Cash & cash equivalents	6,849
Total Assets	**537,080**

Liabilities	**(€m)**
Shareholders' equity	25,079
Minority interests	1,098
Financial liabilities (including subordinated debt)	42,316
Technical reserves – non-life	32,902
Technical reserves – life	329,591
Technical reserves – unit-linked and pension business	67,997
Other provisions	1,950
Payables	10,494
Other liabilities	25,653
Total	**537,080**

4.1 Intangible Assets

Although we have already come across goodwill and other intangibles for industrial companies in earlier chapters, insurers' balance sheets include intangible assets which are unique to insurance businesses, such as goodwill. Insurance companies incur various costs which are intended to produce benefits over the duration of the policy they relate to. For this reason, they are capitalised and amortised over the policy.

The most important of these is the cost of acquiring insurance business, called deferred acquisition costs (DAC). As insurance companies pay sales agents up-front commission for the distribution of contracts which extend over several years, the commissions can be treated as an investment, i.e. capitalised and amortised over the life of the policy. The practice of deferring and capitalising acquisition costs is referred to as Zillmerisation and it impacts on the way technical reserves are calculated. This practice is not permitted by all accounting standards for insurance companies. As a result of acquisition commissions, insurance cash flows might show an outflow the first year, followed by inflows for the duration of the policy. If acquisition commissions are not capitalised, then published accounts would register lower profits or potentially higher losses the faster a company is growing its sales. Notice that Generali has opted to not capitalise acquisition commissions

Other intangible assets include acquisition costs. For example, these might be the costs of issuing new policies. Other costs in intangible assets would include advertising, goodwill and compliance. There will also be other related costs, such as, design and development for new policies, or those related to the restructuring of an organisation, its IT systems and procedures.

Investments

Investments are the largest single asset category in the balance sheet of an insurer (88% of total assets for Generali). They cover a wide range of investment types, which are generally grouped under the following main headings:

- Land and buildings.

  Land and buildings relate to those held for investments purposes (i.e. rented to third parties).

- Investments in affiliated companies.

  Investments in affiliated companies primarily relate to investments in associated companies and joint ventures.

- Financial assets.

  Financial assets represent the largest category of investments for insurers, as insurance companies invest policyholders' and shareholders' funds to generate investment returns. Financial assets include:

  - Equities
  - Bonds
  - Investment fund units
  - Derivatives
  - Loans and deposits

Within the above, some of the investments relate to products where the risk is borne by the policy holders (unit linked investments and pensions business). These investments are separately identified on the face of the balance sheet and we explain these investments further in a separate section to follow.

Valuation and Link with the P&L

- Land and buildings are generally valued at cost less depreciation. However, as investment properties, IFRS also permits them to be recorded at fair value.
- Investments in affiliated companies are accounted for using the equity method (see Chapter 11).
- There are a variety of approaches and classifications for financial assets. It should also be noted that although a new accounting standard for financial instruments (IFRS 9, see Chapter 13) became effective in 2018, insurance companies were granted a carve-out from adopting the new rules until the new insurance standard takes effect in 2021. Insurance companies will continue to apply IAS 39 until then. In accordance with IAS 39, investments are valued in the balance sheet at either amortised cost (for debt instruments which are 'held to maturity') or fair value (for other debt instruments, all derivatives and all equity instruments, except associates and JVs).
- Equity and debt investments which are recorded at fair value can either be classified as 'available for sale' or 'held for trading'. Classification as available for sale results in fair value gains and losses being recorded in equity (until the investment is disposed of, at which point the cumulative gains are 'recycled' to earnings), whilst classification as held for trading results in fair value gains and losses being recording in earnings.
- Fair values are ideally based on latest market prices, but where this is not available, an estimate must be made based on the prices of similar instruments or using an accepted valuation technique.
- Debt investments which will be 'held to maturity', as well as loans and deposits, are recorded at amortised cost. This results in only interest income being recorded in earnings. However, the company is required to disclose the fair values of these investments in the notes to the accounts.
- In addition, the application of the principle of prudence requires companies to impair the value of investments when the amortised cost substantially overestimates the realisable value.

4.2 Unit-Linked Investments and Pensions Business

Unit-linked products are life insurance investment products where the risk of investment returns is borne entirely by the policyholders. The insurer is essentially packaging a pure asset management product in a life insurance wrapper. They are separately identified within investments and described as "Financial assets where the investment risk is borne by the policyholders and related to pension funds".

As is typical of asset management, funds under management have to be completely segregated from the accounts of the asset manager. For instance, when banks offer asset management products, funds under management are not reported in the banks' balance sheet but are instead disclosed in the directors' report. Similarly in the case of insurance companies, funds under management for unit-linked products and pension funds are segregated from other funds. They are, reported in the insurer's balance sheet in a double entry: of Provisions and liabilities where the financial risk is borne by the policy holder (liabilities) and Investments where the financial risk is borne by the policy holder (assets).

Investments of unit-linked and pension business are required to be classified and valued in the same way as other investments (see above). However, interest, dividends and both realised and unrealised capital gains and losses are reported in the P&L as "Income from financial instruments where the investment risk is borne by the policyholders and related to pension funds".

4.3 Reinsurance Technical Reserves – Non-Life and Life Business

Insurance companies are exposed to multiple types of risks, including in particular:

- Underwriting risk, i.e. the risk that claims are higher than expected when pricing the policy.
- Investment risk, i.e. the risk that return on investment is lower than expected and, in particular, lower than that assumed when discounting future commitments in the valuation of insurance reserves (see paragraph Technical Reserves – Life Business).

In order to reduce underwriting risk, the insurance company often transfers (or 'cedes') part of the risk to a reinsurance company; this process allows the underwriting risk to be shared across a number of insurance businesses. There are two types of reinsurance cover:

- **Proportional reinsurance (also known as 'quota share')** A simple proportional reinsurance involves the ceding company transferring a fixed proportion of written premiums and the reinsurer compensating for the same fixed proportion of claims (for example, 20% of premiums in exchange for refund of 20% of claims). Proportional reinsurance treaties might involve a different proportion of reinsured business for each different type of policies.
- **Non-proportional reinsurance**, which can take two main forms:
  - **Excess of loss reinsurance**, where the reinsurer pays the excess of every single claim beyond a specified threshold (for example, any

motor claim in excess of €500,000) or from a single event (e.g. weather claims in excess of $20m for a named storm).

– **Stop loss reinsurance**, where the total claims are calculated for a whole portfolio of similar policies and the reinsurer compensates the direct insurer for any loss in excess of an agreed level (for example, any total claims above 70% of premiums, calculated by portfolios of policies and not by individual policies).

The initial insurer ('direct insurer') remains the key counterpart to the policyholder but can now claim back part of its losses from the reinsurer. As reinsurers undertake a proportion of risk, they must build technical reserves to cover the risk undertaken. Reinsurance technical reserves represent the claim of the direct insurer towards the reinsurer.

Valuation

Reinsured technical reserves are generally reported as a separate asset on the balance sheet. They cannot be netted off against the insurer's technical reserves and have to be valued consistently with gross technical reserves.

4.4 Miscellaneous Assets

Miscellaneous assets include both additional items related to the insurance business and items common to industrial companies.

Miscellaneous assets encompass:

- Tangible assets (including land and buildings used by the company for their own purposes).
- Receivables arising from direct insurance operations, such as credits towards policyholders and insurance intermediaries (brokers and sales people).
- Receivables arising from reinsurance operations, such as credits towards ceding companies or reinsurers.
- Prepayments and accrued income, relating to temporary differences between written and earned premiums as well as paid and incurred expenses.
- Cash and cash equivalents.

4.5 Shareholders' Funds and Minority Interests

Shareholders' funds and minority interests are not specific to insurance companies. Therefore, they are accounted for in exactly the same way as for industrial companies (refer to the other relevant chapters of this book).

4.6 Financial Liabilities Including Subordinated Debt

Financial liabilities include:

- Subordinated debt
- Issued bonds
- Bank borrowings
- Derivative liabilities

Subordinated debt includes debt which, in case of company liquidation, is paid only after all other senior creditors have been paid and only if there are sufficient liquid resources in the company. As such, subordinated debt can absorb part of insurance companies' losses, and therefore can, under specific terms and conditions, contribute to insurers' solvency ratio in the same way as it contributes to banks' capital ratios (refer to the Regulatory Requirements section below)

Valuation and Link with the P&L

- Subordinated debt, issued bonds and bank borrowings are generally valued at amortised cost, with interest expense recorded in earnings. However, insurance companies can choose to designate financial liabilities as fair value through profit and loss to help offset fair value gains and losses on investments.
- Derivative liabilities are required to be recorded at fair value in the balance sheet, with fair value gains and losses recorded in earnings, unless they are designated as cash flow hedges.
- For financial liabilities recorded at fair value in the balance sheet, changes in fair value arise because of a change in the credit risk of the insurance company. However, IAS 39 prohibits this 'own credit' component being recorded in earnings – instead it is recognised in equity (and any residual fair value gain or loss is recognised in earnings).

4.7 Technical Reserves – Non-Life Insurance

As highlighted previously, the technical reserves represent the claims of policyholders in relation to existing policies. Non-life insurance reserves are split between:

- Unearned premiums reserves.
- Reserves for claims outstanding.
- Other non-life insurance reserves.

Prior to IFRS, insurance companies also included 'equalisation' and 'catastrophe' reserves to help smooth profits over time. However, these reserves are now prohibited under IFRS.

Unearned Premiums Reserves

Unearned premiums reserves are generated because most insurance policies sold during the year are still in force at the end of the financial year, except for those which have been sold on 1 January (or those whose cover lasts less than one year). In other words, a proportion of written premiums has yet to be earned because it relates to the following financial year.

The unearned premiums reserves are calculated as the sum of two components:

1. **Reserve by fraction of premiums.** This is simply a temporal pro-rata adjustment of written premiums based on the proportion of cover which has yet to lapse. It is calculated based on a fraction of premiums assuming that premiums are written evenly throughout the year.
2. **Reserve for current risks.** The unearned premium reserve is also intended to cover any potential claim which policyholders might make in the remaining period of the insurance policy (i.e. current risk). These are future claims covered by existing contracts. To the extent that the probability of claims is not uniform over time, the reserve by fraction of premiums might be insufficient to cover current risks. Any potential inadequacy of the reserve by fraction of premiums needs to be integrated by the reserve for current risks.

Reserve for Claims Outstanding

This is the single most important reserve for the non-life insurance business, representing, in the case of Generali, over 70% of total technical reserves. It is also the most difficult to quantify and value.

Outstanding claims are those claims which have already been incurred during the financial year but have yet to be liquidated and settled. This might occur for a couple of reasons:

1. Some claims have been incurred but not yet reported (IBNR) (for example, theft in the second home).
2. Some claims have been reported but might take time to settle, because of a legal dispute between the claimant and the insurer (for example, car accidents causing psychological trauma and loss of income or asbestos claims).

Insurers have to provide for claims outstanding to apply the matching principle and report claims relating to contracts sold during the year.

Whilst in the case of life insurance, the insurer's obligation expires when the contract reaches its maturity (usually there is limited dispute about its amount), in the case of non-life insurance, the insurer's obligation can stay for a long period of time as certain claims take several years to settle (so-called long-tail business).

Valuation and Link with the P&L

- As already discussed, unearned premiums reserves are calculated by fraction of premiums integrated by an additional reserve for current risks.
- The calculation of reserves for claims outstanding is the single most complicated issue for non-life insurers as it involves a high degree of uncertainty and subjectivity. Regulators require insurers to respect the general rule of prudence and to take into account different factors:
  - An all-inclusive definition of cost of claims, including:
  - Requests for compensation.
  - Technical investigations, such as medical examinations.
  - Expenses incurred by the policyholder and policy beneficiary.
  - Recent experience of average costs for similar claims.
- Increases in technical reserves are charges to the income statement which appear in different places according to the reserve, namely:
  - The change in unearned premium reserve is included in the calculation of earned premiums.
  - The change in reserves for claims outstanding is included in the calculation of claims incurred.
  - The change in other technical reserves is reported separately within the operating result from non-life business.

4.8 Technical Reserves – Life Insurance

Although technical reserves for life insurance still represent the claims of policyholders (as is the case for non-life business) the actual calculation of these reserves is very different. This is because the underlying risk is longer term in nature and varies over the duration of the policy. Life insurance reserves are split between:

- Mathematical reserves.
- Reserves for claims outstanding.
- Other reserves.

Mathematical Reserves

Mathematical reserves are by far the largest liability for life insurers, representing in the case of Generali almost 94% of technical reserves

Mathematical reserves are not a cover against uncertain events. They are the necessary cover for the insurer's expected (mathematically calculated) future commitments towards policyholders. They are built over time as premiums flow in and the maturity of the contract approaches and the probability of claims increases. In other words, life insurers cannot freely dispose of the premiums received from policyholders, which instead build mathematical reserves to be interpreted as policyholders' funds

Whilst the probability of claims is constant in most non-life insurance policies (for example, the probability of a car accident in the case of motor insurance), this is not the case for life insurance. For example, in the case of whole life cover which pays the beneficiary upon death of the policyholder, the event triggering the insurance payment becomes more likely as the policyholder ages. However, it would not be commercially viable for insurers to charge an increasing premium towards the end of the policy to reflect the increased risk they undertake. Instead, insurers charge a constant premium made of two changing components:

- A "risk premium" proportional to the probability of claim. For example, in the case of a whole life policy, the "risk premium" will increase over time.
- A "savings premium", which is intended to cover the probability of claim in the remaining period of cover. In the case of a whole life policy, the savings premium will be initially positive and become negative in the second part of the cover.

Every year, mathematical reserves represent the **net present value of commitments to policyholders less the present value of future premiums.** It is calculated by taking into account multiple factors, such as:

- Mortality rates.
- Acquisition and administrative expenses.
- Minimum guaranteed returns promised to policyholders.
- Risk of early surrenders and the penalty received by the insurer in that event.

Reserves for Claims Outstanding and Other Reserves

Reserves for claims outstanding cover claims already incurred but not yet paid.

Other technical reserves include premium reserves for non-life insurance complementary to the life cover, such as health insurance often packaged together with a life policy

Valuation and Link with the P&L

- EU norms require insurers to appoint qualified actuaries to calculate technical reserves. The calculation can be done on the basis of different accepted actuarial methodologies. For example, the prospective method calculates the present value of the difference between insurer's and policyholders' commitments, whilst the recurrent method bases the calculation on the previous year level of mathematical reserves.
- The valuation has to follow the general prudence principle, which implies adopting conservative assumptions in terms of mortality rates, surrender rates and cost ratios. Particularly important is also the assumption relating to the technical rate that is used to discount future commitments. Insurers might assume a high technical rate to show a lower level of technical reserves on the balance sheet. However, regulators monitor the technical rate and require, usually, that the technical rate does not exceed the average return on investments covering technical reserves.
- The unwind of the prudence margin over time can be an important source of earnings for insurance companies.
- Actuarial assumptions have to be revised regularly, to reflect changing demographic patterns and the impact of changing market trends of interest rates and investment returns.

4.9 Technical Reserves – Unit Linked Business and Pension Business

"Reserves for policies where the investment risk is borne by the policyholder and relating to the administration of pension funds" represent the insurer's liability towards policyholders for unit-linked business and pension funds.

Policyholders accept that they will be entitled exactly to what they have contributed into the policy (either through single or regular premiums), plus the investment return achieved by the insurer investing on their behalf in funds selected by the policyholder, less administration and other expenses

4.10 Miscellaneous Other Liabilities

Miscellaneous other liabilities include both additional items related to the insurance business and items common to industrial companies, including:

- Deferred and current tax liabilities.
- Payables from the insurance business including amounts owed to policyholders (for example, pre-paid premiums) and reinsurers.
- Accrued expenses.

5 Income Statement Description

Generali

Income statement	**2017 (€m)**
Net earned premiums – non-life	19,661
Net earned premiums - life	44,943
Total net earned premiums	64,604
Fee and commission income	1,080
Income from investments	15,015
Other income	3,180
Total income	**89,204**
Net insurance benefits and claims – non-life	(12,804)
Net insurance benefits and claims -life	(52,944)
Total benefits and claims	(65,748)
Fee and commission expense	(608)
Expenses related to investments	(2,802)
Acquisition and administration costs	(10,868)
Other expenses	(5,493)
Total expenses	**(85,518)**
Earnings before taxes	3,686
Taxes	(1,173)
Result of discontinued operations	(217)
Consolidated result for the period	**2,295**
Attributable to the Group	2,110
Attributable to minority interests	185

For ease of analysis, in the narrative below we analyse separately the operating result of the non-life and life insurance activities, followed by the non-operating result (taken from the segmental disclosures provided in the annual report, where they are fully reconciled to the aggregated income statement provided above).

6 Operating result from non-life business

The operating earnings for non-life business are calculated as follows:

Net earned premiums	**19,661**
Net insurance benefits and claims	(12,804)
Acquisition and administration costs	(5,472)
Other income and expenses	587
Operating earnings from non-life business	**1,972**

Taking each of these items in turn:

6.1 Net earned premiums

The net earned premiums is represented by:

+	**Gross written premiums**	**20,746**
-	Reinsured premiums	(999)
=	Net written premiums	19,747
-	Change in provision for unearned premiums	(86)
=	**Net earned premiums**	**19,661**

Gross Written Premiums

Gross written premiums are the revenues received from policyholders (individuals, companies or professional associations) for protection against risks in any year.

Net Written Premiums

In order to minimise underwriting risk, the insurer transfers part of the risk to a reinsurance company. As a result, the insurer also pays out a proportion of written premiums to reinsurers.

Net written premiums are calculated as gross written premiums less reinsured premiums and the net level of revenues against the net retained level of risk assumed by the insurance company.

The duration of non-life insurance contracts is typically 12 months and premiums are usually paid annually. Even if all insurance policies ran for a year, by the end of the year only policies written on 1 January would cover risks running through to 31 December of the same year. All other policies would be included in premiums written during the year, even though a proportion of the cover relates to the subsequent year and therefore cannot be considered "earned".

Net Earned Premiums

Earned premiums are calculated to match the risks undertaken during the financial year. Therefore, they include premiums written in the previous year but relating to the current year and exclude premiums written in the current year but relating to subsequent years.

For example, a policy with an annual premium of €1,200 sold on 30 September 2017 would generate €1,200 written premiums and only €400 earned premiums in 2017, as the remaining €800 is unearned in 2017 and will be earned in 2018.

6.2 Net insurance benefits and claims

The net insurance benefits and claims for non-life business is calculated as follows:

+	**Gross claims paid**	**13,331**
–	Reinsurers share	(738)
=	Net claims paid	12,593
–	Change in provision for outstanding claims	170
=	Claims incurred	12,763
-	Change in other insurance provisions	41
=	**Net insurance benefits and claims**	**12,804**

Taking each of these elements in turn:

Gross Claims Paid

Gross claims paid include all claims which have been settled during the financial year under review. Claims include not only compensation to policyholders, but also all related expenses (for example, legal costs).

Net claims paid

As for premiums, claims are initially reported gross of reinsurance, and subsequently reduced by the amount which is passed to reinsurance companies, to determine net claims paid.

Claims Incurred

Claims paid may differ from claims incurred, i.e. claims generated by events occurred during the year but yet to be paid. Incurred but outstanding claims have to be estimated in order to match the cost of claims included in the income statement with risk exposure during the year under consideration.

The adjustment is achieved by adjusting provisions for claims outstanding. Claims incurred are the sum of claims paid and change in reserves for claims outstanding.

The 'claims ratio' is calculated as claims incurred divided by net earned premiums. It is a key financial metric and an important earnings measure.

Change in Other Insurance Provisions

As the change in the reserves for unearned premiums and the change in the reserves for claims outstanding are already included respectively in the calculation of earned premiums and claims incurred (see paragraphs above), change in other technical reserves is a less material residual item.

It includes, for example, the change in other technical reserves due to so-called "portfolio movements", which refer to insurance policies moving in and out of the reinsured portfolio. The change is disclosed gross and net of reinsurance.

6.3 Acquisition and administration costs

These costs include:

- Acquisition costs, such as:
  - Commissions paid to insurance sales people.
  - Advertising expenses.
  - Other sales expenses.
- Administrative expenses, such as:
  - Staff costs.
  - Rents.
  - Other general expenses.
- Collecting commissions paid to agents upon collection of premiums.

Expenses are reported net of reinsurance. In particular, in the case of proportional reinsurance, the reinsurer typically uses the ceding company's infrastructure to distribute the business and to settle claims and therefore shares a proportion of operating expenses.

7 Operating result from life business

The operating earnings for the life business are calculated as follows:

Net earned premiums	**44,943**
Net insurance claims	(52,945)
Acquisition and administration costs	(4,756)
Net operating income from financial instruments	15,621
Other	278
Operating result from life business	**3,141**

Taking each of these items in turn:

7.1 Net Earned Premiums

Net earned premiums for life insurance are calculated as follows:

+	**Gross earned premiums**	**45,662**
–	Reinsured premiums	(719)
=	**Net earned premiums**	**44,943**

Gross earned Premiums

From the policyholders' point of view the premium is the cost of buying a life insurance policy. From the insurer's point of view, it is the key source of revenues.

The premium is calculated as the sum of three components:

1. The "fair premium", equal to the expected value from the life insurance policy, i.e. the present value of the insurance compensation multiplied by the probability of the event triggering the insurance compensation (for example, death of the insured person in the case of a term insurance policy). Here the insurer benefits from access to statistical tables which allow it to calculate with a certain precision mortality rates and survival rates for each policyholder.

2. A safety margin on top of the "fair premium" which ensures that the cost to the policyholder (in present value terms) is slightly higher than the cost to the insurance company (always in present value terms). The safety margin on top of the fair premium can be calculated as a straight percentage. Alternatively, and more likely, it is achieved indirectly by adopting very conservative actuarial assumptions (in terms of mortality rates, surrender

rates and also in terms of the interest rates used to discount future commitments) which overstate the expected present value of the insurance company's commitments.

3. A loading to cover the insurer's expenses connected to the acquisition and administration of the policy. The insurer takes into account the cost of paying upfront commission to sales agents, additional fees for the collection of regular premiums and other administration costs. In addition, there is the risk that the policyholder cancels the policy early on or surrenders it before its natural maturity.

The sum of the "fair premium" and of the safety margin is called "pure premium". The sum of the "pure premium" and the loading for insurer's expenses is the gross written premium that appears in the life insurer's income statement. The policyholder pays also any Government tax on top (i.e. the insurance equivalent of VAT for industrial products).

For life insurance products premiums can be paid upfront (single premium) or at regular (usually annual) rates (regular or annual premiums). This creates a problem of interpretation: gross written premiums are a good measure of revenues but not the best measure of sales. Industry experts often use alternative measures for sales, namely:

- **New business premiums.** I.e. premiums relating only to the sale of new insurance contracts. They exclude regular premiums relating to contracts sold in previous years (existing business portfolio)

  Total business premiums = New business premiums + Existing business premiums

- **Annual premium equivalent (APE) = 1/10 × Single premium + Annual premiums.** This is an approximation of the equivalent amount of premiums if all contracts where regular premiums. It assumes that average single premium contracts have a maturity of ten years and therefore it distributes the single premium over ten years

Net Earned Premiums

As for non-life insurance policies, life insurance products can also be reinsured. Net written premiums are calculated after deducting the premiums ceded to reinsurers.

7.2 Net Insurance Claims

Claims include all payments to policyholders related to the termination of a life policy. A life policy can terminate and generate a payment to the policyholder for any of three possible reasons: (i) the policy reaches maturity (ii) a triggering event (such as death of policyholder) has occurred or (ii) the policyholder surrenders the policy before maturity.

Claims incurred are calculated as claims paid plus the change in technical reserves. These changes in technical reserves include:

- Change in mathematical reserves.
- Change in other technical reserves relating to the traditional business.
- Change in reserves relating to unit-linked and pension business.

Similar to non-life insurance contracts, claims are reported net of reinsurance.

7.3 Acquisition and administration costs

Acquisition and administration costs include:

- Acquisition commissions.
- Other acquisition costs.
- Change commissions and other acquisition costs to be amortised.
- Collecting commissions.
- Other administrative expenses.

With expenses reported net of any reinsurance commission.

Given the timing mis-match between the upfront payment of acquisition commissions to sales people, and the future inflow of premiums (in the case of regular premium policies), acquisition commissions can be capitalised and amortised, as an alternative to General's policy of deducting them upfront.

Whereas acquisition and collecting commissions and costs can be directly attributable to each insurance policy sold and managed, other administrative expenses (including the cost of head-quarters and depreciation of tangible fixed assets) need to be allocated between life business, non-life business and the nontechnical account. Such allocation is usually achieved by analysing the premiums.

7.4 Operating Income from Financial Instruments

Although the operating income from life business primarily relates to the underwriting activities, it does include some income from investing activities. This primarily relates to the investment returns that are attributed to policy holders (e.g. for unit-linked policies).

Note that other investment returns are included in the non-operating result (see below).

8 Non-Operating Result

The non-operating result consists of all other income and expenditure arising in the business. It includes:

- Investment income (i.e. realised and unrealised gains and losses from investing activities).
- Interest expense from company borrowings.
- Central operating expenses (e.g. head office costs).

The investment income included in the non-operating result includes only the net investment income generated by investing non-life technical reserves, shareholders' funds and a proportion of that generated by investing life technical reserves (since the investment returns on some life policies are included in the operating result, as highlighted above).

The result from ordinary activities is the sum of the following components:

+	Operating result – non-life insurance
+	Operating result– life insurance
+	Non-operating result
-	Taxes
=	**Net income**

In addition to the above, some insurance companies provide a separate subtotal for the 'technical result' and 'investment result' for their business. Although these are not accounting defined terms, they allow the company to separately show the profits of their underwriting activities (the technical result) separately from their investing activities (the investment result), whereas the operating results referred to above can include some investment returns.

9 Regulatory Requirements

Insurance companies are subject to extensive regulation aimed at ensuring that they can fulfil their commitments to policyholders, and that in case of poor operating performance there are sufficient funds to absorb losses without endangering policyholders' rights. For EU insurers, the key regulatory framework is Solvency II. Solvency II is divided into three thematic areas known as 'pillars':

Pillar 1 addresses adequacy of assets, technical provisions and capital of a firm. It specifies two sets of capital requirements: the Solvency Capital Requirements (SCR) and the Minimum Capital Requirement (MCR);

Pillar 2 addresses more qualitative areas such as risk management and governance

Pillar 3 addresses transparency by requiring certain disclosures to be provided to regulators and in public reports.

It is worth noting the similarities in this 'three pillar' approach to the regulatory framework for banks under Basel III.

The capital requirements included in Pillar 1 are particularly important as are designed to provide regulators with a so called 'supervisory ladder of intervention': the Solvency Capital Ratio is a higher ratio and - if breached –results in intervention by the regulator to ensure remedial action is taken (e.g. suspending further dividend payments), whilst a breach of the Minimum Capital Ratio can ultimately result in an insurance company having its authorisation withdrawn.

The calculation of the capital requirements is addressed further in the following sections, but at this point it is worth highlighting that they are based on using 'the economic balance sheet' approach to valuing the company's assets and liabilities:

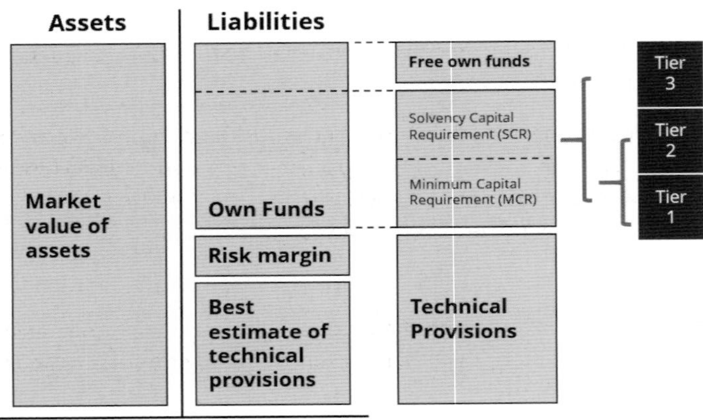

This is different to how the assets and liabilities are calculated under existing accounting rules[23] and the key elements of this approach are:

- The insurance liabilities are calculated using the 'best estimate' of the future liability cash flows (i.e. the insurance claims and benefit payments) calculated on probability-weighted average basis. This calculation uses a risk-free discount rate, but is adjusted to the extent that there is matching between the assets and liabilities, to avoid unnecessary volatility in the difference between the asset and liability value.
- A risk margin is applied to cover the uncertainty in the future cash flows; this risk margin is essentially the difference between the best estimate of the future liability cash flows and the transfer value of the liabilities if they were to be transferred to a third party.
- Own funds are defined as assets in excess of technical provisions. They are split into three tiers, with Tier 1 being the highest quality and most permanent forms of capital (e.g. ordinary share capital, non-cumulative preference shares and long-term subordinated liabilities) and Tier 2 being lower quality (e.g. cumulative preference shares and shorter-term subordinated liabilities). Tier 3 would include any own funds which don't satisfy the Tier 1 and Tier 2 requirements.

9.1 Solvency Capital Requirement

Under Solvency II, insurance companies are expected to maintain own funds at more than 100% of the solvency capital requirement (SCR).

This requirement is often expressed as a solvency ratio:

$$\text{Solvency ratio} = \frac{\text{Own Funds}}{\text{Solvency Capital Requirement}} \geq 100\%$$

The SCR is a risk-based assessment and is calculated on the business assets, technical provisions and other liabilities.

The calculation covers operational risk, market risk, underwriting risk (life and non-life), health risk and credit risk and is calculated using either a standardised formula or an internal model (where supervisory approval is obtained). The calculation is calibrated to assume a 99.5% confidence level on a one-year time horizon.

[23] As explained later in this chapter, the accounting for insurance companies will be changing in the near future and will achieve some alignment between the regulatory approach and the accounting.

For the solvency ratio, own funds include Tier 1, Tier 2 and Tier 3 capital but there are various constraints and limits for the different tiers. For example:

- Tier 1 capital must cover more than 50% of the SCR.
- Tier 3 capital cannot be used to cover more than 15% of the SCR.

9.2 Minimum Capital Requirement

The minimum capital requirement (MCR) is designed to be the minimum solvency threshold for the business, and therefore insurance companies must maintain own funds at more than 100% of the MCR.

$$\text{Minimum capital ratio} = \frac{\text{Own Funds}}{\text{Minimum Capital Requirement}} \geq 100\%$$

Similar to above, the MCR is also a risk-based assessment. The calculation is standardised and applies specific factors (as detailed in the regulations) to technical provisions and written premiums for different lines of business. The calculation is calibrated to assume an 85% confidence level on a one-year time horizon.

For assessing the own funds against the minimum capital requirement, additional constraints are placed on the composition of own funds including:

- Only Tier 1 and Tier 2 capital can be used to cover MCR.
- Tier 1 capital must cover more than 80% of the MCR.

10 Future Developments

The insurance industry will soon be undergoing a radical overhaul of its accounting, with the IASB having released a new accounting standard for insurance contracts in 2017. The new accounting standard, IFRS 17 Insurance Contracts, becomes effective in 2021.

However, it is not only the accounting for insurance liabilities that will change; insurance companies will also have to change how they account for their investments at the same time. This is because insurance companies were granted a carve-out from adopting the new financial instrument accounting standard (IFRS 9, which is discussed in detail in Chapter 13) until the new insurance standard becomes effective. This carve-out aims at minimising disruption for the industry by allowing both standards to be adopted together.

IFRS 17 represents an enormous accounting change for insurance companies; it is the first comprehensive accounting for all insurance contracts and will result in the net cash flows from insurance contracts being on balance sheet at 'current value' (essentially at fair value), which is a significant shift away from the current approach of accrual accounting for insurance premiums, claims and costs.

10.1 IFRS 17 Key Principles

The key principle under IFRS 17 is that insurance contracts should be captured on balance sheet at their current value. The diagram below demonstrates how the calculation of current value is derived under IFRS 17:

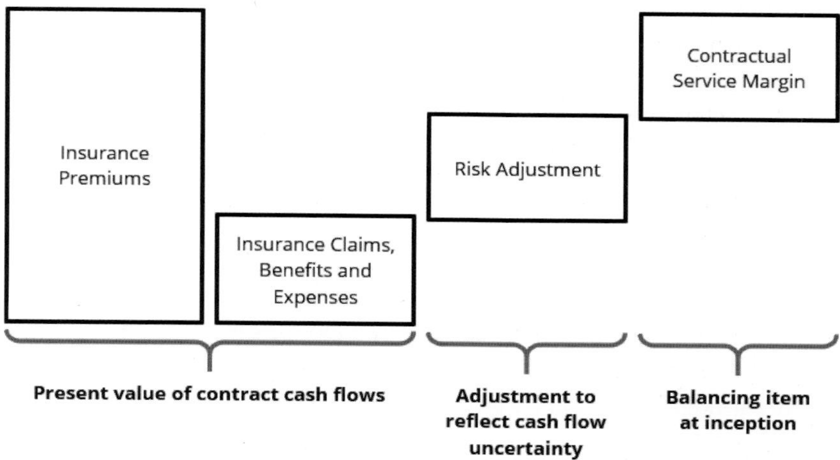

Key points to note from above are:

- The 'contractual service margin' is essentially a balancing item and reflects the expected future profit from the insurance contract as part of the balance sheet value, ensuring that the contract has zero balance sheet value at inception. Therefore, on day 1 of the contract no profit is recognised (though a loss would be recognised if the contract was deemed onerous on day 1).

- The present value of future cash flows is based on 'best estimates' of cash inflows (premiums) and cash outflows (claims, benefits and expenses). Where these estimates change, the contractual service margin is adjusted in the balance sheet, so it doesn't give rise to any immediate gain or loss [24].
- The discount rate for calculating the net present values of the insurance premiums, claims and expenses reflects the risk characteristics of the insurance contract (e.g. duration, currency and liquidity - though it shouldn't reflect the insurer's own credit risk). The discount rate must be consistent with observable market prices and updated at each balance sheet date.
- The risk adjustment is similar in concept to the risk adjustment under Solvency II, reflecting the uncertainty in the expected cash flows.

It's worth noting that there are strong similarities between the balance sheet accounting approach above and the calculation of technical provisions under Solvency II (albeit using different discount rates), since they both seek to capture market consistent 'current values' of insurance contracts.

10.2 IFRS 17 Earnings

The IFRS 17 income statement will look completely different to that under the current accounting; for a start, there will be no gross or written premiums or claims incurred since the contract cash flows are now calculated on a net basis, to derive the contract profit (or contractual service margin).

Instead, the income statement will include the following key elements:

1. Insurance Service Result

The insurance service result aims to show the profit generated from the insurance business each period. It will include:

- **Release of contractual service margin** (i.e. the amount of contract profit that is being recognised). The profit recognised each period is based on the proportion of claims paid out each period, relative to the total expected claims. Therefore, the profit profile over the whole contract will match the profile of cash outflows (so profits are recognised earlier for annuity contracts than for life insurance contracts).

[24] The exception would be if an increase in expected claims or benefits eroded all the contract service margin. At this point the contract is deemed onerous and any further losses are recognised immediately in earnings.

- **Release of risk**. This is released to earnings based on the confidence level for contract cash flows.

2. Financial Result

The investment result aims to show the financing expenses and income of the business each period. It will include:

- **Interest cost on insurance liabilities**. Each year, the present value of the insurance liabilities will increase slightly, as the effect of discounting the cash flows partially unwinds. This gives rise to an interest cost which is included in the investment result.

- **Investment income**. This will include the returns generated on all investments (e.g. equities, fixed income instruments and investment property). As highlighted above, the returns generated from investments in equities and fixed income instruments will be accounted for under IFRS 9.

One further item which we haven't mentioned above is gains or losses arising from changes in discount rates (remember that the IFRS 17 requires discount rates to be updated each balance sheet date). Insurance companies will be able to choose whether to present these gains or losses in the investment result or in 'other comprehensive income'. This choice helps insurers manage earnings volatility.

Solutions to Chapter Exercises

1 Asset Classification (page 11)

	Current assets (✓)	Non-current (✓)	Not an asset (✓)
1. Machinery	☐	☑	☐
2. Telephone bills	☐	☐	☑
3. Vehicles	☐	☑	☐
4. Patents	☐	☑	☐
5. Non-purchased goodwill	☐	☐	☑
6. Debtors (Accounts receivable)	☑	☐	☐
7. Creditors (Accounts payable)	☐	☐	☑
8. Closing stock	☑	☐	☐
9. Equipment	☐	☑	☐
10. Computers	☐	☑	☐

2 Building Balance Sheets (page 18)

Balance Sheet as at 2 March

Assets	€	Liabilities and equity	€
Cash at bank	15,000	Capital	6,000
Motor van	5,000	Liabilities - loan	14,000
	20,000		20,000

As can be seen, the effect of purchasing a motor van is to decrease the balance at the bank by €5,000 and to introduce a new asset – a motor van – on to the balance sheet. The total assets remain unchanged. It is only the 'mix' of assets which will change. The claims against the business will remain the same as there has been no change in the funding arrangements for the business.

The balance sheet as at 3 March, following the purchase of stock, will be as follows:

Balance Sheet as at 3 March

Assets	€	Liabilities and equity	€
Cash at bank	15,000	Capital	6,000
Motor van	5,000	Liabilities - loan	14,000
Stock	3,000	- trade creditor	3,000
	23,000		23,000

The effect of purchasing stock has been to introduce another new asset (stock) onto the balance sheet. In addition, the fact that the goods have not yet been paid for means that the claims against the business will be increased by the €3,000 owed to the supplier, who is referred to as a trade creditor on the balance sheet.

The balance sheet as at March 4, following the repayment of part of the loan, will be as follows:

Balance Sheet as at 4 March

Assets	€	Liabilities and equity	€
Cash at bank	13,000	Capital	6,000
Motor van	5,000	Liabilities - loan	12,000
Stock	3,000	- trade creditor	3,000
	21,000		21,000

The repayment of €2,000 of the loan will result in a decrease in the balance at the bank of €2,000 and a decrease in the loan claim against the business by the same amount.

The balance sheet as at 6 March will be as follows:

Balance Sheet as at 6 March

Assets	€	Liabilities and Equity	€
Cash at bank	17,000	Capital	10,000
Motor van	5,000	Liabilities - loan	12,000
Stock	3,000	- trade creditor	3,000
	25,000		25,000

The introduction of more funds by the owner will result in an increase in the capital of €4,000 and an increase in the cash at bank by the same amount.

Balance Sheet as at 7 March

Assets	€	Liabilities and Equity	€
Cash at bank	22,000	Capital	10,000
		Retained earnings	2,000
Motor van	5,000	Liabilities - loan	12,000
		- trade creditor	3,000
	27,000		27,000

We can see that the inventory (€3,000) has now disappeared from the balance sheet but the cash at bank has increased by the selling price of the inventory (€5,000). The net effect has therefore been to increase assets by €2,000 (€5,000 – €3,000). This increase represents the net increase in wealth (profit) which has arisen from trading. Also note that the capital of the business has increased by €2,000 in line with the increase in assets. This increase in capital reflects the fact that increases in wealth as a result of trading or other operations will be to the benefit of the owner and will increase his/her stake in the business.

3 Impress Inc. (page 25)

a) Balance Sheet as at 1 September

Assets	€	Liabilities and Equity	€
Cash at bank	40,000	Capital	12,000
		Liabilities - loan	28,000
	40,000		40,000

b) Balance Sheet as at 2 September

Assets	€	Liabilities and Equity	€
Cash at bank	30,000	Capital	12,000
Motor van	10,000	Liabilities - loan	28,000
	40,000		40,000

Balance Sheet as at 7 September

Assets	€	Liabilities and Equity	€
Cash at bank	30,000	Capital	12,000
Motor van	10,000	Liabilities - loan	28,000
Stock	6,000	- trade creditor	6,000
	46,000		46,000

Balance Sheet as at 14 September

Assets	€	Liabilities and Equity	€
Cash at bank	26,000	Capital	12,000
Motor van	10,000	Liabilities - loan	24,000
Stock	6,000	- trade creditor	6,000
	42,000		42,000

Balance Sheet as at 26 September

Assets	€	Liabilities and Equity	€
Cash at bank	34,000	Capital	20,000
Motor van	10,000	Liabilities - loan	24,000
Stock	6,000	- trade creditor	6,000
	50,000		50,000

c) Balance Sheet as at 27 September

Assets	€	Liabilities and Equity	€
Cash at bank	44,000	Capital	20,000
		Retained earnings	4,000
Motor van	10,000	Liabilities - loan	24,000
		- trade creditor	6,000
	54,000		54,000

4 Professional Services Inc. (page 34)

1. Overall Profit

Revenues	€
– Costs	240,000
Wages	
Motor van	60,000
Overheads	(120,000)
Profits	60,000

2. It will also be €60,000!

3. Professional Services Inc.

Monthly Net Profit

	January €	February €	March €	April €	May €	June €	July €	August €	Total €
Sales	40,000	40,000	40,000	40,000	40,000	40,000	–	–	240,000
Costs:									
Wages	(10,000)	(10,000)	(10,000)	(10,000)	(10,000)	(10,000)	–	–	(60,000)
Overheads	(20,000)	(20,000)	(20,000)	(20,000)	(20,000)	(20,000)	–	–	(120,000)
Profit	10,000	10,000	10,000	10,000	10,000	10,000	–	–	60,000

4, 5, 6 Professional Services Inc.

Cash Flows

	January €	February €	March €	April €	May €	June €	July €	August €	Total €
Cash in flows	–	40,000	40,000	40,000	40,000	40,000	40,000	–	240,000
Cash out flows									
Wages	(10,000)	(10,000)	(10,000)	(10,000)	(10,000)	(10,000)	–	–	(60,000)
Overheads	(20,000)	(20,000)	(20,000)	(20,000)	(20,000)	(20,000)	–	–	(120,000)
Net cash flows	(30,000)	10,000	10,000	10,000	10,000	10,000	40,000	–	60,000

7. Points to Note:

- Profit ≠ Cash flow.
- Required financing is at least €30,000. This assumes cash received on time.

5 IFS Company (page 39)

(a) 125 Balancing figure (do (b) and (c) first!)

(b) 1,150 Simply a total

(c) 1,150 Must equal (b)!

(d) 1,240

	Opening Accounts Payable	**180**
+	Purchases	?
–	Cash paid	(1,300)
	Closing accounts payable	220
	∴ Purchases	1,340
	Opening stock	300
+	Purchases	1,340
–	Closing stock	(400)
	Cost of goods	1,240

(e) 760 Simple arithmetic

(f) 50 Change in balance sheet cumulative depreciation

(g) (390) Tricky!

	Opening Liability	**30**
+	Wages expenses	400
		430
–	Paid	?
	Closing liability	40

∴ Balancing numbers = 390 paid

(h) 125 Simple total

(i) 700

	Opening Balance	600
+	New building	
	(Cash flow)	100
	Closing balance	700

(j) 500 Tricky!

	Opening Balance	200
+	Sales	2,000
		2,200
–	Received	
	(Cash flow)	(1,700)
		500

(k) 175

	Opening Balance	50
+	Increase in cash	125
		175

(l) 525

	Opening Balance	125
+	Issue of shares	
	(Cash flow)	400
		525

(m) & (n) 1,775 Simply totals

6 Final Exercise (page 42)

Basic Concepts

1. An analyst will want to decide which revenues are from 'core' businesses and which are non-core. This allows an analyst to appreciate that €4.9bn out of €28.7bn of revenues (over 17%) arise from non-traffic activity

2. Gross profit – profit after direct costs only. Operating profit – after all operating costs (direct and indirect; production and non-production)

3. Express the costs as a percentage of sales and conduct a time series comparison:

$$\textbf{2011} \quad \frac{6{,}678}{28{,}734} = 23\%$$

$$\textbf{2010} \quad \frac{6{,}491}{26{,}459} = 25\%$$

These percentages could also be compared with those of other companies in the same sector.

4. Interest typically arises on debt finance. It is called net interest as interest income has been deducted from it (see note 12)

5. As the company is making losses it can use these in future years to offset tax on profits

6. They have helped generate the profits for the period. Where else could they go?!

7. A measure of profit/loss per share

Basic Concepts – Balance Sheet

1. Tangible fixed assets have a physical presence (e.g. buildings) whereas intangibles (e.g. goodwill) do not.
2. Aircraft would typically be fixed assets as Lufthansa will intend to use them on a continuing basis.
3. Provisions are an anticipation of a future liability. They are classified in liabilities, normally in a separate section.
4. Issued share capital is the par (or nominal) value of shares issued. The premium on shares issued (issue price – nominal value) goes to the capital reserve.
5. Net assets = €8,044m
   (Total assets – Provisions and Accruals – Liabilities – Deferred income)

   Total assets = €28,081m

   Equity = €7,949m

Appendix – Lufthansa Case Study

This case study requires resources from the Lufthansa 2017 Annual Report. This can be downloaded from their official investor relations site or Financial Edge's own site, just type the following into your browser address bar to quickly download the PDF:

bit.ly/lufthansa2017

1 Questions

1. What accounting standards have been used in the preparation of these financial statements?
2. Identify the following numbers from the 2017 accounts:
   - Turnover.
   - Operating profit.
   - Total assets.
   - Net assets.
   - Equity.
   - Result of equity investments accounted for using the equity method.
3. Explain the following items in the income statement:
   - Income from joint ventures and associates.
   - Net interest.
   - Profit/loss attributable to minority interests.
4. Explain each of the items that reconcile profit to cash flow.
5. What is the item 'effects of exchange rates' disclosed towards the bottom of the cash flow statement?
6. Complete the attached schedule of ratios (on the following pages) using the last two years of data for Lufthansa.

1. Return on Equity	**2017**	**2016**
Net profit		
Equity		
Return on equity		
2. Operating Profit Margin		
Operating profit		
Turnover		
Operating profit margin		
3. Asset Turnover		
Turnover		
Total assets		
Asset turnover		
4. Fixed Asset Turnover		
Turnover		
Fixed assets		
Fixed asset turnover		
5. Sales per Employee		
Turnover		
Employees		
Sales per employee		
6. Operating Profit per Employee		
Operating profit		
Employees		
Operating profit per employee		
7. Staff Costs per Employee		
Staff costs		
Employees		
Staff costs per employee		
8. Interest Cover in P&L		
Operating profit		
Interest receivable		
Interest payable		

Interest cover in P&L

9. Effective Tax Rate

Tax charge

Profits before tax

Effective tax rate

10. Current Ratio

Current assets

less: Debtors due > 1 year

Current assets due < 1 year

Creditors due < 1 year

Current ratio

11. Quick Ratio

Current assets due

less: stock

Quick assets

Creditors due < 1 year

Quick ratio

12. Stock Turnover

Cost of materials

Stock

Stock turnover

13. Trade Debtors' Collection Period

Trade debtors

Turnover

Collection period (x 365)

14. Trade Payables' Payment Period

Trade payables

Costs of materials

Payment period (x 365)

15. Debt: Equity

Debt (long-term borrowings)

Equity (shareholders' funds + minority)

Debt: Equity		
16. Net Asset Value for Ordinary Share		
Net assets		
No. of ordinary shares		
Net asset value per ordinary share		

2 Solutions

1. International Financial Reporting Standards. There are a number of places to quickly check this if it is in doubt. Looking at the accounting policies notes is one and the audit report is another.

2. For the year 2017:

Turnover:	€35, 579m
Operating Profit:	€3,153m
Total Assets:	€36,267m
Net Assets:	€36,267m -14,030m–12,639m = €9,598m
Equity:	€9,598m
Result of equity investments accounted for using the equity method:	€118m (see note 11 for further details)

3. Result of equity investments accounted for using the equity method is Lufthansa's share of profit under the equity method of accounting. This method is adopted when the parent entity is able to exercise significant influence but not control over the investee. It is a one-line entry rather than a line by line consolidation of the results.

   Net interest is interest income less interest expenses. Sometimes, these are netted off on the face of the income statement but here they have been kept separate. Note 12 provides analysis of these interest figures.

   Profit/loss attributable to minority interests is the profit that has been consolidated in these accounts that does not belong to the shareholders of Lufthansa. This is addressed in chapter 8.

4. The financial statements are prepared using the accruals concept. This means that transactions are accounted for when earned or incurred as opposed to received or paid. For this reason, profit needs to be adjusted to arrive at the cash flow actually generated from operations.

   Depreciation, amortisation and impairment losses: These items have been added back to profit as these are non-cash expenses.

   Fixed asset disposals are deducted because the profit made is not the cash receipts figure. The actual cash flow arising from the sale is shown under investing activities.

Result of equity investments are deducted because it is the dividend income which is the actual cash flow not share of profit. The dividend income is shown under investing activities.

Net interest is added back to profit as it has been accounted for on an accruals basis. The actual cash flows are shown under financing activities.

Income tax paid: This represents is the amount paid in the year. This is not the same as the tax expense for the year which appears in the income statement. The profit figure used is the one before tax so it is just the amount paid that needs to be reflected in the cash flow statement.

Change in trade working capital: This includes changes in inventory, receivables, liabilities and provisions. As it is not subdivided out on the actual cash flow statement here are some example of the logic:

- The *decrease in inventory* is an addition to profit in arriving at cash flows. If inventory has decreased, then more sales are being made and less cash is tied up.
- The *increase in receivables* etc is also seen to be a deduction from profit. If these amounts have increased, then cash is not being collected even though revenue is being generated.
- *Decreases in provisions* are a deduction from profit as they are non-cash profit which will have been added to profit.
- *Increases* in liabilities are an add back to profit as the increase means that cash is not being paid out.

Financial derivatives through profit or loss is a non-cash expense from changes in the market value of financial derivatives and needs to be eliminated when calculating cash flow.

5. The effect of currency translation differences must also be reflected in the cash flow statement. This amount will relate to foreign currency transactions which have generated a difference on settlement. These differences are minimised by the hedging transactions that the group enters into. Foreign exchange differences arising on the retranslation of a subsidiary under the current rate are not reflected in the cash flow statement, as they do not have an effect on the group's cash.

6. Ratio schedule

1. Return on Equity	2017	2016
Net Income	€2,398m	€1,803m
Equity*	€9,598m	€7,149m
Return on equity	24.9%	25.2%

* Note this includes minority interests as the net income used is before deducting profit attributed to minority interests. It could also be calculated by excluding minorities from both.

2. Operating Profit Margin		
Operating profit*/(loss)	€3,153m	€2,190m
Turnover	€35, 579m	€31,660m
Operating profit margin	8.9%	6.9%

* Here we have included an unadjusted operating profit number. Analysts and other users would often strip out exceptional items. Go to notes 9 and 13. Typical items an analyst might exclude would be the profits/losses from disposals.

3. Asset Turnover*		
Turnover	€35,579m	€31,660m
Total assets	€36,267m	€34,697m
Asset turnover	0.98	0.91

* For convenience we have used year end asset figures. Note that averages ((opening balance + closing balance)/2) are often used in practice especially if there has been a large movement in the balances in question.

4. Fixed Asset Turnover		
Turnover	€35,579m	€31,660m
Fixed assets*	€25,237m	€24,504m
Fixed asset turnover	1.41x	1.29x

* Non-Current assets

5. Sales per Employee	2017	2016
Turnover	€35,579m	€31,660m
Employees (Note 8)	128,856	123,287
Sales per employee	€276,114	€256,799

6. Operating Profit per Employee		
Operating profit/(loss)	€3,153m	€2,190m
Employees (Note 8)	128,856	123,287
Operating profit per employee/(loss) per employee	€24,469	€17,763

7. Staff Costs per Employee		
Staff costs (Note 8)	€8,172m	€7,354m
Employees (Note 8)	128,856	123,287
Staff costs per employee	€63,420	€59,649

8. Interest Cover in P&L		
Operating profit/(loss)	€3,153m	€2,190m
Interest receivable	€178m	€64m
	€3,331m	€2,254m
Interest payable	€373m	€282m
Interest cover in P&L	8.9x	7.99x

9. Effective Tax Rate		
Tax charge	789	445
Profits before tax	3,187	2,248
Effective tax rate	24.8%	19.8%

10. Current Ratio		
Current assets	€11,030m	€10,193m
Current liabilities (due < 1 year)	€12,639m	€11,009m
Current ratio	0.872	0.93

11. Quick Ratio	2017	2016
Current assets	€11,030m	€10,193m
Less: Inventory	(€907m)	(€816m)
Quick assets	€10,123m	€9,377m
Current liabilities (due < 1 year)	€12,639m	€11,009m
Quick ratio	0.80	0.85

12. Stock Turnover		
Cost of materials & services*	€19,013m	€17,109m
Stock	€907m	€816m
Stock turnover	20.96x	20.97x

* There would be an argument for adjusting this further to get closer to a 'COGS' number but given the scale of the numbers involved this is perfectly fine.

13. Trade Debtors' Collection Period	2011	2010
Trade debtors (Note 25 – 3rd party only)	€3,901m	€3,191
Turnover	€35,579m	€31,660m
Collection period (x 365)	40.0 days	36.7 days

14. Trade Payables' Payment Period		
Trade payables (Note 37 – 3rd party only)	€3,358m	€3,021m
Costs of materials	€19,013m	€17,109m
Payment period (x 365)	64.5 days	64.4 days

15. Debt: Equity		
Debt (long-term borrowings) (Note 34)	€6,142m	€5,811m
Equity (shareholders' funds + minority)	€9,598m	€7, 149m
Debt: Equity	64.0%	81.3%

16. Net Asset Value for Ordinary Share		
Net assets (excluding Minority Interests)	€9,495m	€7,060m
No. of ordinary shares (Note 30)	471m	469m
Net asset value per ordinary share	€20.16	€15.05

Index

S

T

U

V

W

Z